A Short History
of German Philosophy

A Short History
of German Philosophy

Vittorio Hösle

TRANSLATED BY STEVEN RENDALL

Princeton University Press
Princeton & Oxford

Originally published as *Eine kurze Geschichte der deutschen Philosophie* by
Vittorio Hösle
© Verlag C.H.Beck oHG, München 2013

English translation © 2017 by Princeton University Press
Preface to the English translation © 2017
Published by Princeton University Press, 41 William Street, Princeton, New
Jersey 08540
In the United Kingdom: Princeton University Press, 6 Oxford Street,
Woodstock, Oxfordshire OX20 1TW

press.princeton.edu

This publication has been generously supported by the Institute for
Scholarship in the Liberal Arts at the University of Notre Dame.

Jacket art courtesy of Lebrecht Music and Arts Photo Library/Alamy

Paper ISBN 978-0-691-18312-1

Library of Congress Cataloging-in-Publication Data

Names: Hösle, Vittorio, 1960- author. | Rendall, Steven, translator.

Title: A short history of German philosophy / Vittorio Hosle ; Translated by
Steven Rendall.

Other titles: Kurze Geschichte der deutschen Philosophie. English

Description: Princeton : Princeton University Press, 2016. | "Originally
published as Eine kurze Geschichte der deutschen Philosophie by Vittorio
Hosle (c) Verlag C.H.Beck oHG, Munchen 2013." | Includes index.

Identifiers: LCCN 2016007315 | ISBN 9780691167190 (cloth)

Subjects: LCSH: Philosophy, German--History.

Classification: LCC B2521 .H67 2016 | DDC 193--dc23 LC record available
at http://lccn.loc.gov/2016007315

British Library Cataloging-in-Publication Data is available

This book has been composed in Garamond Premier Pro and Aldus LT Std

Printed on acid-free paper. ∞

Printed in the United States of America

10 9 8 7 6 5 4 3 2 1

IN GRATEFUL MEMORY OF MY MOTHER,
CARLA GRONDA HÖSLE (1929–2015), WHO FOR
HER HUSBAND AND HER CHILDREN'S SAKE
LIVED FAR AWAY FROM HER BELOVED ITALY

CONTENTS

TRANSLATOR'S NOTE

Translations of texts quoted in this book have been taken from the following:

Walter Benjamin, *Illuminations*, trans. Harry Zohn. New York: Schocken, 1969.

Martin Buber, *I and Thou*, trans. Ronald Gregor Smith. New York: Scribner's, 1958, 1986.

Ludwig Feuerbach, *Essence of Christianity*, trans. Marian [*sic*] Evans. 2nd ed., London, 1890.

Johann Gottlieb Fichte, *System of Transcendental Idealism*, trans. Peter L. Heath. University of Virginia Press, 1993.

———, *The Way towards the Blessed Life*, trans. W. Smith, 1849.

Gottlob Frege, "*Concept Script: A Formal Language of Pure Thought Modelled on That of Arithmetic*," trans. S. Bauer-Mengelberg. In *From Frege to Gödel: A Source Book in Mathematical Logic, 1879–1931*. Harvard University Press, 1967.

Hans-Georg Gadamer, "The Anticipation of Completeness." In Georgia Warnke, *The Hermeneutics, Tradition, and Reason*, Stanford University Press, 1987.

———, *Truth and Method*, trans. Joel Weinsheimer and Donald G. Marshall. New York: Continuum, 2004.

Georg Wilhelm Friedrich Hegel, *Elements of the Philosophy of Right*, trans. T. M. Knox. Oxford University Press, 1967; trans. H. B. Nisbet. Cambridge University Press, 1991.

Martin Heidegger, "The Question concerning Technology," trans. in Craig Hanks, ed., *Technology and Values*, Chichester UK: Wiley-Blackwell, 2010.

Karl Jaspers, *Man in the Modern Age*, trans. E. Paul and C. Paul. London: Routledge, 1933.

Immanuel Kant, *Critique of Practical Reason*, trans. Lewis White Beck. New York: Liberal Arts, 1956.

———, *Metaphysical Elements of Justice*, trans. John Ladd. Indianapolis: Hackett, 1999.

———, *The Metaphysics of Morals*, trans. Mary J. Gregor. Cambridge University Press, 1994.

Karl Marx, *The German Ideology*, trans. Salo Ryazanskaya. Moscow: Progress Publishers, 1968.

Friedrich Nietzsche, *The Antichrist*, trans. Judith Norman. Cambridge University Press, 2005.

———, *Beyond Good and Evil*, trans. Judith Norman. Cambridge University Press, 2002.

———, *The Gay Science*, trans. Josefine Nauckhoff. Cambridge University Press, 2001.

———, *Human, All Too Human*, trans. R. J. Hollingdale. Cambridge University Press, 2nd ed. 1996.

———, *Untimely Meditations*, trans. R. J. Hollingdale. Cambridge University Press, 2nd ed. 1997.

Friedrich Wilhelm Joseph Schelling, *A History of Modern Philosophy*, trans. A. Bowie. Cambridge University Press, 1994.

———, *Philosophical Investigations into the Essence of Human Freedom*, trans. Jeff Love and Johannes Schmidt. Albany: SUNY Press, 2010.

Ludwig Wittgenstein, *Philosophical Investigations*, trans. G.E.M. Anscombe. New York: Macmillan, 1953.

———, *Tractatus Logico-Philosophicus*, trans. D. F. Pears and Brian McGuinness. London: Routledge and Kegan Paul, 1966.

All other translations are by Steven Rendall.

PREFACE TO THE ENGLISH TRANSLATION

It is with pleasure and pride that I welcome the English translation of this short history of German philosophy, coming out of such a distinguished American university press only a few years after the original, which was published in 2013. (The only earlier translation is a Korean one, which appeared in 2015.) In Germany, the book has already had a remarkable impact, as the various reviews, both in newspapers[1] and in academic journals,[2] show—reviews of various length, various quality, and originating from various backgrounds. Since not everybody correctly understood the aim of this book, I want to use the occasion of this preface to clarify my purposes, which are even more in need of articulation for an Anglophone public that is probably less familiar than a German audience with certain basic traits of German philosophy, a

---

[1] I name only some of the reviews that I have seen: Achim Vesper in *Frankfurter Allgemeine* 2013–03–09, L 15; Johannes Saltzwedel in *KulturSPIEGEL* 2013–02–25; Felix Dirsch in *Junge Freiheit* 2013–05–10; Thomas Brose in *Christ in der Gegenwart* 64 (2013), 238; Stefan Diebitz in *literaturkritik.de*, no. 5, 2013; Pierfrancesco Basile in *Tagesanzeiger* 2013–08–07; Thomas Meyer in *Die Zeit* 2014–6-22; Anna-Verena Rosthoff in *Der blaue Reiter* 36 (2015). Shortly before the publication of the book, Carsten Dutt interviewed me about it: "Zur Lage der Philosophie," in *Zeitschrift für Ideengeschichte* VI/3 (2012), 58–72.

[2] Again, I offer a selection: Pirmin Stekeler-Weithofer in *Philosophische Rundschau* 60 (2013), 241–242; Jörg Noller in *Philosophisches Jahrbuch* 120 (2013), 448–451; Jens Petersen in *Archiv für Rechts- und Sozialphilosophie* 99 (2013), 434–438; Josef Schmidt in *Theologie und Philosophie* 88 (2013), 585–590; Gregor Sans in *Stimmen der Zeit* 138 (2013), 713–714; Detlef Horster in *Zeitschrift für Individualpsychologie* 38 (2013), 327–329; Reinhard Mehring in *Philosophischer Literaturanzeiger* 67 (2014), 146–152; Ulrich Arnswald in *Zeitschrift für Geschichtswissenschaft* 62 (2014), 843–845. Among non-German reviewers, I mention Robert Puzia in *Roczniki Filozoficzne* 62 (2014), 87–90, and Emma Fleury in *Rivista di storia della filosofia* 1/2014, 185–187. In the following, I respond also to objections in personal letters that I received.

philosophy so markedly different from what the discipline has become, particularly in the United States.

1. The main questions asked by the reviewers have of course been: How is "German philosophy" defined? And: Is it a reasonable enterprise to write about it? Since the definition of a term is to a large degree arbitrary, it is the second question that has to be tackled first, for German philosophy has to be defined in such a way that narrating its history makes sense. But whatever definition is proposed, can it ever make sense? Is it not obvious that German philosophers were influenced by non-German thinkers, both from Antiquity and from the more recent past? And does not focusing on German thought alone discriminate against the two other major modern European philosophical traditions, the French and the British, to which one can add, even if its influence was on a somewhat lesser level, the Italian?

    The answer can only be that of course German philosophy is not an isolated part of world philosophy—no more than any other national philosophical tradition. It would be indeed far more satisfying to write a global history of philosophy, rendering due attention to all the connections that exist between the thinkers of the past. (Such connections are both causal and structural—for certain patterns of thought recur in the history of philosophy, independently of causal connections.[3]) And since philosophy is part of a general culture, the history of philosophy should be written in the context of a comprehensive history of ideas, which encompasses also the history of the sciences and of the arts.[4] The problem, however, is

---

[3] I myself have dealt with the macrostructures of the history of Western philosophy in my book *Wahrheit und Geschichte. Studien zur Struktur der Philosophiegeschichte unter paradigmatischer Analyse der Entwicklung von Parmenides bis Platon*, Stuttgart-Bad Cannstatt, 1984. The third part of the book on philosophy after Plato, however, is far too sketchy; but I still think that the theory captures some basic structures.

[4] James Turner has recently shown in his masterful *Philology: The Forgotten Origins of the Modern Humanities* (Princeton, 2014) how the fragmentation of a unitarian project of philology produced the modern humanities.

that there are not many people who could tackle such a project. The author of this book at least recognizes that it is beyond his forces. For most people, it is necessary and generally acknowledged as legitimate to focus on a segment of the history of philosophy, whether on a single author or on a single epoch, such as the philosophy of the seventeenth century.

But why focus on a single culture? Is this not anachronistic in an age of increasing globalization, and—worse—does it not surreptitiously support nationalistic thinking? I think the last chapter of this book will suffice to answer this charge.[5] We live indeed in an age of increasing cosmopolitanism, and nationalism was perhaps a necessary but certainly an unfortunate episode in human history. However, it remains true that, after the common European identity of the Middle Ages, early modernity led to the formation of separate national cultures in Europe; and these cultures (which now are becoming increasingly permeable to each other thanks to the European Union and the more general process of globalization) were in the late eighteenth, the nineteenth, and the early twentieth century characterized by nationalistic passions. It is this historical fact on which I base my demarcation: I do indeed claim that between 1750 and 1945 German philosophers read, certainly not exclusively, but in large measure, the work of colleagues writing in German and that these frequent interactions explain why certain philosophical traditions could develop within Germany that are distinguishable from the philosophical styles in neighboring countries. Nothing in the book denies the enormous impact of foreign authors on some of the most creative German philosophers of the classical age. As I state several times, Kant's originality, to name only one example, is inexplicable without Hume and Rousseau. While he could read French, Kant had to rely on transla-

---

[5] Anyone interested in my own normative attitude toward nationalism as a political principle may look up my work *Morals and Politics* (Notre Dame, 2004), 476ff., 590f., 766ff.

tions to gain access to Hume, but fortunately even in the era of national cultures the work of translators bridged the divides between the various cultures. Still, the influence of these two thinkers led only to a transformation, not a rejection of Kant's early Leibnizianism; Kant's mature system retained quite a few of the traits of his Leibnizianism, and these radically distinguish it from contemporary British empiricism.

At least for the two hundred years between the mid-eighteenth and the mid-twentieth century there existed a German culture quite different from its neighbors; and German philosophy was part of this culture, perhaps even its center. This is the relatively uncontroversial—or "weak," as one reviewer put it, thesis of the book. While I do not at all hold that this difference has survived into the twenty-first century, I advance arguments in favor of the stronger thesis that the formation of a special German spirit begins long before the eighteenth-century cultural revolution, and that it has its roots in German mysticism and particularly in Lutheranism. On this issue there will be less consensus, for even if I can point to continuities between Meister Eckhart, Nicholas of Cusa, and Jakob Böhme on the one hand, and German idealism on the other, there is little doubt that in these earlier centuries there existed also much thinking that did not deviate in any striking way from mainstream European philosophy.

2. It is the intensity of reciprocal influence that justifies my demarcation of a special area within the larger field of the history of philosophy. This explains why the only criterion I use for considering something as "German" is the use of the German language, for after the loss of Latin as an academic lingua franca and before the rise of English to serve a similar function, people's reading was preferentially shaped by texts in their own language. Neither ethnic, nor political, nor geographical categories play any role whatsoever in my definition of "German." Austrians and German-speaking Swiss thus fall under my definition of "German," even if this may not

be politically correct, and, conversely, medieval and early modern German philosophers who wrote exclusively in Latin do not belong to the German philosophy that I am studying here. As long as someone writes in German, he is potentially a subject of this history, and when he ceases to write in German, he is no longer a candidate for inclusion. This is the reason why I include György Lukács and Roman Ingarden, even though some Hungarian or Polish readers may not appreciate my decision, and this is why the book, while dedicating several pages to both Frege and Wittgenstein, mentions only briefly Carnap and Popper, and ignores almost completely authors like Hannah Arendt or Leo Strauss. For they all switched to the English language after their emigration. From that moment on, they ceased to belong to German philosophy as here defined.

A fortiori I had to exclude Søren Kierkegaard from this book, for he did not write even a single essay in German.[6] But, one may ask, is he not deeply rooted in German culture, in Lutheranism and, philosophically, in Kant and Hegel? He is, certainly, but so were many others, and this is not a book about philosophers influenced by classical German thought. While I do claim that there are some traits common to most German philosophers that distinguish them from most philosophers of the other European nations, this is an empirical thesis that can only be verified after one's concepts are defined. And, again, my defining criterion for "German" is the German language. Needless to say, a history of Lutheran philosophy would be a worthwhile project, and while there would be quite an overlap with my own history, several of my heroes, such as Hermann Cohen and Max Scheler, would have no place in it, while various Scandinavian philosophers would have to be included. But as interesting as this project may be, it is not the one pursued in this book.

---

[6] A colleague lamented the absence of Spinoza. But while certainly Dutch as a Low Franconian language blends into Low German, Spinoza wrote in Latin—like other German authors ignored in this book. The Dutch *Korte Verhandeling* was a translation made by Spinoza's friends, not by himself, of a Latin original.

3. I have provoked some irritation by using the term *Sonderweg* (special path) to point to the specific differences of German philosophy from other traditions. The term, as is well known, was already used in the late nineteenth century in an affirmative sense to point to the intermediate position of Germany between the liberal West and the autocratic East; after 1945, however, the term gained a negative connotation and was mainly employed by historians who claimed that there was a strong continuity between earlier German history and the rise of National Socialism. In the last decades, criticism of the Sonderweg thesis has become prevalent both among German and foreign scholars—I mention only David Blackbourne and Geoff Eley's *The Peculiarities of German History* of 1984. The two crucial arguments have been, first, that the differences between Germany on the one hand and France and Britain on the other have not been so deep as to justify the term (although Germany never became a parliamentary monarchy, the nineteenth century brought a far-reaching embourgoisement) and, second, that there is no reason to regard the British or the French way as the standard course of development leading to modernization. While I agree with both criticisms, I do not think that they are relevant to my use of the term. For I simply maintain that German philosophy, already with Meister Eckhart and increasingly with Leibniz and Kant, became quite different from the neighboring traditions.

This implies neither that British or French philosophy are superior to German (in fact, I suggest the enduring attractiveness of the specific German approach), nor am I committed to some version of the thesis "From Bismarck to Hitler" or even "From Luther to Hitler." With regard to Hegel, for example, I explicitly argue that his political thought belongs to constitutional liberalism and has absolutely nothing to do with totalitarianism. What I do claim, however, is that a robust theory of resistance is lacking in German political thought, and it is only on this level—the last of the three levels that I distinguish while discussing the contribution of German thought to the rise of National Socialism—that I see a connection with classical German philosophy. Given the Holocaust, I have also dutifully mentioned instances of anti-Judaism and anti-Semitism among German philosophers, but I have never averred that they are more frequent than, say, among French philosophers. If the *Sonderweg* thesis is constructed to mean that there was an inexorable causal connection between the mindset of Germany in the nineteenth century and the rise of National Socialism—without taking into account a huge number of individual events, such as the defeat of 1918—then the thesis seems to me no less than absurd. What I do agree with, however, is that both Nietzsche and Wagner contributed considerably to the formation of the National Socialist Weltanschauung, even if this inevitably irritates both the postmodern admirers of the philosopher and fans of German opera.

4. Despite all the remarkable variety among German philosophers, I do indeed maintain that there are certain features that are common to many of them and that had an enduring impact on the German spirit. What are they? To my mind, the most striking are rationalist theology, a commitment to synthetic *a priori* knowledge (ultimately based on the trust that God has created the world in a rational way), a penchant for system building, the foundation of ethics in reason and not in sentiment, and the combination of philosophy and philology. Kant's revolution in ethics is a fascinating example of how the German "spirit" (if I may use an easily misunderstood word) builds on common European developments but gives them a new turn. For Kant's revolution shares much with the general universalistic transformation of ethics that occurred all over eighteenth-century Europe but still differs from it thanks to his abrupt turn against the eudaemonist tradition and thus against empiricism. Needless to say, not all features mentioned are instantiated in every philosopher—for example, there is not much of a rationalist theology in Nietzsche, but there is quite a lot of philosophical sensibility toward the challenge of philology

and history. And the radicality of Nietzsche's thought is distinctly German and ultimately Lutheran. The great key to success for Britain, on the other hand, has always been its openness to substantial innovation while maintaining old traditions: Anglicanism is dogmatically Calvinist, but its liturgy remains Catholic; and the country that first beheaded a king, introduced parliamentary monarchy, and initiated the Industrial Revolution has been able to maintain one of the world's most stable monarchies.

My interest in the German tradition is not simply historical. I do think that German philosophy was the most productive and original philosophical tradition of modern Europe and that many of its foundational ideas remain valid. What I particularly admire in this philosophical tradition is the way it permeated culture at large, and thus my book often draws connections to other German developments, especially in literature, but occasionally also in the other arts, in science, and in politics. I have now lived long enough in the United States to say that such an interpenetration of general culture and philosophy is quite alien to this great country. Here, philosophers understand themselves mainly as smart puzzle solvers— which is indeed noble work, but rarely inspires society at large or even other disciplines or the arts. Philosophy as a Weltanschauung was more than that, and even when it did not meet the necessary standards of rigor, its cultural impact was huge, and it contributed to the almost religious awe in which Germans have held products of high culture. It was particularly the specific German version of objective idealism that inspired a philosophical religiosity alien to American culture, where religion is often anti-intellectual and philosophy anti-religious (the short period of Transcendentalism excepted). For many Europeans, two of the most striking features of the contemporary political debate in the US are, on the one hand, the entanglement of political and cultural wars (which render it difficult to reach compromise even in such practical matters as establishing a budget) and, on the other hand, the unhealthy polarization between "religious" and "secular" culture. The secular culture presents itself in two versions: the naturalist one (often based on a specific reading of Darwin) and the constructivist one (which dominates the humanities). Both reject transcendent ideal norms, and while naturalism at least adheres to some objectivity, it offers quite a reductive concept of objectivity. The religious culture, on the other hand, is largely rooted in philologically and theologically naïve conceptions, which in Germany had already become impossible in the nineteenth century, no doubt due in large part to the rigorous study of the classical languages in the *Gymnasium*. The lack of an intellectually sophisticated religiosity is, I believe, one of the main reasons for the level of the general culture in the US, which contrasts considerably with the exceptionally good institutions of higher learning of which the country rightly boasts.

5. Clarifying the concept of "German" that I utilize is one of the prerequisites for embarking upon the project of narrating the history of German philosophy. The other is the elucidation of the concept of philosophy. This is a much more arduous task, for philosophy is not as clearly demarcated as, say, mathematics. I understand philosophy—admittedly in a vague way—as the intellectual endeavor that tackles the ultimate principles of the various disciplines, whether they are general categories such as truth, goodness, and beauty, or more limited to regional areas, such as the nature of time or life. This explains why I have not hesitated to touch upon authors who were not philosophers but whose work in specialist disciplines caused important changes in philosophical reflection, such as Johann Joachim Winckelmann, Max Weber, and Albert Einstein. However, I only touch upon them; and to the complaint of some reviewers that Weber or Freud would have deserved many pages, I can only answer that the elaboration of their specific sociological or psychological theories transcends the task of a history of philosophy.

Another reproach has been that I do not mention at all certain philosophers who deserve at least an honorable mention, such as Hans Blumenberg (whom I consider more a historian of ideas than a philosopher), and treated others far too quickly, such as Karl Jaspers or Ernst Bloch (who in my eyes were important in their time but did not leave classic works behind). At least no reviewer has complained of the absence of any really great name. It was my explicit desire to focus on the most important figures and to avoid as much as possible mere name-dropping; and—an added difficulty—I had to write this history within the three hundred pages granted to me by the German publisher. This inevitably meant that I could not write as much on secondary figures as I would have loved to—it is in fact often harder to write a book of three hundred than of five hundred pages. That my choice of secondary authors as well as of the amount of words dedicated to each of them is partly subjective I do not deny; and the indefinite article used in the title of my book already pleads guilty to this charge. I am aware that my history is only one possible account. Still, I want to mention some of the criteria that determined my selection.

As a negative criterion, I decided to avoid living figures. The jury is still out on them (I personally believe that some figures still unknown internationally may gain more attention after their deaths than others who have already garnered acclaim), and the inclusion of some at the expense of others is always invidious. I made, however, two exceptions, namely for an octogenarian and a nonagenarian philosopher. Jürgen Habermas has for more than a half century been such an important figure in the intellectual life not only of the Federal Republic of Germany, but also worldwide, that his exclusion would have deprived the penultimate chapter of one of its most forceful presences. Habermas, however, is unintelligible without Karl-Otto Apel, whose inclusion is a simple matter of fairness when dealing with Habermas.

My positive criteria have been four: first, the pure quality of the philosophical work; second, its impact on the history of philosophy; and third, its capacity to express certain basic ideas of the time and of German culture in a paradigmatic way. The fourth criterion rests on whether the author helps us make sense of the development of German thought—for a history must be more than an agglomeration of data, it must narrate a process that follows a certain logic. It is this fourth criterion that justifies my dedicating an entire chapter to Schopenhauer—for without him the transition from Kant to Nietzsche could not be grasped. And Nietzsche's impact on later philosophy, as well as his capacity to express the German crisis of the late nineteenth century (and thus to prepare the catastrophe of the twentieth) are so extraordinary that he, too, cannot be handled in less than a chapter, even if, as the reader will surely notice, I am not one of his admirers. At least, I have showed him respect by trying to write about him in a way somehow similar to the one in which he spoke about the philosophers of the past.

But is not a judgment about the quality of a philosophy, which, unlike its impact, cannot be measured by quantitative data, utterly subjective? I do not believe so. I hold that a fruitful history of philosophy, like that of a science, can only be written by someone who is familiar with the issues at stake and not afraid to make judgments about the possible truth of a philosophical theory. Since the great philosophers of the past collectively, but often also individually, covered all of the subdisciplines of philosophy, an intelligent historiography of philosophy has become more difficult in a world where the purported need for professionalization leads graduate students to early specialization. In my own work, I have tried to avoid it, but it is to the reader to decide whether this enabled me to access German philosophy in a way that renders at least some justice to its astonishing wealth.

I finish by mentioning that this English version, besides correcting some errors, offers three differences with regard to the German original. The original thirteenth chapter has been divided into two, because one of the two anonymous reviewers rightly suggested that Heidegger belongs in a different philosophical league from Gehlen or Schmitt. While Heidegger doubtless was a National Socialist philosopher, and indeed the most talented of them, he was far more than that, and it is unfortunate that in the last decade the discussion of Heidegger's political entanglements has supplanted the analysis of his theories, which in the US had for many decades been studied on their own. Second, in the Heidegger chapter I added a paragraph on Kierkegaard. The latter does not belong in a history of German philosophy in his own right, but it is useful to refer to him when one wants to understand Heidegger, keeping in mind that I also mentioned Descartes and Spinoza in the chapter on Leibniz. Finally, in the penultimate chapter I name the main figures who emigrated from Germany in her darkest time.

I do not want to end this preface without thanking Steven Rendall, who has now translated my fourth book into English, for his excellent work and the smooth cooperation on the intricate issue of rendering some philosophical German terms.

A Short History
of German Philosophy

Does German Philosophy Have a History? And Has There Ever Been a "German Spirit"?

Does German philosophy have a history? The question seems absurd, because every child knows that the Germans are the people of poets and thinkers, or at least they once were. German philosophy is no less famous worldwide than German music and poetry. Yet it is not at all easy to answer the question in the affirmative. There have undoubtedly been many famous German-speaking philosophers, but that does not imply that there is a history of them that can recounted in a meaningful way. There are, after all, many philosophers whose names begin with a "P," but a history of philosophers whose names begin with P does not strike us as a particularly meaningful project. Nor is it hard to see why: an intellectual connection is lacking. The history of an individual can be recounted to the extent that one is aware of constants and coherent developments in his life, and a history of several people can be recounted to the extent that they are connected by a common topic. A history of ancient Platonism from Plato to Proclus is the history of people and institutions characterized by a special relationship to Plato and on that account distinguishable from other people and institutions. But is there something—for instance a method or a theme—that is common to all German philosophers, and only to them? Was the development of German philosophy at least a self-contained process governed by its own laws?

To begin with the last question: the answer is clearly "no." Anyone seeking meaning and coherence, anyone seeking truth in the history of philosophy, must consider the history of European philosophy, at least, as a unified whole. Schelling—who concluded the lectures he delivered in Munich in 1827, "On the History of Modern Philosophy," with a lecture entitled "On National Differences in Philosophy"—sees in religious seriousness and *apriorism* something that distinguishes German philosophy from the two most important neighboring philosophies, the French and the English. However, he emphasizes that "the truly universal philosophy cannot possibly be the property of a single nation, and so long as any philosophy does not go beyond the borders of a single people, one can be safe in assuming that it is not yet the true philosophy." When the French philosopher Victor Cousin, who had made Hegel and Schelling known in France, was accused by patriotic countrymen of bringing the enemy into his homeland, he rightly replied that in philosophy there is no homeland other than truth. In fact, Nicholas of Cusa cannot be understood without the Catalan Ramon Llull, Leibniz without the French philosopher Descartes and the Dutch philosopher Spinoza, or Kant without the Scotsman Hume and the French-speaking Swiss Rousseau; and for all three of them, ancient philosophy was, in different ways, a point of reference for their own thinking. Indeed, for the Christian philosophy of the Middle Ages the influences of Islamic and Jewish thought were also important. For example, Meister Eckhart, like Thomas Aquinas, frequently grappled with Maimonides and Averroes, and also with the Persian Avicenna—and he did so more often than most philosophers today debate thinkers from other cultural groups in our own globalized world. In short, the extraction of a separate history of German philosophy underestimates the real referential relationships in the world republic of thought, and it therefore seems as wrong-headed as a history of German mathematics, which obviously exists only as a dependent part of world mathematics. It is equally difficult to find traits that are common only to German philosophers, or at least to all of them. To be sure, almost the whole of German philosophy in the eighteenth century was determined by the reception, or at least by the conscious criticism, of the decisive ideas of the Enlightenment. But as its best modern historian, Jonathan Israel, has shown, the Enlightenment was a thoroughly European phenomenon. Not only were its ideas found in most Western European countries, but the reception-history relationships, the real intellectual-history configurations, transcended national borders. And, conversely, individual German philosophers stood far apart from one another—what connects Kant and Nietzsche, for example? Would it not be much more natural to relate both of them to Hume than to each other?

Thus the suspicion arises that "German philosophy" is an artificial construct that owes its existence to nothing other than the need of the German nation and the German nation-state to create an intellectually ambitious identity. It can hardly be an accident that in the first half of the nineteenth century books with titles like *Deutscher Sinn und Witz* (German thought and wit, 1828) and *Geist deutscher Klassiker* (The spirit of the German classics, 1850) were still rare, but became more common in the second half of the century in connection with the unification of Germany (*Deutscher Geist und deutsches Schwert* (The German spirit and the German sword, 1866); *Deutscher Geist und deutsche Art im Elsass* (The German spirit and German ways in Alsace, 1872); *Deutsches Herz und deutscher Geist* (The German heart and the German spirit, 1884), and downright proliferated in the first half of the twentieth century. And writings that make use of the "German spirit" are not limited to books of the kind that one can today only handle gingerly with forceps, such as that of Arthur Trebitsch, the well-known anti-Semite of Jewish descent who supported Hitler and was admired by him, *Deutscher Geist—oder Judentum: der Weg der Befreiung* (The German spirit—or Jewry: The path to deliverance, 1919). First-rate scholars such as Ernst Troeltsch, as edited by Hans Baron, and Ernst Robert Curtius wrote on the German spirit.

The fact that in the meantime people have ceased to talk about the German spirit cannot be attributed to the catastrophe of National Socialism alone. After the war, an effort was still made to grasp the German spirit; its most important document is Thomas Mann's novel *Doktor Faustus. Das Leben des deutschen Tonsetzers Adrian Leverkühn, erzählt von einem Freunde* (Doctor Faustus: The life of the German composer Adrian Leverkühn, told by a friend, 1947). Today, such an effort no longer seems in accord with the self-conception of an age that is forming supranational units such as the European Union and whose essence is globalization. And yet this epochal change means only that it has become absurd to talk about *current* German philosophy as an independent entity that is more than a number of objects related only externally. It does not mean that this also holds for the past. Precisely because the German spirit, if it ever existed, is part of the past, we can now examine with greater distance and objectivity the question as to what it was. An intellectual historian who studies the various European cultures since the end of the Middle Ages can scarcely avoid the impression that certain ways of questioning and approaching the world are more strongly developed in some European cultures than in others. To be sure, in every culture there are always exceptions that stand closer to the mainstream of another culture than to its own, but that does not change the fact that in most cultures there is something like a mainstream worldview that often deviates from those of other cultures. This is rapidly changing in the age of the Internet, in which one communicates with people in other continents more quickly and more often than with one's own next-door neighbors.

In an oral culture, however, all direct, intellectually fruitful interactions take place with people in one's physical proximity, and this also holds for the majority of such interactions after the rise of writing, even down into the twentieth century. To be sure, books from other cultures and correspondence with scholars from other lands played an important role in the Middle Ages and the early modern period, but they were fewer in number than interactions with members of same culture. Indeed, it is obvious that the course of modern history was in no way determined by a steady increase in intellectual globalization. The advances in systems of communication and transport that characterize the modern age were accompanied by the loss of Latin, the common language used for academic purposes in the Middle Ages and the early modern period. Thanks to the emergence of English as a new common language for academic purposes, the present is in many respects closer to the Middle Ages than to the nineteenth century. We must not forget that Hume did not know German, nor Kant English; even in the 1820s, very few British intellectuals could read German. Until the eighteenth century, French was the modern *lingua franca* for educated Europe, though it was not as dominant as Latin had been in the Middle Ages. But Edward Gibbon still wrote his first book in French; Hume persuaded him to compose his *magnum opus* in English, predicting that it would have a significant future after the British victory in the Seven Years' War. It is *a priori* probable that language barriers, deliberately strengthened by the rise of the nation as the primary factor in identity, produced national cultures in the era of nation-states. This is all the more relevant to the history of philosophy, because philosophy is connected in complex ways with culture as a whole, not least because a clarification of the ultimate goals of both individuals and the collective takes place within its framework. Hence there is much to be said for the working hypothesis that although the German philosophy of the Enlightenment shares common traits with European philosophy of the period, it acquired a specific configuration that distinguishes it, beyond the simple use of the German language, from that of neighboring countries. This hypothesis is rendered all the more plausible by the fact that almost all the hegemonic German intellectuals came from a religious denomination that hardly existed in the most heavily populated European states: Lutheranism, which shaped the German spirit more than any other factor. The Lutheranism in which they were brought up is also one of the traits shared by Kant and Nietzsche. In addition, the transition from one thinker to the other took place quickly; and the only mediating figure required for it was Schopenhauer, another German. (Because of the enormous importance of Lutheranism for the formation of the German spirit I considered for a time bringing in Søren Kierkegaard, who was often in Berlin and quoted Shakespeare, for example, in German. But I decided against doing so because Kierkegaard wrote nothing in German and cannot be understood by drawing on Kant and Hegel alone, without knowledge of his specifically Danish environment).

Thus the objective of this book has been outlined. My goal is to provide a brief survey of German philosophy—a sort of aerial view, as it were—and thereby to bring out peculiarities that distinguish this philosophy from those of other European nations. We will see that *reflection on the concept of Geist (spirit) is a crucial part of the German spirit*. Despite all the changes in German philosophy, plausible lines of development will be made clear; without them, a history really cannot be written. The audience to which this book is addressed is not primarily composed of professional philosophers, but rather of educated general readers—it is intended to be of interest, for example, to mathematicians and lawyers, and therefore it occasionally touches on their disciplines. But I have foregone footnotes and cited no secondary literature, even though I owe much to it. I have often modernized spellings in quotations, most of which can easily be found on the Internet. In citing posthumously published texts, I give the usual titles, even if they date from a later time. Here we are concerned with the main lines, not with scholarly details; I hope the reader will be encouraged to read the classics of German philosophy, rather than spend too much time on another book of secondary literature. Heinz Schlaffer's *Die kurze Geschichte der deutschen Literatur* (A short history of German literature) provided me with a model, and of course I had constantly in mind Heinrich Heine's incomparably astute work *Zur Geschichte der Religion und Philosophie in Deutschland* (*On the History of Religion and Philosophy in Germany*). The influence on my first chapter of Hagen Schulze's brilliant historical essay "Gibt es überhaupt eine deutsche Geschichte?" is obvious. My book does not presuppose an extensive knowledge of philosophy and deliberately avoids presenting complex technical arguments. Since philosophy inevitably consists partly, but not wholly, of such arguments, this book is more a history of ideas than a history of philosophy; I am concerned especially with the historical changes in consciousness that are triggered by philosophy and/or conceptualized by it. Thus this book falls into the domain of German studies, understood as the general study of German culture and not solely of German literature. I repeatedly point to other achievements of German culture, particularly in the literature and the human sciences, that differ from the achievements of other cultures and that can easily be related to German philosophy. I am no less interested in interconnections between the history of German philosophy and political history. The religious presuppositions of the German spirit play a central role as well—I seek to understand the path that leads from German mysticism to the Reformation, the transformation of Lutheranism into classical German philosophy, and the de-Christianization of Germany in the nineteenth century.

The present book may be useful also to those who want to understand what specific role German culture played in the context of the modern age in Western Europe. This was one of the two criteria of selection that determined this short overview. But what was the initial body of material from which I made the choice of those works that might best shed light on the special path taken by German philosophy? What complicates this seemingly simple question is the fact that Germany was politically unified only in the second half of the nineteenth century, and that even today states exist outside the German Federal Republic that are wholly or partly German-speaking. Language, in view of what was previously said about it as a connecting link, seems to me the most meaningful criterion of definition. This means, first, that Austrian but also Hungarian philosophers writing in German, such as György Lukács, should be counted as part of German philosophy; and second, that philosophers who wrote only in Latin, even though they lived in territories that are now part of modern Germany or were in their time part of the Holy Roman Empire of the German Nation, should be excluded. From this it follows that the overwhelming majority of medieval philosophers from Germany do not belong to German philosophy in the sense defined here. In fact, they neither differed sufficiently from other medieval philosophers to constitute, through their ideas, a distinct subgroup, nor did they have an important influence on classical German philosophy. Meister Eckhart, the first creator of a German philosophical language, is the central exception to this rule. Thus, for the most part, German philosophy in the sense we have given the term here extends from 1720 to 2000; I concentrate on the especially innovative period between 1770 and 1930. However, I also mention works not written in German by thinkers who wrote primarily in German but who occasionally still used either the old language of Latin for academic purposes (Latin continued in use for formal academic occasions down to the nineteenth century), the European cultural language of French, or the new academic language, English. Neither Kant's Latin works, nor Marx's *Misère de la philosophie*, nor Hans Jonas's *The Phenomenon of Life* can be left out of a history of German philosophy. Qualifying works written in Latin were a requirement of the German university; despite his exile in France, Belgium, and Great Britain, and the surrender of his Prussian nationality, Marx remained rooted in German culture, on which he exercised an enduring influence. Jonas helped translate his aforementioned book into German, and ultimately wrote his last great work in his native language. I have even discussed here two philosophers who wrote in German only occasionally. One is Leibniz, who wrote most of his works in Latin or French (for an academic and a nonscholarly but educated audience, respectively). His thought represents a starting point for Kant's philosophy, and indeed without Wolff's creation of a highly sophisticated German technical language for philosophy, German philosophy in the linguistic sense defined here would not exist at all; Wolff, however, was inspired by, among other people, Leibniz. In addition, I could not envisage ignoring Nicholas of Cusa.

It might be replied that the problem disappears if a territorial or ethnic criterion is substituted for a linguistic one. No one doubts that Nicholas of Cusa and Leibniz were born and grew up in the territory of the Holy Roman Empire, or that German was their native language. But apart from the fact that Kant never set foot on the territory of the Holy Roman Empire, to which Prussia proper did not belong, it can also be objected against such a criterion that it creates artificial boundaries: so long as there is a common language for academic purposes that transcends state borders, any drawing of boundaries in accord with political structures is rather arbitrary. The assumption that there is something that binds German philosophers together and that this is what we have in mind when we make use of the concept of a German spirit, is valid from the outset only if a causal mechanism links the representatives of this spirit, and that mechanism is and remains the especially intensive reception that is made possible by language—and in fact, for philosophy, by the language used for academic purposes, rather than by the native language. Not peoples, but individuals and their attributes (in fact often socially shared) are ontologically prior. Only on the basis of an increase in socially shared attributes such as a common language, religion, and political rule can something like a people be formed—or in the event of their decline, be dissolved.

A history of Germany cannot begin with the unification of Germany in 1871; the widespread desire for a common state was an outgrowth of the strong German national consciousness that had developed since 1800. This consciousness was partly engendered by developments in neighboring countries, and partly expressed the feeling that, since about 1760, German-speaking culture had taken a path that distinguished it from other European cultures. This new path did not emerge as the result of a return to earlier periods in German history; a comprehensive interest in the German Middle Ages or even in early Germanic history did not develop until the nineteenth century. Goethe knew Greek, Latin, Italian, French, and English literature incomparably better than he knew Middle High German literature; indeed, despite his enormous gift for languages, he did not take the trouble to learn to read Middle High German. To put the point provocatively, one can say that the German spirit did not exist before 1750, even if it rested on earlier developments, and especially on Lutheranism. But even if Lutheranism combined the religious with the national in a way that was unknown to the Middle Ages, it was first of all a religious movement and only secondarily a national one. The dating of the German spirit proposed here is also valid for the external perspective: only since the early nineteenth century (Madame de Staël's famous book on Germany was published in 1813) did Europe begin to take a specific interest in German culture, and not just in the German nation as the traditional bearer of the Holy Roman Empire, that august relic from the Middle Ages. It was, among other things, that special and honorable role that made Germany's rise to the status of a modern nation-state like France, Spain, or England so difficult. Until the collapse of the Empire, Germany was politically both more and less than the other great European states. The Empire's Christian-universalist project, which we citizens of the European Union now look back upon with more respect than did the age of nation-states, guaranteed that Germany would be more deeply entangled in the past and at the same time that its thought would be more utopian than that of France or England, for example.

If from our perspective at the beginning of the twenty-first century, when the political and cultural focus of world development seems to be turning away from Europe after two and a half millennia, we look back on the last thousand years, we can say (albeit over-simplifying to a considerable degree) that of the great European nations, Germany was the last that exercised a certain intellectual hegemony. In the High Middle Ages, Italy and France were Europe's leading cultures; in the sixteenth century, Spain was the foremost power, in the seventeenth primacy passed to France, which had to yield it to the United Kingdom in the eighteenth. (In the seventeenth century, the Netherlands played an important secondary role.) The writers in other European nations who are considered the greatest in their respective national literatures come, like Dante, from the Middle Ages, or like Camões, Shakespeare, and Cervantes, from the early modern period. By contrast, in the sixteenth century, drama in Germany did not rise above the level of Hans Sachs, and Germany produced its first literary masterpieces only around 1800. (Russia was the only major European country to follow even later.) The history of German culture is thus the history of the most belated Western European culture, at least in the areas of literature and philosophy—in the plastic arts, first-rate work was already done by Tilman Riemenschneider and Albrecht Dürer around 1500, and in the seventeenth and early eighteenth centuries Heinrich Schütz and Johann Sebastian Bach won international recognition for German music. The simultaneity of brilliant literary and philosophical achievements is one of the reasons for the special attraction of classical German philosophy. The latter took up questions raised by modern science and the Enlightenment, as did other European philosophies of the time, but it developed at the same time as a poetry of original greatness was forming, a poetry of a kind that hardly still existed in neighboring Western countries. The well-known view mentioned above, to the effect that Germans are the people of poets and thinkers, was first shaped in the nineteenth century to mark the high level of culture among Germans in general; but it can also be understood as indicating a connection between philosophical and poetic development so close that it had before this existed only in Greece. It is exemplified by the youthful friendship of Hegel, Schelling, and Hölderlin.

But the true reason why it makes sense to produce a new account of the history of German philosophy at the beginning of a century that will no longer be a European one is the extraordinary quality of this philosophical tradition that is surpassed only by that of the Greeks. This is a massive value judgment, and the reader should be forewarned: he will find much in this book—which is half essay, half history—that deliberately interprets German philosophy in light of its culmination in German idealism. Inevitably, this decision is shaped by its author's own philosophy. Every historian has to select, and my second criterion of selection is in fact the *quality* of a philosophy. I make no attempt at completeness here; I concentrate on the greatest thinkers and ignore academic philosophers who were influential only in their own time. What Horace said about poets—that neither humans nor gods allow them to be mediocre—holds to an even greater degree for philosophers. In addition, only the German classical philosophers shaped a German culture that endured over generations. Here we will be dealing solely with those thinkers who achieved truly important insights or at least threw light on peculiarities of German culture. These are the philosophers without whom the development of that culture cannot plausibly be explained. But in what does the importance of a philosopher consist? Philosophy is concerned with truth, and so, quite logically, we assign high rank to a philosopher when he or she has recognized certain truths for the first time. Philosophy is however such a complex enterprise, and its truth so many-layered, that we also have to recognize as important a philosopher who had the courage to pursue, all the way to the end, an idea that later turned out to be false. Working out phenomena, the ability to conceptualize one's own time, reflections on the foundations of philosophical claims to validity, subtleness in the construction of concepts, precision in the analysis of arguments, an eye for the essential in the results of scientific[1] research, the construction of bridges between different spheres of reality, and the writing of dense, sometimes also literarily brilliant texts are all philosophical virtues that only seldom appear combined in a single individual. Fairness also requires us sometimes to acknowledge the greatness of two thinkers who are diametrically opposed in method and content.

But aren't value judgments inevitably subjective? There is a point of view that says that they are, and this viewpoint is itself a philosophical position that was formed only belatedly. At least by the end of this book the reader will know how it was arrived at and why it is not self-evident. But if the reader wants to know what drives the author of this book, then it must be admitted that

---

[1] The English terms "science" and "scientific" are used to translate German *Wissenschaft* and *wissenschaftlich*, respectively. As Joel Weinsheimer and Donald G. Marshall note in the preface to their translation of Gadamer's *Truth and and Method*, the German terms suggest "thorough, comprehensive, and systematic knowledge of something on a self-consciously rational basis." This contrasts with the more limited English meanings of "science" and "scientific," which should here be understood in the special German sense. —Trans.

my motive is personal. I was born and grew up in Italy, learned German as a foreign language, and a large part of my youth, in which I benefited from a Lutheran training in religion, was spent enthusiastically appropriating German language, literature, philosophy, and human sciences. Having in the meantime become an American married to a Korean, for more than a decade I have been living and teaching at the leading Catholic university in the United States. My perspective on Germany is no longer an internal one, but rather that of a foreigner who wants to understand two things: what factors helped German philosophy rise to be one of the two most fascinating in human history, and how, despite this philosophical tradition, the moral and political catastrophe of 1933–1945 could happen.

This book has benefited enormously from critical readings by my father, Johannes Hösle, and by my friends Karl Ameriks, Roland Galle, and especially Carsten Dutt, during the time they spent at the Notre Dame Institute for Advanced Study; I wish here to offer them my hearty thanks.

৯ 2 ৯

The Birth of God in the Soul: The Beginnings of German-language Philosophizing in the Middle Ages in the Work of Meister Eckhart and Nicholas of Cusa's Consummation and Demolition of Medieval Thought

The first histories of German philosophy began with Lessing (Arnold Ruge's *Geschichte der deutschen Poesie und Philosophie seit Lessing*, 1847 [History of German poetry and philosophy since Lessing]) or with Leibniz (Eduard Zeller's *Geschichte der deutschen Philosophie seit Leibniz*, 1873 [History of German philosophy since Leibniz]). It is true that in the introduction to Zeller's book the German philosophy of the Middle Ages and early modern period is mentioned, but only in a cursory way. Conversely, most histories of medieval philosophy have little to say about German philosophy. The dominant view has always been that the intellectual centers of medieval philosophy were Paris and Oxford, and that from a philosophical point of view, Germany was a mere province. It had nothing to compare with the famous French cathedral schools of the twelfth century, and a glance at the history of European universities suffices to make clear how late Germany was in establishing its own exemplars of this, the most important institution of higher learning that the Middle Ages produced. The oldest European university, in Bologna, was founded in the late eleventh century; in the twelfth century Paris and Oxford followed, and in the early thirteenth century Cambridge, Salamanca, Montpellier, Padua, Toulouse, Orléans, and others (some of these institutions had only one faculty). A small country like Portugal got its first university in 1290. In Central Europe, by contrast, the first universities were not founded until the fourteenth century: in 1348 in Prague, 1364 in Cracow, 1365 in Vienna, and 1386 in Heidelberg. Everywhere, the language of instruction was Latin, and therefore Germans were able to study abroad long before universities were founded in the German Kingdom of the Empire. But that does not alter the fact that from a scientific point of view, Germany was on the periphery of Europe until the fourteenth century.

Philosophy is not bound to the institution of the university: In the Middle Ages, before universities emerged, it was possible to do concentrated study at monastery and cathedral schools, and sometimes also at princely courts. Indeed, a few of the most important modern German philosophers, such as Leibniz, Schopenhauer, and Nietzsche, were not professional teachers of philosophy at universities, and the same goes for the most original German philosopher of the Middle Ages, Nicholas of Cusa. But contact with an institution such as a university no doubt abetted efforts to achieve universality. Therefore it is not surprising that the number of important philosophers active in medieval Germany is small—only Albertus Magnus, Meister Eckhart, and Nicholas of Cusa achieved the status of classics. In recent decades, however, a deepened interest in less well-known German philosophers of the Middle Ages has developed and found expression in the publication, by Kurt Flasch and Loris Sturlese, of a separate corpus of the works of German medieval philosophers. We owe to Sturlese a learned book published in 1993, *Die deutsche Philosophie im Mittelalter*, which covers the period between 748 and 1280. Sturlese sees his approach as "regional history of philosophy," and in fact he discusses with great erudition most of the figures who dealt with philosophical questions on the territory of what today is Germany.

But does this really prove that there was a German philosophy during the designated period in the Middle Ages? Aren't we looking rather at medieval philosophy *in* Germany—*in Germaniae partibus*, as Gilbert of Poitiers once put it? The difference goes back to an issue discussed in the first chapter. Of course, an author can draw boundary lines wherever he wishes; thus one could write a history of philosophy from 807 to 1305 between the Greenwich meridian and the circle of longitude 9.5° east. But one cannot assert that such a delimitation is determined by objectively relevant differences, that is, that it represents a natural classification. Certainly, philosophizing took place on German soil, and Albertus Magnus (c. 1200–1280) can with some legitimacy claim to be among the most important thinkers of the High Middle Ages—along with Anselm of Aosta or of Bec or of Canterbury, Thomas Aquinas, and Bonaventura. In the Middle Ages he was probably the most revered thinker from Germany (he was sometimes called "Albertus Teutonicus" [Albert the German]), as both his byname, "the Great," and the many legends that gathered around him prove. But what is specifically German in his philosophy? Hardly the language in which he writes; it is exclusively Latin. And although he spent most of his life in Germany, he studied in Padua, where he entered the Dominican order in 1223, and he lived and taught in Paris from 1243 to 1248. It is true that his thought, and especially his doctrine of reason as the divine element in humans, influenced a series of German Dominicans, such as his pupil Ulrich of Straßburg, and also Dietrich von Freiberg, Meister Eckhart, and Berthold von Moosburg—but his most influential student by far is Thomas Aquinas, an "Italian" who studied with him in Paris and Cologne. To be sure, with the establishment of the Dominicans' *Studium generale* in Cologne in 1248, he created an institution from which the University of Cologne was able to proceed in 1388; and the series of lectures on Aristotle he gave for a decade in Cologne (beginning in 1250) did indeed permanently change the history of philosophy in the Middle Ages. After Albert, theology had to cope with a conception of philosophy and science that was independent of theological categories; and in fact Albert's own descriptions of the natural world, of minerals, plants, and animals, were important and admired in the Middle Ages. But already in 1259, a commission charged with reforming the Dominicans' program of studies in Valenciennes had admitted a few newly discovered philosophical texts to the training curricula of theologians. Among the members of this commission were, in addition to Albert, Thomas

Aquinas, and Pierre de Tarentaise (later Pope Innocent V); it was international. That is the decisive point: the order to which Albert belonged was international, despite its division into provinces; the university system of his time was international; and the language of philosophy was international. Earlier, I made a point of mentioning all three of the places with which Anselm's name is associated; one lies in what is now Italy, one in France, and one in England. Anselm was a European—like Alcuin, who was born in northern England, and Eriugena, who was born in Ireland, both of whom made their careers on the continent under the Carolingians—and much the same can be said about Albertus Magnus. He therefore does not yet fall under the concept of German (that is, German-language) philosophy used here, but is instead a highpoint in its prehistory.

The first thinker to whom we owe philosophical texts in German is the Benedictine Notker Labeo (c. 950–1022), who was the director of the monastery school in St. Gallen. He was not himself an original philosopher, but he translated Aristotle (from the Latin) and Boethius into Old High German, in the process helping to standardize its spelling. We recognize in his work the first steps toward a German language for academic purposes, even though Notker's was a language that capriciously mixed Latin and Old High German. Early on we find works of popular science in Middle High German—around 1190, the "Lucidarius" (Donor of Light), a work in prose that disseminated knowledge of theology and the natural sciences. Mechthild of Magdeburg (c. 1207–1282) wrote a work in the vernacular that describes mystical experiences, " Ein vliessende lieht miner gotheit" (usually translated "The Flowing Light of the Godhead," it is extant only in a High German translation from the Low German original). But the first writer to express *his own* philosophical ideas in the vernacular was the Dominican Meister Eckhart (c. 1260–1327/28). For this reason, and also for two others, it is in my opinion still meaningful to consider him the first German philosopher. First, some of his ideas uncannily anticipate ideas that appear in the philosophy of religion in later German tradition and that considerably deviate from the Christian mainstream, as his contemporaries already sensed: toward the end of his life an inquisitorial trial was instituted against him, first in Cologne, and then, after he had appealed to the Apostolic See, in Avignon;

in 1329 seventeen of his theses ended up being posthumously condemned as heretical, and eleven were declared suspicious in John XXII's bull *In agro dominico*. Apparently people saw similarities between his teaching and that of the Brethren and Sisters of the Free Spirit, who were said to have freed themselves from the dogmas and moral norms of the Church in the name of freedom of the spirit; in 1310, the Beguine Marguerite Porete, the author of a mystical treatise in Old French, was burned at the stake. Second, although Meister Eckhart did not significantly influence the development of German idealism, we know that the young Hegel excerpted passages from Eckhart's writings and from Tauler's. In 1823/24 Franz von Baader read Eckhart out loud to Hegel, and the latter is supposed to have reacted with admiration: "There we have it, what we want." Hegel quoted Eckhart in his lectures on the philosophy of religion, and as early as 1864 Joseph Bach celebrated Eckhart as the "father of German speculation." In 1868, the Hegelian Adolf Lasson devoted another study to Eckhart. An essential relationship with Eckhart thus began to make itself felt quite early in the history of classical German philosophy.

The use of the vernacular for philosophical purposes did not occur first in Germany. Around 1274 the lay scholar Ramon Llull wrote in Catalan, and in the first two centuries of the fourteenth century Dante composed his *Convivio* (*Banquet*)—and, of course, his masterwork, the *Divina Commedia* (*Divine Comedy*), certain passages of which are a philosophical didactic poem—in Italian. Unlike Llull, Dante and Eckhart were also completely fluent in Latin. Since Eckhart, unlike Dante, was a trained theologian (he took a Master's degree in Paris in 1302 and twice taught there), he wrote a large number of his works in Latin, but also many others in German—mainly sermons, a large number of them delivered in nunneries, but also a few treatises. *Die rede der underscheidunge* (*The Counsels on Discernment*), which he wrote in Erfurt at the end of the thirteenth century, contains ethical teachings that Eckhart, in his capacity as the vicar of his order's province of Thüringen, conveyed to his brethren in German. This he did contrary to custom and despite the fact that they could certainly understand Latin. More important theoretically is *Daz buoch der goetlichen troestunge* (*The Book of Divine Consolation*), presumably a late writing that together with the sermon "Von dem edeln menschen" ("The Nobleman") composes the *Liber benedictus* (*Benedictus*). At its end Eckhart explicitly justifies the use of the vernacular: only in the vernacular can one reach the uneducated. Whether the work "Von abgescheidenheit" ("On Detachment") was written by Eckhart himself or only inspired by him, is a matter of debate; it is not mentioned in the papal bull.

What is it, then, that is innovative in Eckhart's philosophy, beyond his creation of a German philosophical vocabulary? Simplifying somewhat, we can say that *it combines a rationalistic system with new interest in an unmediated relationship to God.* The notion that reason can and must legitimate belief was very widespread in the early Middle Ages (think of Eriugena and Anselm). However, Eckhart's Dominican brother Thomas Aquinas taught that the proper articles of belief escaped reason; his view soon became canonical for Catholicism and supported the Church's claim to power, which thereby no longer depended on its dogmas having a rational foundation. In contrast, Eckhart insisted that the enlightened could know what cruder minds could only believe (Sermon 39 Quint). In the fourteenth and fifteenth centuries this rationalistic position was found only rarely outside Germany—especially since the *via moderna* of Nominalism, which was flourishing in England, but also influenced Luther through Gabriel Biel, definitely abandoned the Platonism of the Church Fathers, and fostered an empiricist theory of knowledge. Eckhart shared an interest in a direct relationship to God with those called mystics, who are found everywhere in Christian Europe, and indeed also in other religions. He encountered mystically inclined thinkers in, among other places, the nunneries that he supervised pastorally. But in Eckhart's case, we can speak at best of philosophical mysticism, because he argues in a highly complex way and is in no way satisfied with evoking or describing religious experiences. As he sketched it out in the "Prologus generalis" ("General Prologue"), the basic structure of his never-completed masterpiece, *Opus tripartitum* (*Three-part Work*), makes the nature of his rationalism clear. The first of the three works was supposed to contain general theses, the second problems, and the third interpretations of the Old and New Testaments (together with a few sermons). What is crucial is that philosophical theses stand at the beginning, and that they guide the discussion of particular questions as well as the Bible interpretations. The Scriptures are to be interpreted *naturali ratione*, with natural reason, as Eckhart explains at the end of the previously mentioned prologue and also at the beginning of his "Expositio sancti evangelii secundum Johannem" (Interpretation of the Holy Gospel according to John). The Scriptures can be correctly understood only through the spirit; philosophy, on the other hand, is the measure of theology. The connection of the interpretation of Scripture to the spirit is an old strategy that goes back especially to Origen, a thinker highly esteemed by Eckhart; its goal is to avoid the repeatedly arising awkwardnesses of a literal interpretation. The doctrine of the four-fold meaning of Scripture (which sees allegorical, tropological [moral] and anagogic meanings alongside the literal meaning) was the foundation for the whole of medieval Bible interpretation. But Thomas Aquinas, among others, emphasized that the literal meaning of the Bible must always be the starting point. In contrast, Eckhart skips with sovereign aplomb over the literal meaning and reads his own metaphysical and ethical convictions into the text. A famous example is his splendid Sermon 86, in which Eckhart interprets the passage in Luke (10:38ff.) about Mary and Martha. Hardly any reader of the Gospels can seriously doubt that Jesus here prefers Mary over her bustling sister, and on a superficial acquaintance with Eckhart one might assume that he himself would laud Mary's pious listening to Jesus. But he manages not only to represent Martha as superior, but also to interpret Luke's Jesus as actually criticizing Mary and praising Martha.

Eckhart's conception of God is no less novel. In one of the four extant Parisian *Quaestiones disputatae* (*Work of Questions*), he examines the question, "Utrum in deo sit idem esse et intelligere" (Are being and knowing identical in God?), and defends the thesis that in God knowledge grounds being. Being is the vestibule, but reason is the temple of God, we read in Sermon 9. In this sense, in *The Book of Divine Consolation* God is called "the spirit of all spirits." This is (in a way that is not really plausible) connected with a negative theology according to which God stands over being, a theology that ultimately goes back to Plato and Neoplatonism. Therefore Eckhart insists that, at his center, God is a pure unity that transcends his Trinitarian structure. But the superordination of knowledge over being foreshadows the basic operation of idealism, even if Eckhart has in mind not humans, but God: God must think not only the world, but also himself, before he can be meaningfully described as existent. The creation of the world must not be understood as a one-time act but rather as on-going, since God is timeless. Man's real task is to attain unity with God, for the lowest point of man's soul is higher than the highest point of the heavens. Things are more valuable in the soul than in the world (Sermon 17). Through love for God, man can almost become God—we find this view expressed in several passages in the sermons that are condemned in the papal bull. Eckhart speaks of the birth of God, in which God gives birth and is born, and repeatedly suggests that God is dependent on men's subjective appropriation: "The eye in which I see God is the same eye in which God sees me" (Sermon 12). Of course, Eckhart accepts the doctrine of the Incarnation and Christ's role as a model; but he teaches, in a certain continuity with the Gospel according to John, that Christ's status as the son of God is attainable by every person. For God it is more valuable to be spiritually born in a good soul than to be physically born from the Virgin Mary (Sermon 22). Indeed, in the text "On Detachment," with reference to John 16:7, Christ's death is said to be useful because the apostles took too much pleasure in the bodily appearance of Christ; only his death made them receptive to the perfect bliss of the Holy Spirit. The inner appropriation of the spirit seems more important than the relationship to Christ. To be sure, it is still a long way to Hegel's philosophy of spirit, but it is fascinating that in his early theological writings Hegel also highlights the same passage in John and interprets it in an analogous way.

There can be no doubt as to the sincerity of Eckhart's intellectually very subtle religiousness. And we can doubt even less that a few of his statements that offended naïve beliefs are persuasively deduced from plausible propositions. What raises the *Book of Divine Consolation* so far above the usual representatives of the consolation genre is its comprehensive metaphysical perspective. The injunction to subject oneself to God and the rejection of speculation on contrafactual courses of the world remind us of Spinoza; but whereas the latter, like the Stoics, seeks to be freed from affects, Eckhart affirms the depths of pain as a path to God. One ought not wish to be rid of pain, but rather to accept it inwardly. If one's whole life and knowledge are in God and as God, then one can no longer be afflicted by either the creature—or by God. A person in whom God acts can no longer complain about harm, but only about the fact that he is still complaining. Prayers asking for something, such as health, are unseemly; the heroism of the pagans teaches us that natural virtue is already capable of self-sacrifice. A fortiori, someone who is God's son should not think of rewards. Indeed, since God has in a certain way willed my sins, I should not will that I had not committed them. With God, I must will not only my punishment (a thief who inwardly accepts his execution will be saved), but in some cases even my own damnation. This idea is incompatible with the notion that moral conduct strives for a reward, if not in this world, then in the next. Contrafactually, Eckhart admits the assumption that it is righteousness that has the sufferings of Hell as its consequence, and he firmly asserts that one must nonetheless be righteous (Sermon 6). Anyone who loves God because of the advantages connected with him loves him the way one loves a cow (Sermon 16 b). The idea of a radical love of God is one of the elements that in Kant ultimately led to the collapse of the two-thousand-year-old tradition of eudemonism. Other ethical ideas of Eckhart's also anticipate Kant— for instance, his notion that what counts is the will, not the external act. For Eckhart, what matters is an inward orientation toward God; Hell consists in its lack, not in fire and brimstone (Sermon 5 b). To be sure, in the twelfth century Abelard had already worked out an ethical intentionalism, but when Eckhart points to the divinity of the inner act, which cannot be comprehended by time or space, the modern reader inevitably thinks of Kant's conception of the noumenal ego. And Eckhart's association of autonomy and theonomy also points to Kant. The good man loves God, but since God loves in him, he loves himself precisely insofar as he renounces everything that is perishable. The disentanglement from everything creatural, the detachment and releasement (gelâzenheit) that he proclaims, is grounded in the monastic ideal of renouncing the world, though this does not exclude active commitment to one's neighbor, or indeed to utter strangers. However, the greatness of Eckhart's ethical thought should not lead us to overlook the fact that it lacks the extraordinary concreteness of Thomas Aquinas's comprehensive ethical system; there is nothing in Eckhart that corresponds to Thomas's doctrine of natural law. The elaboration of a concrete doctrine of norms and institutions on the basis of an ethics of autonomy was first achieved by Kant and German idealism.

The condemnation of Eckhart did not prevent the dissemination of his writings. On the one hand, his pupils Johannes Tauler (c. 1300–1361) and Heinrich Seuse (1295 or 1297–1366), who was even beatified in 1831, pursued Eckhart's ideas in a less radical vein, more edifying than philosophical. On the other hand, his personal fate inspired a Middle Dutch dialogue, probably written around 1340 and usually described as "antihierarchical," in which Eckhart converses with a layman and sharply criticizes the clergy's patronizing and persecution of simple people. It is not hard to discern here a sensibility that anticipates the Reformation, and in fact Luther admired Tauler. However, his favorite book from the age of German mysticism was the anonymous one he called the *Theologia deutsch*, also from the fourteenth century, which despite the presence of many an idea of Eckhart's, Tauler's, or Seuse's, is directed primarily against the Brethren and Sisters of the Holy Spirit, defends Christological orthodoxy, and vehemently rejects the subordination of faith to knowledge. In this turn against rationalism in the philosophy of religion, the book is as distant as possible from Eckhart, but it is in accord with Luther. The path from Luther to German idealism was to consist in a return to Eckhart's rationalism.

Discussing Nicholas of Cusa (1401–1464) between Eckhart and the Reformation is not really in accord with the principles I developed in the first chapter. None of his treatises and dialogues were composed in German, and only one of his almost 300 sermons was written down in (Moselle-Franconian) German (although some sermons drafted in Latin were delivered in German). Moreover, it can hardly be claimed that Nicholas had an enduring influence on later German philosophy—Lessing worked on a translation of one of his works, but Hegel did not know even his name. However, Nicholas himself was clearly influenced by Eckhart, whose genius he praised (even if he wanted Eckhart's works kept away from the general public, thinking them useful only for initiates) when Johannes Wenck reproached him for his proximity to Eckhart and pantheism. Moreover, the originality, the quality, and even the intellectual affinity of his philosophical theology with that of Hegel are so striking that it would be odd to ignore him in a history of German philosophy. Indeed, Nicholas was probably the most multitalented German of the Middle Ages—a philosophical theologian who could think at the highest level in the domains of law, mathematics, and the natural sciences, and whose legacy still finances a retirement home in his native town. On the one hand, he was among the very few people of his time who anticipated the modern age; on the other hand, he maintained a distance from the most important European movement of his period, humanism, even as he appropriated its achievements very early on, and in this we can glimpse something of what characterizes the special path followed by German philosophy. The Reformation was in part an antihumanist movement, and some of its concerns are clearly present in Nicholas, even if in the course of his career he became a cardinal, the prince-bishop of Brixen, and a counselor to the pope in the Curia. The fact that such a career was possible for a man of his intellectual openness, who showed an unmistakable preference for authors condemned as heretical or suspected of heresy, speaks for the intellectual condition of the Catholic Church in the fifteenth century. In post-Tridentine Catholicism we no longer find any comparably important intellectuals in high Church offices. For although the Council of Trent restored the Church's moral seriousness, which the Renaissance papacy had largely lost and which in his own time Nicholas had called for in vain in the Curia, it resulted in an intellectual narrowing and a scientific atrophy from which the Catholic intellectual world began to recover only with the Second Vatican Council.

Nicholas began his studies in Heidelberg, but he took his degree in canon law in Padua, and in Italy absorbed the spirit of the early Renaissance. He formed a lifelong friendship with Paolo dal Pozzo Toscanelli, the eminent astronomer and cartographer who encouraged Columbus to sail westward toward India. Benefitting from a humanistic education, he discovered, among other things, manuscripts of previously unknown comedies by Plautus. His studies in the history of law permitted him to declare that the Donation of Constantine was a forgery before Lorenzo Valla did the same. And he laid the foundation for his later career through activities at the Council of Basel, where he initially supported the conciliarists who set the council's authority over that of the pope; but in 1436 changed sides. His first work, *De concordantia catholica* (*On Catholic Concordance*), published in 1433, defended the conciliarist position: that the council could depose a pope who violated his duties. Nicholas also elaborated a philosophy of the state that justified rule largely on the basis of consensus. In this, he was strongly influenced by Marsilius of Padua, whom he never cites, however; for this most revolutionary medieval political philosopher had been excommunicated. But the maxim "Quod omnes tangit, ab omnibus approbari debet" (Whatever concerns all must be approved by all) was hardly new, having been first formulated in the canon law of twelfth-century Cologne. According to Nicholas, the pope did not have the right to install or depose a monarch without the consent of the people. The third book of the work provides detailed recommendations regarding the reform of the Empire, whose weaknesses it clearly recognizes. It argues for a strengthening of the central power, and contains the first formulation of the electoral system that was proposed by Jean-Charles de Borda in the eighteenth century and is named after him.

In 1437 the papist party sent Nicholas to Constantinople; he returned accompanied by the Byzantine emperor and the patriarch, who in view of the threat posed by the Ottomans agreed at the Council of Ferrara and Florence to a (short-lived) union with Rome. However, the journey produced more than just this significant diplomatic success; it was, or at least so he claims, on his way home that Nicholas conceived, in a moment of sudden intuition, the philosophical project to which he gave expression in his subsequent philosophical-theological works, from *De docta ignorantia* ("On Learned Ignorance," 1440) to the retrospective *De venatione sapientiae* ("On the Hunt for Wisdom," 1463). In what does the originality of his first theoretical work consist? It is striking, first of all, that Nicholas, unlike Thomas Aquinas, for instance, but very much like Ramon Llull, whom he had studied with great care, cites only a few authoritative sources (assuming a broad convergence between the Bible and pagan philosophy). He argues on the basis of reason, and thus pursues a rational theology, even in matters involving the specifically Christian dogmas of the Trinity and the Incarnation, which according to Aquinas cannot be grounded in reason. Nicholas tries to clarify the immanent trinity of God before the Creation by means of triadic groups of categories; and the Incarnation is also made comprehensible within a triadic scheme. Thus the structure of *De docta ignorantia* seems at first to be modeled on that of Aquinas's *Summa theologiae*: the third book of both works deals with Christ, whose central philosophical significance is for Nicholas beyond doubt. But in his first book Aquinas discusses God and the Creation, including the Fall, whereas the second presents general and particular ethical norms. Nicholas, who had hardly any interest in ethics, instead devotes his first book exclusively to God before the Creation, whom, following Anselm, he interprets as the absolute maximum. The second book deals with the universe, which he interprets as the contracted or limited maximum. Christ is introduced as the synthesis of the first two concepts, that is, as both absolute and limited maximum; the Church as the community established around Christ concludes the third book. God, the universe, and Christ and his church appear as three steps in an inherently coherent development. God is essentially the unified ground of the world, which with Christ returns to its origin. The Incarnation has as its primary task not vicarious satisfaction, but rather the completion of the structure of being.

As an image of the Trinitarian God, the universe gains a new dignity, and the result is the project of an *a priori*, theologically grounded natural philosophy. This project goes back to Plato's dialogue *Timaeus*, which enjoyed great popularity in the Christian West of the twelfth century. However, Nicholas develops on this basis not only a holistic natural philosophy, according to which the world in no way consists of independent particular substances, but also the most important medieval critique of the geocentric system. It was a philosophy that exercised an enduring influence on such fathers of modern cosmology as Giordano Bruno and Johannes Kepler, even though it was hardly based on empirical observations. Nicholas's insight into the principle of the relativity of movement destroyed the Aristotelian worldview, with its strict distinction between the sublunary and the stellar worlds, and the universe, as a result, lost both its boundaries and its hierarchical structure. The planets no longer move in perfect circles, the Earth is not a perfect sphere, the stars consist of the same elements as the Earth, and many of them are probably inhabited by rational beings. What is fascinating about Nicholas's critique of the Aristotelian worldview is that he bases his scheme on the Christian spirit: an infinite God is incompatible with the finite ancient cosmos. In truth, modern science is indebted not so much to a "secularization" of Christianity as to taking seriously what is specifically Christian, as against the antique, and especially against Aristotelianism—just as did Eckhart's ethical revolution, which took on new intensity in the modern period. However, it must be conceded that there were tensions between the new science and Christianity: if there are rational beings on other stars, the modern reader asks himself, what is the source of the special status of human nature, on which the argument for the Incarnation is based?

The title *De docta ignorantia* implies that our knowledge of God is limited, and in fact Nicholas began as the representative of an at least partially negative theology. Since there is no proportionality between the finite and the infinite, only learned ignorance of God is possible, in whom the greatest and the smallest coincide, because nothing is opposed to him. However, Nicholas proposes a new method of coming closer to God. One begins from finite mathematical figures, rises to infinite figures, and from there finally moves on to the infinite as such. In this connection, Nicholas anticipates ideas from both projective geometry and the set theory created by Georg Cantor, who recognized in Nicholas a forerunner of his defense of actual infinity. In his later works, however, Nicholas seems to defend a more optimistic view of the knowability of God. Thus, already in his second major theoretical work, *De coniecturis* ("On Surmises," c. 1442), we find an epistemological distinction between understanding (*ratio*) and reason (*intellectus*). This distinction goes back to Plato and the Neoplatonists, but it plays no role in the writings of Aquinas and most other medieval theologians. For Nicholas, reason is capable of achieving knowledge that is denied to the understanding, which is limited by the law of contradiction. In contrast, in God opposites coincide; indeed, God is beyond their coincidence. But Nicholas cannot explain how unity unfolds into multiplicity. *De coniecturis* describes a four-stage emanation inspired by Neoplatonism that moves from divine unity through spirit and soul to the sensory and physical world—a model that deviates from the triadic one that sees the universe returning to its origin via Christ. Nicholas plays with various systemic conceptions but is unwilling to commit himself to any one of them.

Of particular importance are the works *Idiota de sapientia, Idiota de mente*, and *Idiota de staticis experimentis* (The layman on wisdom, The layman on mind, and The layman on experiments done with weight-scales), which date from 1450. What is dramatically interesting in these dialogues is their representation of a layman as clearly superior to an orator and a philosopher, respectively, who stand for the humanistic tradition. In the last dialogue, the layman calls for an experimental science that is as quantitatively precise as possible, that would, for example, be able to predict the weather. Alchemy and astrology are depreciated. Nicholas thus anticipates the scientific revolution of the seventeenth century; and his holistic convictions do not prevent him from investigating concrete correlations between physical magnitudes. Of special importance is his praise of the human mind, which is now no longer understood as the unfolding of the divine unity, but rather as the latter's direct image; the mind is thus detached, discontinuous with the soul and the physical world. The divine mind wants to create itself again, as it were, in the human mind, and paradoxically, the human mind is precisely more perfect insofar as it is not too similar to God, because through that alone is a process of convergence with God made possible, in which the mind manifests its vitality. In this connection Nicholas develops a revolutionary philosophy of mathematics: the human mind creates mathematical structures. This constitutes a break with an almost two-thousand-year-old Platonic tradition, but it is compatible with the assumption of the preexistence of mathematical structures, insofar as human creativity merely imitates that of the divine mind. By creating numbers out of itself, the mind also finds what subsists timelessly in the divine mind. In his last work, *De apice theoriae* (On the summit of contemplation, 1464), Nicholas defends a far-reaching epistemological optimism: everything exists for the sake of the mind, but the mind itself exists in order to contemplate possibility-itself—that is the last of the many names of God that Nicholas seeks to introduce.

In 1453, after the fall of Constantinople, Nicholas wrote the interreligious dialogue *De pace fidei* ("On Peaceful Unity of Faith"), which more than three centuries later fascinated the author of *Nathan der Weise* (*Nathan the Wise*). Lessing, however, assumed that all three monotheistic religions were of equal value, a view that Nicholas was far from sharing. His anti-Judaism is evident (and influenced, unfortunately, a few of his decisions regarding church policies); and his *Cribratio Alchorani* (Sifting the Quran) of 1460/61 recognizes as positive in the Quran only what is also found in the Gospels. Nonetheless, this dialogue is important; it continues a long medieval tradition that goes back to Anselm and his pupil Gilbertus Crispinus and to which Abelard and Ramon Llull made the most important contributions. What is new in Nicholas's work is that it brings in a much larger number of representatives of religions. The conversation described takes place "in the heaven of understanding," under the guidance of the *logos*, Peter's and Paul's. This seems already to presuppose the truth of Christianity and deviates markedly from earlier interreligious dialogues. But here the *logos* is the reason presupposed by all. Nicholas seeks to ground a philosophical religion (superior to the many popular religions) by reflecting on reason and its presuppositions. For Nicholas, the unity of religion is compatible with a plurality of rites; sacraments, obviously, are devalued. Justification depends not on works but solely on faith—which must, however, find expression in works. Here Nicholas anticipates a crucial issue in the Reformation; a dissolution of Christianity into Platonism, as in the Florentine Neoplatonism of the late fifteenth century, is alien to him.

Whereas in *De genesi* (On Genesis, 1447) Nicholas rejects the chronological data in the Pentateuch as not binding, some of his theological arguments presuppose the historicity of the events reported in the Gospels, for instance, the Resurrection. We will see how in the late eighteenth century a new formulation of Christianity was attempted that no longer shares this presupposition. Paradoxically, it was precisely the Protestant Revolution that led to this critical result. But Hegel's idealism, which also emerged from this crisis, was to develop a metaphysics and natural philosophy that is surprisingly close to that of Nicholas, but replaces the third part of the system of *De docta ignorantia* with a general theory of the mind that goes still further than the conception of the mind in Nicholas's dialogues. Hegel also devoted one of his first works to the now truly moribund Empire. But before doing so he studied the historical development of Christianity with a thoroughness for which all the presuppositions were lacking in the fifteenth century.

The Change in the Philosophical Situation Brought about by the Reformation: Paracelsus's New Natural Philosophy and the "No" in Jakob Böhme's God

From a philosophical point of view (the only one that concerns us here) Martin Luther's Reformation was both an advance and a retreat. Throwing off the authority of the Catholic Church and of Scholastic philosophy allowed new free spaces to open. A few medieval thinkers had already taken advantage of them, but they were now generally available to every individual Christian. At the same time, however, this increase in autonomy could be justified only by binding every Christian directly to the divine word. Unmediated recourse to the Bible was objectively plausible, for if the Catholic Church traced its authority back to the God who became a man, while at the same time reserving for itself a monopoly on the interpretation of Christ's words, the circular nature of this grounding was only too obvious: Christ legitimates the Church, but the Church declares what Christ actually taught. It is rather astonishing that it was so long before the call for independent access to the word of God became historically potent. External factors were indispensable: on the one hand, the Church's loss of moral credibility as a result of the behavior of the Renaissance popes and bishops; on the other hand, the German princes' perception that the Reformation offered them an opportunity to throw off the emperor's dominion. Luther could prevail, or even survive, only because his sovereign supported him, and not for religious reasons alone.

In his great study *Die europäischen Revolutionen* (The European revolutions), Eugen Rosenstock-Huessy (1888–1973), one of the last German universal scholars in the humanities and social sciences, spoke of a "princely revolution" in connection with the Reformation. The formation of religiously autonomous small states with their own local universities (whereas the University of Paris had been a European university) and an officialdom devoted to the sovereign and enjoying great prestige was one of the most important results of the German Reformation. In the seventeenth century, as in the Middle Ages, England got along with only two universities, but this did not in the least hinder its rise to become the economically and politically most advanced nation in Europe, while Germany had about forty universities, despite its late adoption of the institution. Princes and professors/pastors/officials were the pillars of the new order, and while the princes disappeared in 1918, Germany is still basically, even in its Catholic areas, a professors-and-officials state such as exists nowhere else in the world. Although on most questions Lutheranism occupies a middle position between the Catholic Church and the Reformed denominations that freed themselves from medieval ideas much more decisively than Luther did, there is one issue on which Calvinism stands closer to Catholic doctrine than to Lutheranism, namely the right of resistance, to which both Catholicism and Calvinism cling. Luther, by contrast, radically rejects this right, and however much he believes he is authorized by Scripture to reject the right to resist (Romans 13), seen from the outside it is clear that this rejection was the price he had to pay for the protection of the princes. The peculiar combination of an emotional commitment to freedom of conscience with an insistence on subservience, even to unjust rule, long remained one of the distinguishing marks of Lutheranism in Germany. (Characteristically, a defense of the right to resistance—by corporative groups, not individuals—is found in the Calvinist Johannes Althusius (1563–1638), whose conception of a federal corporative state with subsidiarity deviates sharply from the thinking of

Jean Bodin, who justified French absolutism, and legitimated the Netherlands' battle for freedom).

But this half-autonomy did not characterize Lutheranism solely with respect to politics. Luther's masterful translation, which made the Scriptures freely accessible and raised the new High German language to the level of other European languages, at the same time shackled interpretation to the letter of the Bible. The old doctrine of the fourfold meaning of Scripture had led to far-fetched interpretations that no longer had anything to do with the text; that was now over. But at the same time the fourfold doctrine had allowed exegetes to further develop the tradition in the sincere belief that they were remaining true to its real meaning; and now that, too, was over. Or rather, it became significantly harder to continue in that tradition. It could not be wholly abandoned because, first of all, Scripture was needed to legitimate the new economic and social order, which differed even more radically than that of the Middle Ages from the order praised in the Sermon on the Mount; and second, because for more than two hundred years Lutheranism strove to avoid recognizing that between the Christologies of the Gospels (which deviate from one another) and that of the *Credo* there are enormous differences—Calvin himself had Michael Servetus burned at the stake because of his discovery that the doctrine of the Trinity had hardly any basis in the New Testament. In order to understand the true meaning of the Bible, it became necessary to devise new hermeneutic techniques that left behind those of the Middle Ages; the study of Hebrew and Greek now received a religious consecration, so to speak. The emergence of the methods of modern humanistic studies was decisively encouraged by Lutheranism, even if at the price of a repression of theology's philosophical validation. The latter affected Melanchthon less than it did Luther himself, for Luther had an unphilosophical mind, and was thus hardly a great theologian (and certainly no saint). But he had what people call "character," and, for better or for worse, through the creativity of his religious as well as his linguistic achievements he contributed more than almost anyone else to the separation of the German nation from the common European family. Because Luther did not collaborate in Calvin's and Zwingli's further innovations, German Protestantism (along with that in the Scandinavian countries) persisted in an intermediate position between the old and the new worlds of which the Romanic and the Anglo-American countries are the leading examples.

Certainly the appeal to the subjective certainty of faith helped people shake off heteronomous authorities and thus to acquire great personal integrity. But unfounded certainties do not become truths just because someone totally relies upon them. Indeed, the obsession with one's own justification could lead to a spiritual narrowness of the kind that characterized Lutheranism until the rise of Pietism. Luther's antihumanistic streak led to the view that he had kept alive for another two centuries the Middle Ages that the Renaissance had already vanquished; but this overlooks the fact that the fourteenth and fifteenth centuries were intellectually significantly more multifaceted than were the first two centuries of Lutheranism. Certainly Christian anti-Judaism, in its full abomination, goes back to the Middle Ages; but the higher clergy and the emperor had repeatedly tried to restrain it. Luther, on the other hand, expressed the *vox populi* directly, and gave—especially in "Von den Juden und ihren Lügen" ("On Jews and their Lies")—anti-Judaism a consecration that continued to be influential through its transformation into modern anti-Semitism from the end of the nineteenth century to 1945 (consider just Veit Harlan's film, *Jud Süß*). The belief held by most medieval theologians, that no non-Christian could be saved, is hardly tolerable, but then what can we say about the teaching of the Wittenberg professor Abraham Calov, who maintained that no Catholic, and not even a Reformed Christian, could be saved—indeed, that even Lutherans who, like Georg Calixt, did not follow him on the last issue, were to be damned as heretics? God's plan for salvation shrinks to the area around Wittenberg. The revolt against orthodox Lutheranism that, prepared by Pietism, began at the end of the eighteenth century and produced classical German philosophy, preserved one trait of Lutheranism: the unconditional will to sincerity and the refusal to profess things in which one no longer believed. And paradoxically, the lighter ballast of Scholastic tradition facilitated a new beginning in philosophy that was denied to Catholicism, which, although philosophically more interested, was controlled by the hierarchy.

In the sixteenth century a spiritualist tradition was already being established that was partly inspired by the Reformation, and partly broke with the latter's dogmas and hence was prosecuted by Lutheranism. Its main representatives were Hans Denck, Sebastian Franck, and Kaspar Schwenckfeld, for whom it was the spirit that was now crucial and no longer the Scriptures. (In Thomas Müntzer [1489–1525] this is connected with a revolt against corporative society and violent action on behalf of the peasants in the Peasant War, for which he paid with his life.) The natural philosopher Theophrastus Bombastus of Hohenheim, called Paracelsus (1493–1541), who around 1516 received a doctoral degree in medicine, probably from Ferrara, also belongs to this line of thought. He must be mentioned in this book because despite his many travels throughout the Mediterranean world, he not only wrote his numerous works in German (often only the titles are in Latin), but in 1527 even gave lectures in German at the faculty of medicine in Basel (which was one of the reasons he was expelled)—long before the legal philosopher Christian Thomasius (1655–1728), who at the end of the seventeenth century was the first successfully to introduce lectures in German at a university. The young Goethe read Paracelsus, and it is plausible that a few of Paracelsus's essential traits, along with traits of the skeptical magician Heinrich Cornelius Agrippa of Nettesheim (1486–1535), were incorporated into the character of Goethe's Faust. The symbolic figure of the German essence, Faust was inspired by Paracelsus's contemporary Dr. Johann Georg Faust, to whom Paracelsus was, however, vastly superior in intellect.

If we try to classify Paracelsus's philosophical-scientific ideas, we find that they belong, like most of the innovative ideas of the sixteenth century, to the time of fermentation between the collapse of Scholastic science and the emergence of the new science in the seventeenth century. The polemic against traditional medicine, especially the humoral pathology that derived from books rather than from direct experience, is conducted in a churlish manner reminiscent of Luther and with bombastic self-praise. He was responsible for significant individual discoveries, for example concerning the influence of external factors on health, and programmatic ideas, but Paracelsus by no means grounded his assertions through a precise experimental method (nor did he contribute to the mathematicizing and quantifying of the natural sciences). He did not yet distinguish astrology and magic from genuine science; and he claimed that the doctrine of signatures, to which Jakob Böhme also adhered, made it possible to infer the inner qualities of natural substances from their external appearance. Although the Renaissance worldview begins by grasping nature as a largely self-enclosed causal web, its holism is detrimental to the isolation of individual causal factors, without which scientific progress is not possible. Paracelsus's *Paragranum* teaches four pillars of medicine: philosophy, astronomy, alchemy, and *proprietas* (a kind of ethics of medicine). Elements pointing to the future are here interwoven with others that are unscientific by modern standards. Alongside an important call for founding medicine in chemistry and mineralogy, we find the idea that the human microcosm corresponds to the macrocosm, that is, that individual organs correspond, for instance, to the planets. In his reflections on natural philosophy Paracelsus assumes, in addition to the four classical elements, three principles (sulfur, mercury, and salt), which he interprets as an expression of the divine Trinity. (Joachim Jungius [1587–1657], one of the founders of modern scientific thinking in Germany, argued against both the four classical and the three alchemical principles.) According to Paracelsus, God manifests himself in the forces of nature, so that all sciences are particles of theology. Free will is not possible; even the villain can act only because God authorizes him to do so. The highest achievement is the abandonment of one's own will in God.

Paracelsus's religious ideas are especially fascinating. He was buried as a Catholic, but his criticism of the institutionalized Church—indeed, of all religious confessions—is severe. He believes in a Church in the Holy Spirit, which has no dwelling, rejects any forceful conversion as "the Devil's," teaches the salvation of all children, even those that have not been baptized, and praises, in an appendix to the early drafts of a commentary on Matthew, "the islands of naked people"—he thinks it would have been better if the European ships that came to these islands had sunk and left the pagans unconverted, because the natives will quickly forget Christ and only the knavery will remain. In his political ideas Paracelsus stood close to the radical wing of the spiritualists, whose exemplar was Thomas Müntzer. But in "De magnificis et superbis" (On the magnificent and the proud), in which he proposes that Paul's theory of political authority should be understood as applying only to his own time, he also warns expressly against rebellion, which can lead to significantly more evils than existed before. As a Christian ideal, however, Paracelsus advocates a far-reaching equality of estates and active intervention on behalf of the poor. Nobility is not established by God; rights to land are always lent only by the emperor; everyone has a duty to work; property without labor is theft; a father should bequeath to his children only work equipment. He rejects the death penalty; only defensive wars are morally permissible.

The honorary title of the first epoch-making German philosopher of the modern period belongs to Jakob Böhme (1575–1624), who was early on considered the *teutonicus philosophus* par excellence. To make clear German culture's relative backwardness and at the same time its special potential for religious philosophy, a glance at the neighboring countries is instructive: French philosophy shines in the late sixteenth century through the person of the highly cultured skeptical essayist Michel de Montaigne, and in the first half of the seventeenth century through René Descartes, who sought to provide an unshakeable foundation for metaphysics and science; in England, the statesman Francis Bacon developed the methodological bases of the modern empirical sciences. By contrast, his contemporary Böhme, who came from what was then the most stimulating German cultural area, Silesia, was a cobbler who had never studied and therefore could not write Latin, but who had experienced mystical visions and wanted to provide a deeper foundation for his traditional Lutheran piety (inspired by the Bible) through a philosophical account of the development of God, nature, and redemption through Christ. He might well be called, after the well-known naïve painter, the Henri Rousseau of philosophy—a naïve thinker who in fact read, in addition to the Bible, Paracelsus and other Renaissance spiritualists, yet articulated in an enormously expressive and creative language that was hardly influenced by the philosophical tradition his fascination with nature and his religious anxieties and hopes, producing a simultaneously confused and magnificent image of reality. Böhme's urge toward speculation drove him beyond the ecclesiastical Lutheranism that persecuted him pitilessly in Görlitz even after his death, although he considered himself a pious Lutheran and stood closer to the Middle Ages than to German idealism. His interpretation of the history of Creation in the *Mysterium Magnum* (Great mystery) is at bottom closer to the commentaries on the six-days' work produced in the Middle Ages than it is to Nicholas of Cusa's *De genesi*; his descriptions of the horrors of Hell, for instance in the sixth point of the *Sex puncta theosophica, oder von sechs Theosophischen Puncten hohe und tiefe Gründung* (*Sex puncta theosophica,* or high and deep foundation of six theosophic points; English title: *Six Theosophic Points*), make us think of Hieronymus Bosch transferred inwardly, so to speak. His Christology, too, is traditional, indeed, his veneration of Wisdom as the virginal-female side of God expresses elements of Catholic rather than Lutheran religiousness. Böhme's originality soon won him a group of admirers, and after his death his influence extended to the Netherlands, Scandinavia, and even England (to my knowledge, no other thinker was translated from German into English in the seventeenth century). Around 1670 the important Cambridge Platonist Henry More wrote a treatise against Böhme, the *Philosophiae teutonicae censura* (Critique of German philosophy). Around 1800, Böhme was rediscovered not only by the German idealists, but also by William Blake.

Böhme's first work, *Aurora oder Morgenröte im Aufgang* (Aurora or the rising of dawn, 1612; English title: *The Aurora*) was preceded by a long phase of fermentation, on which he reports in the twelfth of the *Theosophische Sendbriefe* (Theosophic epistles): "Although I dealt with it twelve years, and I was pregnant with it in myself, and there was a strong urge in me, before I could bring it into the outside: until it afterward fell on me like a driving rain." Böhme boasts that he has not learned from books, "but rather from my own book, which was opened in me." This book has, he says, "only three sheets, and they are the three principles of eternity; in them I can find everything that Moses and the Prophets, and also Christ and the Apostles said." He declares expressly that he passes his time "in weakness and childishness, in the simplicity of Christ," as if in a pleasance.

Böhme sought a theosophy, that is, a knowledge of God that would make possible an understanding of nature on the basis of God's Trinitarian being. To be sure, he is not a rational theologian—instead of arguing rigorously, he often turns against reason in the name of the spirit. His conceptual world mixes categorically different levels—metaphysical principles, categories of natural philosophy, and especially alchemy, angels, and devils; his numerous works are full of repetitions. But in the later works he achieves more systematic stringency; his last book, which unfortunately he was not able to complete before he died, *Quaestiones theosophicae, oder Betrachtung göttlicher Offenbarung* (*Quaestiones theosophicae*, or Contemplation of Divine Revelation) is perhaps his most rigorous. Despite all his defects, Böhme incontestably raises with unprecedented courage a question that traditional theology likes to shun: Whence come suffering and evil into the world? The classical answer, as we find it in Aquinas, is the doctrine of privation: the bad and the evil are a lack of being. But suffering and malevolence certainly seem to be more than mere lacks, and if God is the creator of everything, then they must also have their ground in him. Böhme considers unavoidable the recognition of a negative principle in God himself, and on the basis of the cooperation of the positive and negative principles (in his last work, these are called, in an abstract manner, the "Yes" and the "No"), he tries to understand God's manifestation in the external world, which is nothing more or less than the unfolding of the divine being and constitutes Böhme's third principle, which binds together the Yes and the No. His crucial idea here is that without opposition nothing becomes apparent. God "would be unknowable in himself, and in him there would be no joy or significance or sensibility without the No," we read in the third of the 177 originally planned theosophical questions. Although in God the positive and negative principles represent only two centers of a single unity, the separation of the two has a consequence. It yields Heaven and Hell, which are called "love-fire" and "wrath-fire": "In the love-fire they are one, but as separated they are two." But unlike later dialecticians, whom he anticipates more than almost anyone before him, Böhme does not see a necessary process in the fall of the angels and the fall of man, but rather interprets them, as Origen did long before him, as results of the free will of the angels and of man. By giving the No priority over the Yes and seeking to be a lord in the No, Lucifer separates himself from God and gives himself over to the wrath-fire. God, who in the light is an *Ichts* ("being"), is in Hell a *Nichts* ("nothing"), that is, not present. It is true that the Devil's wrath is an expression of the negative divine principle, but it should not be thought that God's wrath hardens him from the outside; instead, wrath is his inner essence. "Reason speaks much about God and his omnipotence, but it understands little about God and his essence, what and how he is: it detaches the soul entirely from

God, as if it were only a separate being . . . ; and that is the great harm of the blindness due to which people quarrel and dispute and never arrive at what is truly fundamental." The reunion of Yes and No takes place through Christ, and Böhme attributes his own insights to the spirit of Christ.

The Silesian noble and mystic Abraham von Franckenberg, with whom Böhme corresponded, drew Böhme's writings to the attention of Johannes Scheffler (1624–1677), who is famous under the name Angelus Silesius ("the angel from Silesia"), and who was then studying in Leiden. Oddly enough, Böhme's work contributed to Scheffler's conversion to Catholicism. Far more important than the fanatical anti-Protestant works that he then wrote, are his epigrams in alexandrine verse collected in a volume that was entitled, from its second edition on, *Cherubinischer Wandersmann* (*The Cherubinic Pilgrim*). These epigrams are not only one of the most important examples of the German baroque lyric but also express, with unsurpassed concision and often in paradoxical ways, central ideas of the Christian mystics, including Meister Eckhart and Johannes Tauler, in particular the identification of the soul devoted to God with God himself. "Ich bin so groß wie Gott, er ist als ich so klein; / Er kann nicht über mich, ich unter ihm nicht sein" ("I am as great as God, he is as small as I; / He cannot be over me, I cannot be under him").

⚜ 4 ⚜

Only the Best Is Good Enough for God: Leibniz's Synthesis of Scholasticism and the New Science

Gottfried Wilhelm Leibniz (1646–1716) was not only the most multitalented German of all time, but also humanity's last universal savant; he was creative in logic, epistemology, metaphysics, the philosophy of religion, mathematics, the natural and engineering sciences, jurisprudence, and historiography. There is hardly any other author one might read whose works provide such an effective antidote to pride in one's own intellectual achievements, important though they may be. The intelligent reader soon comes to realize that Leibniz's ability to find simple, if also sometimes counterintuitive, solutions for complex problems in any and all fields is quite beyond his own reach. Indeed, he senses that this all-illuminating mind is rooted in a personality that not only devoted its intelligence to moral ends, as did Plato, but was by nature good. Although he was not free from vanity, Leibniz always made a sincere effort to recognize the partial truth in other positions. An ability to synthesize characterizes most important intellectual achievements. In Leibniz, who possessed this ability in the highest degree, it was (and this is not always the case) the expression of an irenic temperament on account of which he used the pseudonym "Pacidius" (the peaceable). Research on talent treats multi-talentedness and child prodigies as its two best-known anomalies; Leibniz was both. When he was eight years old he began to read his way through the Latin works in his late father's library, and right up to his death he continued to write on the most diverse subjects, combining the greatest precision in the detailed problems he examined with a sovereign overview of the whole of human knowledge, indefatigably striving to put his ideas to practical use. And this he did in the service of the most important princes of Europe (at the end of his life they included the Elector of Hanover, the Prussian King, the Emperor, and the Russian Czar). He formed a genuine friendship with three princesses as well, especially with Sophie of the Palatinate (or of Hanover), whose elder sister Elisabeth had corresponded with Descartes. Even if he lacked true political talent, Leibniz, who had taken a doctoral degree in civil and canon law at the age of twenty (in Altdorf, because the university in his native city of Leipzig had refused to grant him a degree because of his youth), was often active as a diplomat. He tried, for example, to reunite the Christian denominations, which, after Europe's religious wars, was undoubtedly an important task.

Certain philosophical theories must emerge, because they are grounded in the nature of human reason; but from Leibniz we can learn that this does not exclude secondary causes. And it follows, therefore, that we can freely grant that among the decisive factors that favored the rationalistic turn in philosophy in the seventeenth century, there were two circumstances that have special interest for us. The first is the existence of several mutually exclusive Christian denominations with similarly authoritative claims to truth, which prompted the search for an authority that was not based solely on an appeal to authorities. The second consisted in the physical and moral evils that the religious civil wars caused, which absolutely had to be ended. And both of these factors also explain why an effort to ground religion in reason was particularly important precisely in Germany, and why it was pursued with such religious energy. On the one hand, the Empire was confessionally divided, unlike almost all the other European powers—which therefore had less need for philosophy. On the other, it had not (and after 1648 it was clear: *definitely* not) achieved the political unity that characterized the neighboring states, which had become sovereign. However, a structure resembling a monster—that was how Samuel Pufendorf (1632–1694), an important teacher of natural law and an opponent of Leibniz, described it in *De statu imperii Germanici* (On the condition of the German Empire)—calls for special measures, and Leibniz's extreme rationalism provided just such. Moreover, we who have inevitably participated in the expressive revolutions of the *Sturm und Drang* movement and Romanticism should not look down on the intricacy and elaborate courtliness of the late seventeenth- and early eighteenth-century forms of expression that characterize Leibniz's letters and distinguish them so sharply from Luther's *Tischreden* (*Table Talk*) for instance, to whose immediacy the *Sturm und Drang* returned. People have to protect themselves, and after the atrocities of the religious wars it was a splendid achievement of the post-Westphalian *ancien régime* that it protected Europe from similarly brutal wars for almost a hundred and fifty years. Anyone who has lived in the twentieth century should look back with humility on this achievement.

Leibniz's *oeuvre*, which has still not been published in its entirety and was only insufficiently available to Hegel and Schelling, has incontestably gained prestige in the twentieth century. Bertrand Russell's book on Leibniz (1900) contributed, through his insight into the connection between Leibniz's logic and metaphysics and his criticism of that logic, to the development of analytical philosophy. Nonetheless, for thinkers who, like present-day analytical philosophers of religion, would like to articulate the basic ideas of classical metaphysics in a way that is logically more precise and not incompatible with modern science, Leibniz's ideas are the most important source of inspiration. In view of the awe-inspiring beauty of his mind, one fears being driven by resentment when one points to its limits, and yet three of them are obvious. First, his polymathic interests, along with the pleasure he took in personal contact and activity, prevented him from writing a truly comprehensive, literarily refined major work such as Descartes's *Meditations*, for instance; his peaceable spirit too often led him to argue *ad hominem*, that is, taking into account the assumptions and cultural background of his respective conversation partners. His most original ideas are found in private sketches, essays for select acquaintances such as the *Discours de métaphysique* (*Discourse on Metaphysics*, 1685/86), and in letters, and not in his two most extensive works: the *Nouveaux essais sur l'entendement humain* (*New Essays on Human Understanding*), which he completed in 1705 but which were published only in 1765 and probably strongly influenced Kant, and the *Essais de*

Théodicée (*Essays in Theodicy*, 1710), which oppose Locke's radical empiricism and Bayle's fideism, respectively. Second, until the end of his life Leibniz continued to be something of a child prodigy: his belief in the rationality of the world made him overlook phenomena whose cryptic nature is not incompatible with his system, but easily make it existentially implausible. The first impression made by some of his writings is that of a certain childish naïveté, and even if the acuity of his arguments quickly shows that this naïveté is on the highest level and arouses the suspicion that consummate intellectual greatness is not possible without naïveté—indeed, that God himself may be naïve, this only modifies the initial impression without refuting it. Leibniz's logical precision contrasts most sharply with Böhme's visions, and yet we cannot deny that Böhme felt the irreducibility of the negative, even and especially in God, much more strongly than did Leibniz, who attributes only positive attributes to God, and no "No." Third, Leibniz also lacks the sense for cultural phenomena that German culture first acquired in the course of the eighteenth century, though not without having been inspired by Leibniz's metaphysics of perspectivism. It is true that Leibniz's interest not only in the philosophy of language, but also in the history of language, is noteworthy, but the aesthetic sensibility of classical German philosophy is as foreign to him as Kant's moral revolution: his ethical ideas, which were developed only incidentally, are anything but original; indeed, they are probably not even consistent, since they vacillate between Aristotelian eudemonism, basic Christian convictions, and Spinoza's ethics of perfection.

If we compare Leibniz with Kant, his is more a European than a German mind (as was true also of Pufendorf, who long taught and worked in Sweden). His mathematically and scientifically most productive phase occurred in Paris, where he lived from 1672 to 1676, entering into contact with Christiaan Huygens, among others, and where he would gladly have stayed. He joined the Royal Society in London in 1673, the Accademia Fisico-Matematica in Rome in 1689, the Académie des Sciences in Paris in 1700, and shortly thereafter became the first president of the Kurfürstlich-Brandenburgische (soon to be: Königlich-Preußische) Societät der Wissenschaften. His travels also took him to the Netherlands, where he met Spinoza and others, and to Italy, among other places also to the Curia, where a position as *Custos* at the Vatican Library was offered him—though on the condition that he convert to Catholicism. This was a condition that the ecumenical Lutheran who had worked at the beginning of his career for the Catholic archbishop of Mainz, Johann Philipp von Schönborn, was not prepared to fulfill. He wrote an enormous number of letters (around 15,000) to about 1,100 correspondents from Madrid to Stockholm, from Oxford to Moscow, and even to Beijing, from whence missionaries strengthened his marked sinophilia. At the end of his life, he would have been only too glad to follow his prince, who became George I of Great Britain in 1714, to London; but as a punishment for the slowness of his work on the history of the Welfs he was left behind in provincial Hanover; disappointed, he considered moving back to Paris. The great majority of his writings are in French and Latin, but a few treatises are in German, including *Unvorgreiffliche Gedancken, betreffend die Ausübung und Verbesserung der Teutschen Sprache* (Unprejudiced thoughts on the use and improvement of the German language, c. 1697), in which he made an obvious effort to help raise German to the rank of a language suited to academic purposes. This text alone, like Leibniz's contribution to the first German scientific journal, the *Acta eruditorum* launched in 1682, along with his participation in the founding of one of the first two German academies (Leibniz did not belong to the older Leopoldina), and his forty-year-long relationship with the Welfs make it indispensable to discuss him in a history of German philosophy. Hardly any other German has helped so much to draw attention abroad to German science and philosophy—both respectful, as in the case of his correspondent Nicholas Remond, and scornful, as when in *Candide* Voltaire ridiculed the Leibnizian Pangloss and his doctrine of the best of all possible worlds.

Like Descartes, Leibniz has a place among the greatest philosophers as well as among the most productive mathematicians. Shortly after Newton but (largely or probably wholly) independent of him, Leibniz founded infinitesimal calculus, on which he was the first to publish; he developed the binary system and made important contributions to the theory of functions, matrices, and determinants, as well as to probability theory and combinatorics, and even to the beginnings of the calculus of variations; programmatic ideas about topology and game theory, and on the axiomatization of arithmetic are also found in his work. His contributions to mathematical notation were especially momentous (and notation is much more important than the layman thinks). The controversy regarding who first invented the infinitesimal calculus, which was pursued especially disgracefully by Newton, led to the latter's inferior notation being retained in England, which long held back the development of English mathematics. In physics, Leibniz conceived, with the *vis viva* (vital force) the double of kinetic energy, and understood that it was preserved in certain systems; he opposed this early form of the law of the conservation of energy to the Cartesians' and Newton's law of the conservation of momentum, which led to a long controversy in which the young Kant also took part (in his first book). It lasted until, in the course of the eighteenth century, it was realized that both laws of conservation were valid; they follow, as Emmy Noether demonstrated in 1918, from the homogeneity of time and space. In geology and biology Leibniz pondered the transformation of the species; as an engineer he invented, among many other apparatuses, a calculating machine that could carry out the four elementary arithmetical operations. To be sure, he was not the first German who made a decisive contribution to modern science; the laws of the movement of the planets discovered by Johannes Kepler (1571–1630) were as important for the formation of the Newtonian theory as Galileo's discovery of the law of falling bodies. But in *Mysterium Cosmographicum* (The cosmographic mystery) Kepler was still motivated by Pythagorean-Platonic ideas that are not compatible in any simple way with modern scientific method.

Leibniz, in contrast, entirely appropriated the methods of science, and even wrote an admiring letter to the old materialist Hobbes—though at the same time he continued and transformed the Scholastic tradition in such a way that it became compatible with modern science. Leibniz, like almost all original thinkers of the seventeenth century, declined to pursue a university career (which was offered him early on), but unlike his greatest colleagues, Descartes and Spinoza, he was very familiar with Scholastic philosophy, which was still cultivated even in Protestant universities. In a letter written to Remond in 1714, he describes, perhaps understating his age, how as a fifteen-year-old he turned away from the Scholastic substantial forms and toward modern, mechanistic natural science, but later returned to the metaphysical tradition, because the ultimate grounds of the sciences were to be found only in the latter. It is undeniable that a combination of science and theology characterizes modern natural science in general. But Descartes is a voluntarist; that is, he sees natural laws, and even the axioms of mathematics, as arbitrary postulations by the divine will; they are facts that cannot be further explained. Leibniz, on the other hand, is a rationalist—he sees God's being and his Creation as determined by reason. And that means that it must in principle be possible to grasp the basic structures of reality through *a priori* reflection. Why are natural laws the way they are? Why is there mind in the world? Why are there beings that act in accord with moral ends? According to Leibniz, these questions point beyond science to metaphysics, which however only pursues further the way of thought essential to science, which consists in inquiring into the grounds of phenomena—in this case, the laws of nature themselves. The physical search for efficient causes and the metaphysical search for final causes, which are also presupposed in every human action, are compatible, indeed complementary, enterprises.

This rationalism, which deviates so markedly from the empiricism championed in England, was rooted in different assumptions regarding the nature of God. And these assumptions played a crucial role in giving German culture its special status, even if after Herder the central focus of interest was the connection between God and the laws of the humanities, not the laws of the natural sciences. Precisely because Leibniz assumes that natural laws are themselves determined by God, he can maintain—against Henry More, for instance, and with Spinoza—that every event must be determined by secondary efficient causes. The repression of prescientific religious belief, *in the name of a more complex concept of God*, was probably Leibniz's most important contribution to the German spirit. In England, far into the nineteenth century, a more naïve form of religiousness persisted that believed it recognized the hand of God in very limited natural goals that purportedy could not be explained scientifically; but at the same time, because of its empiricist foundation, science in England was more quickly disengaged from theological and metaphysical bases. In Leibniz's work, the silly notion that religion has its place where gaps appear in the sciences was replaced by the more complex idea that only a metaphysical and theological grounding could deprive natural laws of their brute facticity. *God is not a gap-filler endangered by every new triumph of science; instead, he is the foundation of the sciences, whose advancement is a religious duty.* Analogously, Leibniz's early-Enlightenment program for improving the world expresses a Christian philosophy; in science and technology we imitate God's creative power. The opposition of reason and religion that runs through the French Enlightenment of the eighteenth century, which identified religion with the Catholic Church, would have been incomprehensible to Leibniz, and a like opposition never gained a footing in German culture even after him. *On the contrary, the acutest critic of Christianity, Nietzsche, shows his German roots by the fact that he simultaneously wages war on reason—which would again have been incomprehensible to Voltaire.*

What are Leibniz's central philosophical ideas? In very simplified terms, modern philosophy can be seen as a contest between "ancientizing" authors and modernizing authors. The leader of the latter is Descartes, who starts from the undeniability of the *cogito* ("I think") as an unshakable foundation, whereas the other camp seeks to integrate subjectivity into a complex order of being in which it is a part, not the starting point. Modernizers think primarily epistemologically, ancientizers ontologically. From his analysis of the ego Descartes concludes that the physical (*res extensa*, "extended thing") and the mental (*res cogitans*, "thinking thing") are different in kind, and thus bestows on modern philosophy a problem that was alien to the ancients but is the driving force behind the modern development. Descartes believed, in complete accord with common sense, that physical and mental states could cause one another, but his royal correspondent Elisabeth already expressed doubts about this, given the differing nature of the two substances, and the interactionist conception became even more questionable in the course of the seventeenth century as it was understood that momentum is a vector and not a scalar magnitude. In view of the law of the conservation of momentum, Descartes's idea that the mind could determine the direction of the (physical) animal spirits collapsed. The most important thinkers of the second half of the seventeenth century sought an alternative to this conception. But in doing so they did not challenge the fundamental irreducibility of the mental to the physical; Leibniz lent it support with a famous simile: someone who could move around inside a person's brain as if it were a mill with all its gears and pulleys would nonetheless never be able to know which mental states corresponded to the brain states.

For the ancientizer Spinoza, the ontological proof stands at the beginning of philosophy; it proves the existence of a single substance—"God or nature"—that has an infinite number of attributes, of which only extension and thought are known to us. All the modes of these attributes occur with necessity on the basis of preceding modes and general laws; in this process, mental and physical events run in parallel, are two aspects of a single underlying reality, and do not affect one another causally. From this it follows that everything is animated. Leibniz takes over from Spinoza significantly more than he allows to be seen, given Spinoza's bad reputation. For Leibniz as well, God always acts through secondary causes; and Leibniz is also a determinist (not a fatalist) who defends freedom only insofar as it is compatible with a thoroughgoing determination. In addition, he, too, is a parallelist and a pan-psychist who rejects any interaction between the physical and the mental. At the same time, his deviations from Spinoza are important (and not only in political philosophy, where he does not adopt the Dutchman's democratic ideas). What bothered Leibniz in Spinoza was first of all his power-centered positivism, which is clearly expressed, for instance, in his theory of international relations, and which follows from the fact that according to Spinoza all value judgments are subjective: in the perspective of ultimate reality everything that happens is equally good. This dissolution of the normative difference between good and evil seems to be the consequence of pantheism, since it can provide no transcendent standard external to actuality. In contrast, Leibniz stands much closer to traditional Christian theology and ethics, despite his fascination with modern science and despite his agreement with Spinoza that divine omnipotence implies omnicausality. In addition, he can provide a good foundation for his intuitions because he is an incomparably better logician than Spinoza, indeed with the *calculus ratiocinator* he outlined the idea of a symbolic logic long before Boole, De Morgan, and Frege. Leibniz was more interested in proving propositions than in justifying conceptual systems, though he had important ideas about that, too—for example, how through combination one can move from elementary concepts to more complex ones.

Spinoza's modal concepts are completely unsatisfactory. What does he mean by "necessity"? According to a certain interpretation of his theory, he seems to claim that natural laws are logically necessary; but since this is unacceptable, he may also only mean that natural laws are nomologically necessary, which is nothing more than a tautology. One of Spinoza's problems probably consists in the fact that he does not distinguish between logical and nomological necessity—the logically necessary holds in all possible worlds, while the nomologically necessary holds only in worlds with the corresponding natural laws—because he does not have access to the concept of possible worlds and perhaps even deliberately rejects it. This concept is undoubtedly complex: it was alien to the ancients, having first been developed in the thirteenth century. Leibniz begins by distinguishing between rational truths and factual truths; the former, to which he assigns all the truths of mathematics (but not the *cogito*), are derived by analysis from the law of contradiction; they hold in all possible worlds, and are therefore logically necessary. Factual truths, by contrast, hold only in the actual world. But why did God create this world and not another one? Even if other worlds were logically possible, there must have been a reason for his choice, because according to Leibniz the principle of sufficient reason is as important for metaphysics as the law of noncontradiction: even—and precisely—free action has a reason. (Leibniz's principle includes reasons and causes.) As omnipotent, omniscient, and omnibenevolent being, God cannot not create the best of all possible worlds. Therefore factual truths are, though contingent, *a priori* knowable for an infinite mind. Leibniz posits as a logical principle that all a subject's predicates are analytically contained within it. The fact that Caesar crossed the Rubicon follows from the concept "Caesar"—even if it is a contingent factual truth that this concept was instantiated in our world. From this it follows that there is no transworld-identity, to use the modern term. Someone who had all Caesar's other qualities, but who had not crossed the Rubicon, would not be Caesar, not even himself in another world. That is averred in Leibniz's controversy with Antoine Arnauld, which returned anew in the debate in modern analytical metaphysics between David Lewis and Alvin Plantinga. However, Lewis can no longer make the actual world stand out, because he lacks all axiology: it is just one of an endless multitude of real worlds.

Leibniz does justify the special status of the actual world axio-logically; he presupposes that value criteria are something given for God, and are thus in no way dependent on his arbitrary will, and further, that there is only one world with maximal value. This last supposition is questionable—the young Kant sought in vain to justify it and eventually gave up on the project. However, Leib-niz's idea can be pertinently formulated without this presuppo-sition in the following way: God must create *one* of the worlds with maximal value. But even this theory does not correspond to the tradition; according to Thomas Aquinas, for instance, there can be no world with maximal value any more than there can be a number larger than all other numbers. Whatever world God cre-ates, he could always create a better one, and therefore one could say—to exaggerate a little—that it does not matter which one he finally decides on. This is in accord with the medieval concept of suffering from being in the world; and, as Hume rightly empha-sizes in his *Dialogues on Natural Religion*, it is in accord with an age of Enlightenment and the belief in progress that religion now emphasizes the good in the world, especially since it is not easy to understand where evil comes from, if the world was created by a good God. And in fact Leibniz's metaphysical optimism (which is compatible with optimism in the philosophy of history, since according to him the possibility of an increase in value, that is, of progress, is inherent in the best possible world) in no way isolates him in his time. Shaftesbury's *The Moralists* (1709) expressed a similar enthusiasm with nature, as Leibniz recognized in his lau-datory review of the work, which he had not yet read when he wrote the *Theodicy*.

But even if his religiousness is similar to Shaftesbury's in char-acter, Leibniz's theory is far more precise. In it, we immediately sense the mathematical mind: for God, the world is a kind of solution to a problem in the calculus of variations, namely a func-tion, for which the functional assumes a minimum of negative and a maximum of positive value. The support complex mathe-matical concepts provide for enthusiasm about the world seems to be the culmination of a justification of the world that began with the Renaissance, even if, from the perspective of common sense, it seems to add something doctrinaire to the justification that soon came to be regarded as typically German. And yet Leibniz is not simply the most eloquent advocate for God and his world. Indeed, it would seem likely that God saw fit to bring forth such a brilliant advocate because God's position in intellectual history had become threatened, a threat based, paradoxically, on an argument advanced by the advocate himself. In the *Essais de Théodicée*, Leibniz had soared to such heights of abstraction only because he had at the same time made the problem of theodicy immensely more difficult: according to him, God's existence would be refuted if it could be shown that a world better than the actual one were possible. Leibniz was the first to tie God down to a single world: if he did not create the best possible world, then he cannot exist. It no longer sufficed to show that the good far outweighs the bad (even if Leibniz asserts that it does, because this is implied by his much stronger thesis); only the best is good enough for God. In view of the suffering it contains, the optimistic qualification of our world is immediately counterintuitive; and humanity certainly did not need to wait for the Lisbon earthquake and Voltaire to sense this: the Thirty Years' War, before whose end Leibniz was born and which Grimmelshausen so strikingly described, was more than enough. So then, why did Leibniz assert something so counterintuitive? Because in his view, its negation leads to atheism. But why did he defend the alternative "either the actual world is the best possible, or God cannot exist"? Because in his view it follows from the previously designated attributes of God.

Even a skeptic like Hume did not deny that in view of our limited capacity for knowledge, our world is compatible with a divine plan. What he did deny is that the existence of a creator with the attributes of the theistic God can be proven on the basis of this world. Leibniz, however, does not commit this error, because the so-called physico-theological proof appears in his work only in the special form of preestablished harmony, a concept that we will examine further later on. His other proofs are not inductive, but *a priori*, and since he is sure of them, he can set up his alternative with full confidence of victory; however, if one begins to doubt them, the alternative could encourage atheism. For Leibniz, the ontological proof, in both its versions (God as a necessary and as a perfect being), is central, and as Mersenne had already done in his criticism of Descartes, he understands that God's possibility has to be proven before his necessity can be inferred from it. In order to achieve this, he emphasizes that God has only simple and positive attributes that cannot contradict each other. The cosmological proof, which argues from the contingency of actuality to a necessary being, presupposes the principle of sufficient reason—but this ultimately presupposes the ontological proof as well, since otherwise it would be possible to question beyond God. In addition, Leibniz uses the proof on the basis of eternal truths, which according to him can subsist only in a divine mind. Russell considered this proof scandalous, since Leibniz himself presupposed that the eternal truths are something given for God; they could then not also presuppose him. But perhaps the divine mind and those truths can be understood as only two aspects of a complex unity, especially if a few of these truths are based on the principle that performative contradictions are to be avoided.

In any case, Leibniz believes that on this basis he can serenely interpret all the world's evils—metaphysical, physical, and moral—as compatible with the best possible world: any alternative world would have less good or more evil to offer. The arguments regarding this compatibility, derived *a priori*, and which Leibniz seeks to make plausible in detail, are partly very old and already to be found in the Church Fathers. Leibniz first modifies the theory of privation, according to which evil is a lack of being, to the effect that every finite existent necessarily contains a negation, precisely because God in his perfection can exist only once. Again, this follows from his other metaphysical principle that what cannot be distinguished must be identical; that is, there cannot be two things that are similar in every respect (differing only in their position in space and time). Whereas the converse of the principle is undisputed (if "two" things are identical with one another, they must be alike in every respect), Leibniz's principle—against which Kant, for one, objected early on—is not compelling, even if Leibniz uses it in many of his arguments—for example, in his debate with Samuel Clarke over the nature of space and time, which according to Leibniz represent only relations between things. Second, Leibniz points to the fact that only certain evils make certain goods possible, and he emphasizes, third, that human freedom is a good for the sake of which God accepts certain evils. However, since Leibniz is a compatibilist (that is, he thinks that with God's choice of a world all acts are already established), the reference to freedom does not really represent a new argument compared with the second one: in Leibniz, freedom is not—as it is in Origen, who shaped the modern conception of will more than almost anyone else—something that happens against God; instead, it is part of his plan. How could it be otherwise, given the presupposed omnipotence and omniscience of God? (However, God does not want certain acts directly, but accepts them only for the sake of a higher good.) What is lacking in Leibniz is a concrete attempt to name exhaustively the positive values that God aims to achieve with his Creation, and to make the basic structures of reality plausible on the basis of those values. Leibniz limits himself to abstract ideas such as the simplicity of natural laws, the principle of plenitude, and the principle of continuity, according to which all compossible intermediate stages must be realized, and finally a hierarchy of beings that culminates in the city of God, the community of rational spirits, whose happiness God seeks as the monarch of the world, after he has created it as its architect. The German idealists were the first to attempt to determine more precisely the basic structures of reality on the basis of the concept of the absolute.

The differentiation in the concept of necessity and the moralization of the concept of God constitute Leibniz's first deviation from Spinoza. The second concerns the concept of substance. Whereas Spinoza is a radical monist, Leibniz assumes, like most philosophers in the tradition, a plurality of substances. He calls them "monads," and thus one of his late essays, which outlines his system, is entitled "Monadologie." However, Leibniz's concrete metaphysics is the most peculiar part of his system. It had, in fact, almost no followers, even though his assumptions could certainly be made plausible on the basis of his logical principles. For Leibniz, everything that truly exists is a substance that, as such, must be characterized by a complete individual concept. As a good Lutheran, Leibniz is not a realist with regard to universals; truly existing are only the individuals, which are, however, to be distinguished conceptually from each other: here Leibniz draws on Duns Scotus's category of *haecceitas*. Thus there is not only a concept of the human being, as Plato would have it, but also a concept of Plato or Leibniz.

What is ontologically decisive for a substance is that it constitute a unity and thus be indestructible; and therefore matter, which is infinitely divisible, cannot be a substance. Furthermore, a substance must be an active center of force. This is connected on the one hand with Leibniz's critique of the Cartesian doctrine that mere extension is the fundamental category of the physical world. He rightly recognizes that force is not reducible to extension, but on the other hand he connects this insight with the questionable conviction that every active center of force must be at least an elementary form of subjectivity. This leads to pan-psychism— everything is animate, including any and every particle of matter, no matter how small, and each particle contains an infinite plenitude of other subordinate monads. The world of bodies is derivative; it consists of well-founded phenomena, with regard to which all monads are in agreement, but only the monads and their ideas are truly real—even if a correlated body belongs to the ideas of each monad (with the sole exception of God). According to Leibniz, the activity of a monad, the series of its perceptions and volitions, is determined solely by the monad and by God himself; there can be no interaction among monads. Leibniz also rejects an occasionalism such as Malebranche's; that is, the theory that God intervenes in a given monad whenever a second seems to refer internally to the first one. Instead, he defends a preestablished harmony: even if the windowless monads play out their inner programs alone, they are nonetheless so constructed that they correspond precisely to one another. Each monad expresses a possible perspective on the whole universe, and represents it in each moment, along with its own earlier and later temporal development. Leibniz emphasizes that there are also "petites perceptions" (small perceptions) that constitute, as it were, the background noise of clear perceptions; contrary to Descartes, Leibniz thus recognizes something like preconscious mental states.

Leibniz's perspectivism therefore does not lead to relativistic consequences, because it is bound up with a hierarchical order of monads. In it, perceptions and volitions gain in complexity; for instance, rational beings have, in addition to perceptions, apperceptions; that is, they are aware of their perceptions. And they reflect not only on themselves, but also have access to the necessary truths that are innate in them. Conceptual knowledge is superior to sensual representation because of its greater clarity. And the more rational a monad is, the more active and free it is. The increase in one's own rationality constitutes happiness, and whereas the medieval tradition in the West interpreted the beatific vision in the afterworld as an unsurpassable state, at the end of "Principes de la Nature et de la Grâce, fondés en raison" ("Principles of Nature and Grace, Based on Reason") Leibniz emphasizes his eschatological hope that there will be continual progress. "Thus our happiness will never consist, and should not consist, in a complete enjoyment in which there is nothing to be desired and that would make our spirit dull, but rather in an eternal progress toward new joys and new perfections." When Goethe's Faust accepts his damnation in the event that he ever asks to linger, even for an instant, he is hardly a traditional Christian, but he is certainly, even more than an heir of Paracelsus, a Leibnizian.

According to the criteria established at the outset, Christian Wolff (1679–1754) should have no place in this book, because this industrious but not really original mathematician, philosopher, and jurist never wrote a work of classical rank. Schelling said remembering him was "boring," and indeed, Wolff's writings are often painful to read because of their superfluously elaborate proofs. And yet he deserves to be mentioned for three reasons. First, despite what is often said, it is not true that he merely systematized Leibniz's philosophy. What he in fact did was integrate Leibnizian ideas into his own philosophy, which drew on the most diverse sources ranging from the Scholastics to Descartes. He adopted in particular Leibniz's rationalism and the central role of the principle of sufficient reason, but he rejected other doctrines of Leibniz's, such as the monadology and the dismissal of the distinction between essential and nonessential properties; and even though he corresponded with Leibniz from 1703 on, his knowledge of the latter's still widely unpublished *oeuvre* remained limited. Nonetheless, his pupils already spoke of a Leibniz-Wolffian philosophy. His adoption of Scholastic categories explains his popularity in the Catholic Enlightenment: though he himself was a Lutheran, he had grown up in Breslau, which was bi-confessional. Second, Wolff has the merit of being the first to have composed a comprehensive philosophical system in German, which therefore had enormous influence on the curricula of German universities in the eighteenth century, replacing the old Scholasticism. It is true that in a later phase Wolff also worked out his system in Latin—because only in that language could he gain international attention; but the step toward using German for academic purposes had finally been taken, however late in comparison to other great European nations. (Perhaps it is more than an accident that the creator of the Russian academic and literary language, Mikhail Lomonossov, studied with him.) The shift to the vernacular supported the Enlightenment's goal of communicating "reasonable ideas" (thus begin the titles of several of his works) to a broad audience.

Third, one of the greatest scandals in the history of German philosophy is connected with Wolff's name. In 1723 he was forced to give up, at Frederick William I's command, his professorship in Halle and leave Prussia within forty-eight hours if he wanted to avoid being hanged. In truth, this only contributed to his fame; he was given a professorship in Calvinist Marburg and became celebrated all over Europe. In 1740 Frederick the Great called him back to Halle. How did he come to be expelled? In 1721, Wolff had delivered in Halle, as prorector, a celebratory speech on the practical philosophy of the Chinese, in which he expressed his admiration for their morality—a morality that was precisely *not* theologically founded. This praise sprang from the widespread sinophilia of the seventeenth and eighteenth centuries; at the same time, it expressed the conviction that morality could exist without religion (even if Wolff, in the long annotations to the expanded printed version of 1726, did not deny that specifically Christian norms rested on Revelation). His theological colleague Johann Joachim Lange was enraged; and the fact that Wolff, like Leibniz, was a determinist also played a role in the denunciation that Lange and other theologians mounted against him. Thus he was said to be a fatalist who depreciated individual responsibility, for example that of soldiers who were thinking about deserting—and that of course alarmed the Soldier King. The theological-philosophical controversy, which ran its course over several years, contributed to the emancipation of philosophy from theology in Germany and is also important because Lange was a representative of Pietism, whose center was the Francke Foundations in Halle. Since the Reformation, Pietism had been the most original religious movement in Germany: without its rejection of rigidified Lutheran orthodoxy and its emphasis on the individual examination of conscience and the elevation of feeling (which had to become manifest in active social commitment), the German cultural revolution around 1770 would not have taken place. And the man who shared Wolff's notion that ethics could, indeed must, be grounded without theology (though his philosophy cannot be understood without reference to his rebellion, which reminds us of Lange's, against Leibniz's and Wolff's determinism) was also brought up in a Pietist household: Immanuel Kant.

The German Ethical Revolution:
Immanuel Kant

In many respects, Kant (1724–1804) is the antithesis of Leibniz. While the latter was cosmopolitan and could be called the last European philosopher of German ancestry, Kant, who never left Prussia proper, the eastern part of the kingdom, was not at all nationalistic (during the Russian occupation of Königsberg he was a loyal subject of the Empress). But he was nonetheless a German, through and through. Because of him and the philosophers inspired by him, the study of the German language, in which he wrote all his important works, became almost obligatory for philosophers in every country for a century and a half. At the same time, Kant took Britain's empiricist tradition much more seriously than had Leibniz, who, unlike Kant, could speak English. Second, while Leibniz, who was the son and grandson of professors, avoided academia, Kant, of lower middle class ancestry, remained connected with the university almost his whole adult life, with the exception of the six years he spent as a private tutor; and the university, in consequence, acquired national and international prestige as a place in which not only guild interests but also intellectual innovations had their place. Humboldt's reform of the university in the early nineteenth century built on this prestige. Third, while Leibniz created the infinitesimal calculus at the age of twenty-something and had completed his philosophical system before he turned forty, Kant was a late bloomer. He published his first epoch-making philosophical work, the *Kritik der reinen Vernunft* (*Critique of Pure Reason*) in 1781, when he was fifty-seven; up to that point, the greatest recognition for his work in philosophy came for the *Untersuchung über die Deut-lichkeit der Grundsätze der natürlichen Theologie und der Moral* (*Inquiry Concerning the Distinctness of the Principles of Natural Theology and Morality*, 1764), which received a (second) prize from the Berlin Academy of Sciences. In this Kant is the exception, not Leibniz: system-building in one's middle twenties and thirties is as common in philosophy as is first-rate work in mathematics at the same ages. Thus Kant's pupil Johann Gottfried Herder achieved prominence before his teacher, who was twenty years older. Brilliance is entirely compatible with soundness; but Kant lacked the former. And since brilliance, even if sound, easily blinds the uninitiated, beginners in philosophy are strongly urged to study Kant. It not only sharpens reasoning power, but also communicates the moral seriousness without which philosophy is seldom more than a matter of puzzle-solving.

In order to work out his ideas, Kant needed, as we have said, a great deal of time. It is true that his ideas developed much more continuously than was long thought. But without the silent decade before 1781, which passed almost without publications—indeed, even without appearances on talk-shows or blogging—Kant today would be known only to experts. Unmolested by university evaluation committees, he took the time he needed to restructure and ground his philosophy. It is in fact still dazzling how in the following seventeen years, using the time that remained to him in his own unique way, he produced a multitude of also architectonically perfect works on the most diverse problems. In this process, he constantly developed further his conception of philosophy; the counterbalancing *Kritik der Urteilskraft* (*Critique of Judgment*) of 1790 was not at all foreseen in 1781; it revoked earlier assumptions and at the same time created a systematic unity of Kant's philosophy that was not at all what he had intended at the outset. (In Kant's obituary, Schelling therefore says that his philosophy was produced "more atomistically than organically.") Kant looked back on his recently completed writings so little that he did not notice transpositions of whole passages in the *Prolegomena* and the *Rechtslehre* caused by the compositor. Fourth, while philosophy was only one of the areas in which Leibniz excelled, Kant was *not* a creative polymath, but rather only a broadly cultured philosopher, thanks in part to his

comprehensive lecturing activities. Nonetheless, he had published a few studies in natural science that were important, especially for their concept formation, the *Monadologia Physica* of
1756, for example; in 1754 he even proved a change in the Earth's
rotation. But Kant was extremely creative in all areas of philosophy, including ethics, which Leibniz had neglected, and aesthetics, which Leibniz had ignored. Comparable creativity had not
been seen since Plato and Aristotle. This is the fifth difference:
even if Kant continues the seventeenth-century project of justifying modern science philosophically, he is most revolutionary
in ethics, in which the dyed-in-the-wool metaphysician Leibniz
had hardly any interest. In its concrete demand for equality in
rights and duties, Kant's ethical universalism was largely in accord
with the European Enlightenment, but he gave it a metaethical
grounding and built upon this foundation a complex metaphysics of ethics that lent German culture a special attractiveness:
British utilitarianism, for instance, not only differed materially
from Kant's ethics (although it, too, produced a universalistic
ethics), but failed completely to understand the desideratum of
a metaphysics of duty. The exceptional level of German legal culture in the nineteenth and parts of the twentieth century is due to
a philosophical training that has up to now been rejected by common law jurisprudence, guided as it is by individual cases. (We
have only to consider that the United States to this day does not
grant universal suffrage for elections to Congress.) The German
Basic Law of 1949 was written in a Kantian spirit.

Heine already understood what Kant's philosophy represents
in terms of the history of consciousness. On the one hand, in his
theoretical philosophy Kant destroys the old metaphysics (only
the old one, because the three Critiques do the preliminary spade-
work for a new metaphysics, and in no way seek to put an end to
all metaphysics). The fact that today the average intellectual considers the idea of a proof of God or a demonstration of the immortality of the soul as absurd, even though the most important
minds of the seventeenth and early eighteenth centuries adhered
to them, goes back, in the German-speaking world, to Kant. In
the British world something analogous was accomplished by
Hume, but the differences are noteworthy. Hume presented
his critique of the most popular proof of God's existence, the
physico-theological proof, in his *Dialogues on Natural Religion*,

but in a way so literarily subtle and so ironic that although the first reviewers (and also Kant) understood the work's true intention, in the course of the nineteenth century it was interpreted by many British intellectuals in such a way as to suggest that Hume had absolutely left room for this argument. However, there can be no mistake about the thrust of Kant's attack, even if, or precisely because, he writes so much less elegantly than Hume: in his view, none of the traditional proofs of God is valid. Indeed, in his most anti-Leibnizian work "Über das Mißlingen aller philosophischen Versuche in der Theodizee" ("On the Failure of All Attempted Philosophical Theodicies," 1791), Kant declares that even all doctrinal solutions to the problem of theodicy have been unsuccessful. Leibniz's joyful affirmation of the world has been replaced by a more gloomy view, especially of human nature, which Schopenhauer will soon render darker still. The sarcastic tone of the young Kant became increasingly bitter as he became older.

On the other hand, in his practical philosophy he opened up a new mode of access to God, and he did so, paradoxically, precisely by detaching the foundations of ethics entirely from any hopes of an afterworld. Against the notion, already criticized by Meister Eckhart, that one should behave well in order to be rewarded by God, but also against the ancient theory that moral conduct is what leads to personal happiness, Kant emphasizes that the value of a moral act consists in its being performed as an end in itself. Ethics is not a science of hypothetical imperatives that teaches that one must use certain means *if* one is to achieve certain goals, on Earth or in Heaven; instead, ethics is based on a categorical, that is, unconditional imperative that is owed to practical reason's self-legislation, not to heteronomous factors such as a voluntaristic God or moral feelings, which are in principle changeable. It is significant that Kant also rejects an ethics of feeling as heteronomous; this distinguishes him from Rousseau, and especially from Hume, both of whom strongly influenced him, and who undertook analogous attempts to justify our moral convictions in the framework of the French and British Enlightenments after the breakdown of Christian dogmatics and the rise of modern science. By aligning ethics with reason, Kant permanently shaped German culture in ways that endure to this day and probably also helped play down the emotional aspects of morality. His anti-eudemonism justified and strengthened Germans' readiness to sacrifice affective bonds in developing a constitutional state based on the rule of law, a condition to which many traditional cultures have not yet ascended. And even though it entails a grotesque misunderstanding of Kant, he probably fostered the German vice that consists in trampling one's own and others' happiness, just to assure oneself of one's capacity to meet one's obligations, sometimes even when there is no need to do so—think, for example, of Innstetten in Fontane's novel *Effi Briest*. Although in his political philosophy Kant, like most of his European contemporaries, thought in terms of contract theory (and even considered a devils' state possible), his ethics implicitly questioned the Anglo-American individualistic philosophy of the state; human dignity is not, even for oneself, negotiable, and law cannot be reduced to a factual balance of interests.

At the same time, with eudemonism the possibility of grounding ethics empirically collapses, because the categorical imperative is valid *a priori*. Pointedly, one can say that in terms of theoretical grounding, the categorical imperative is in Kant the functional equivalent of the ontological proof of God's existence in Leibniz. Though Kant's explicit rejection of any ethics that considers itself a doctrine of happiness is new, it does have rhetorical, theological, and poetic predecessors. Of a soldier who sacrifices himself for his country one cannot simply say that he has made his choice for his happiness; the rhetorical tradition's epideictic oratory praised such heroic behavior as noble, and distinguished it from useful and just behavior. A question intensely debated in the Middle Ages and the early modern period was whether the love of God was reducible to self-love; think only of Fénelon. In particular, however, reflection on the phenomenon of the tragic contributed to an overcoming of eudemonism, especially since from the seventeenth century on this reflection led to a higher valuation of the concept of the sublime, which Kant endorsed in his *Beobachtungen über das Gefühl des Schönen und Erhabenen* (*Observations on the Feeling of the Beautiful and the Sublime*, 1764). What is so magnificent about Kant is not, as Heine thought, that in his ethics he comforted his servant Martin Lampe with God, but rather that he raised every human being, including Lampe, to the level of a tragic hero—a level that had up to the eighteenth century been reserved exclusively for aristocrats. What bourgeois tragedy since Lessing had expressed on the stage, Kant conceptualized:

every human being can come into a situation in which he is obligated to sacrifice his own happiness, and it is only this that gives him dignity. The possibility of a natural being's having dignity, however, points to God as the one who has created nature in such a form that a moral being with a chance of achieving its goal can exist in it. The idea of grounding the relation to God internally, in the moral law, while having skeptical reservations with regard to the presence of God in nature, is a philosophical expression of Protestantism, and especially of Pietism. What constitutes Kant's special status in German intellectual history is that he found a balance between the Enlightenment and Pietism, though in fact the latter was inclined to be hostile to the former—a balance whose perfect expression was his own personal and intellectual integrity. *He thereby opened German religiousness not only to all scientific influences, as Leibniz had done, but also to the wish to transform society, and conversely he gave enlightenment an ethical, indeed almost religious impulse*—for example, in his essay "Beantwortung der Frage: Was ist Aufklärung" ("An Answer to the Question: 'What is Enlightenment,'" 1783)—that had long since disappeared from the work of the contemporary French *philosophes*. According to Kant, summoning everything before the tribunal of reason is a religious duty. This explains the enormous seriousness of Kantian philosophizing, which sometimes seems almost naïve and is largely a stranger to irony: Kant's approach lent wings to tragedy, but it was detrimental to comedy, a genre in which German literature is underdeveloped.

The third aspect of Kant's project, which fascinated his contemporaries, was building a bridge between theoretical and practical philosophy that gave new latitude for human freedom and the autonomy of the human spirit. While it is true that the young Kant still defended, as had Leibniz and Wolff, a compatibilist conception of freedom, the mature Kant, like Lange, rejected this conception, which he called the "freedom of a turnspit." To be morally responsible, my action cannot be a necessary consequence of natural laws and initial conditions. But at the same time Kant assumed that the causal principle is a necessary presupposition for science, indeed, for ordered experience, and he was likewise increasingly convinced that the causal principle could not be derived from the law of contradiction, as Wolff and Baumgarten had tried to do. A trenchant critique of their argument, which anticipates the observations of modern analytic philosophy, is already found in his work *Principiorum primorum cognitionis metaphysicae nova dilucidatio* (*A New Elucidation of the First Principles of Metaphysical Cognition*, 1755). But not until he had studied Hume, presumably around 1770—that is, at about the time when the *Sturm und Drang* writers were enthusiastically discovering English literature—was he convinced that all such attempts were doomed to fail; in fact, that even a grounding based on experience had no prospect of success, because it could never reach beyond the present. Kant's masterstroke consisted in securing for the causal principle a validity that neither dogmatic metaphysics nor Hume's skeptical empiricism had been able to provide, and at the same time preserving human freedom. According to him, causality and, analogously, the other categories—even space and time—proceed from us; we bestow them on reality. It is noteworthy that according to Kant and Hume (but not yet according to Leibniz), similar causes have similar effects; this points to analogies between theoretical and practical reason, whose essence is their universalizability. Our reason is so constructed that without the categories we could not experience the world at all; therefore they are valid *a priori*. *The unity of the world is no longer based on God, but rather on the unity of self-consciousness.* But that does not in any way mean that things-in-themselves, which are inaccessible to us, are really so structured. We have to seek causes in the phenomenal world for every change, but without excluding the possibility that in the true, noumenal reality, which is not shaped by our schematized categories, causality based on freedom exists. Paradoxically, we are free precisely because we prescribe causality to phenomena—for that is our spontaneous positing. Though this idealism emphasizing the conditions of the possibility of experience, which Kant called "transcendental," distressed Heinrich von Kleist and led him to place feeling over limited reason, other German intellectuals found in it something liberating and elevating. It gave them the courage to believe in a metaphysically understood freedom, indeed, to adopt a worldview that depreciated external reality in favor of the human spirit, and also of faculties such as the imagination, on which the Enlightenment thinker Kant cast a critical eye. But without him, Romanticism would not have existed. Kant's interest in the metaphysics of freedom may also have been part of the reason why there continued to be less interest in political freedom in Germany than in France and England.

Kant's solution to the problem of freedom, making compatibilism and incompatibilism compatible through the theory of the two worlds (phenomenal and noumenal) is such a daring exploit that it is easy to see why his delight in it caused him to overlook the fact that it is absolutely untenable. For how can Kant say that things-in-themselves affect us if causality is limited to phenomena? Kant's talk about the realm of unknowable noumena seems without significance even by his own criteria. An almost too eerie part of Kant's theory is particularly fateful. Kant undoubtedly belongs to the Cartesian, modernizing strand in modern philosophy. But on one point he makes a radical break with Descartes. According to the latter, our stream of consciousness is given us as undoubtedly certain. For Kant, the temporality of our consciousness is itself only a subjective transformation of what we are in ourselves; it belongs to the phenomenal, not the noumenal ego, which may very well be timeless, and to which we have no access except through the empty point of the "I think" or through our practical reason; German idealism was to begin from both. Fourth, the depreciation of the stream of consciousness given us directly and the assumption of a true ego standing behind it were ideas that inspired Schopenhauer's metaphysics of the will. The crucial intermediate link between Descartes's *transparent consciousness* and the theory that quite different forces are at work behind our conscious life is paradoxically Kant's theory of the opposition between the phenomenal and the noumenal egos (along with his theory of genius in the third *Critique*).

According to Kant, the judgment "every change has a cause" is a synthetic *a priori* judgment. Thus it neither proceeds from experience, nor can it, like analytic propositions, be grounded in the law of contradiction. Being synthetic *a priori* is a property of judgments, and thus concerns the level of validity; this is something completely different from the genetic question that tormented Descartes, Locke, and Leibniz, viz., how do we arrive at the knowledge of certain propositions? Is that knowledge innate, or does it arise from certain experiences? Kant himself considered the discovery of synthetic *a priori* judgments and the explanation of their possibility as his most important philosophical achievement and, in the *Prolegomena zu einer jeden künftigen*

Metaphysik, die als Wissenschaft wird auftreten können (*Prolegomena to Any Future Metaphysics That Will Be Able to Come Forward as Science*, 1783), he connected with it the hope that now a metaphysics could finally be constructed that would be as enduring as the edifice of contemporary science, whose finality Kant did not doubt.

This hope proved deceptive, but it had consequences. First, it motivated a new generation of young philosophers who had been convinced that the theory of things-in-themselves was untenable to create some of the most audacious metaphysical constructions in the history of philosophy, now that they could start out from the knowability of the intelligible ground of reality. In his *Metaphysische Anfangsgründen der Naturwissenschaft* (*Metaphysical Foundations of Natural Science*, 1786), Kant himself had tried to ground a few of the basic principles of Newtonian theory in the synthetic *a priori* judgments of the first *Critique*. Though the latter are definitely formulated in such a way that this derivation can succeed, the claim that Kant took Newtonian physics as the starting point for the first *Critique* contradicts his own interpretation; what he attempted to construct was, on the contrary, an *a priori* theory of experience as such. In the "Opus postumum" (written in a heroic struggle as his intellectual powers were beginning to decline and left unfinished), Kant tried to justify philosophically even more detailed physical theories; it is tempting to see in this work a basic metaphysical attitude that is related to the system-building of the German idealists. Second, whatever the right interpretation of this last work might be, even today we must keep in mind that the question of the existence and ground of synthetic *a priori* knowledge is a fateful question, perhaps *the* fateful question, in philosophy, and that a concern with it has been one of the essential characteristics of German philosophy that clearly distinguishes it from English philosophy. Kant did not succeed in adducing a common property of all judgments that he considered synthetic *a priori*. But had he done nothing more than ask this question, he would have been assured a place of honor in the history of thought. Kant, however, sought not simply to list the synthetic *a priori* judgments he considered valid, but also to ground them, precisely in the so-called transcendental deductions. Fifth, this striving to ground *at any price* also permanently shaped German culture and distinguished it as particularly thorough in comparison to neighboring cultures. In the *Prolegomena*, Kant attacked the appeal to common sense. It was, he insisted, "a witness whose authority is based only on public rumor." Instead, he stressed that metaphysics "must be a science, not only as a whole, but also in all its parts, otherwise it is nothing at all." Kant's reply to Hume differs in theoretical philosophy from that of the Scottish common-sense school, and especially that of Thomas Reid, who referred all philosophizing to common sense as its starting point. Reid's influence on Anglo-American epistemology was enormous. The epistemologists who, like Roderick Chisholm, for instance, argue for unproven and unprovable evidence as the starting point for any knowledge, emulated him, and it cannot be denied that they have arguments (not mere evidence) for their position, even if in the event that their evidence is challenged they have little else to offer and can only shrug; for evidence cannot be further discussed. Kant and the German tradition following him (Schelling and Hegel call common sense "the local and temporary limitation of a race of human beings") followed another, riskier, and yet intellectually more exciting path.

A few of Kant's precritical writings have already been mentioned. His first work, *Gedanken von der wahren Schätzung der lebendigen Kräfte* (*Thoughts on the True Estimation of Living Forces*, 1746–), begun during his student days, claims to have caught "Herr von Leibniz making errors"—just as conversely the *Critique of Pure Reason* seemed to the old Kant in 1790 "the true apology for Leibniz." It is simply not the case, therefore, that Kant began as a Leibnizian and ended as an opponent of Leibniz. From the outset, he was testing his strength against him, and Leibniz remained a positive point of reference right to the end. (Kant ultimately conceived the noumenal world on the model of Leibnizian monads.) Especially important is the young Kant's insight that Leibniz's "proof" of the three-dimensionality of space is circular, an observation that points forward to his later theory that mathematical judgments are synthetic *a priori*, not analytical. The anonymous *Allgemeine Naturgeschichte und Theorie des Himmels* (*Universal Natural History and Theory of Heaven*, 1755) is Kant's most important contribution to the natural sciences. Though he offers only a few mathematical formulae, Kant, who had in the meantime made a careful study of

Newton, nonetheless anticipates Laplace's nebular hypothesis (the theory of the emergence of our solar system out of a condensation of the original nebula). Kant thus has to justify himself theologically for having tried to explain scientifically not only the movement of planets, but also their genesis; on the astronomical level, his project is analogous to Darwin's. Kant declares that God's existence is suggested "because nature, even in chaos, cannot proceed other than in a regular and orderly way." Like Leibniz, he argues that a causal explanation of the world according to natural laws does not exclude the possibility that the structure of the world serves the ends of rational beings; conversely, a mere reference to purposiveness, such as is occasionally found in Newton's work, is not yet a sufficient explanation, but rather "lazy world-wisdom." Indeed, Kant sees in the infinitude of the cosmos—as did Nicholas of Cusa, who was unknown to him—an appropriate expression of the incommensurability of God, whose Creation continually proceeds in accord with the principle of plenitude, sometimes even by destroying parts of the universe. Kant also hypothesizes the existence of rational beings on other celestial bodies, who are morally superior to humans. In this scheme, humans are compared to lice (even and precisely a figure like Alexander the Great); except for their eschatological hopes, they would be the most contemptible of all creatures. The noble human being must rise above this universe, despite its infinitude, find a source of bliss within himself, and in this way attain grandeur. If we subtract the concept of happiness, the conclusion of the *Naturgeschichte* anticipates the famous passage at the end of the *Critique of Practical Reason*, "Two things fill the mind with ever new and increasing admiration and awe . . . the starry heavens above me and the moral law within me."

Der einzig mögliche Beweisgrund zu einer Demonstration des Daseins Gottes (*The Only Possible Argument in Support of a Demonstration of the Existence of God*, 1763), is Kant's most important precritical work. It is true that several of its ideas are already found earlier (for instance, in the two works published in 1755, the view that the physico-theological proof cannot prove God's omnipotence and that the ontological proof is invalid), but this is the first time that the problem of the proofs of God's existence is systematically developed. The position of the first *Critique* is almost already achieved. Kant considers the argument from purposiveness in nature (which he here still calls the "cosmological argument" but later the "physico-theological argument") natural, but not compelling: at best it proves the existence of an architect, not a creator of matter. It does not allow us to conclude God's omnipotence and omniscience; indeed it does not even allow us to conclude that there is only one God—as Hume had argued independently of Kant, and as the Indian philosopher Ramanuja had already argued in the eleventh or twelfth century. Kant shares the feeling of most intellectuals in continental Europe at his time, namely that the leap from limited goals in nature to the Creator is improper, and he quotes with approval Voltaire's taunt that we have noses so that glasses can be set upon them. In England, however, thanks to the *Bridgewater Treatises*, the physico-theological tradition persisted almost to Darwin's day. For that reason, Kant was interested in a formal-teleological principle such as Maupertuis's "principle of least action," and he stressed that a teleological view of the world could not be excluded even if we succeeded in explaining the order of the world in purely mathematical terms: God could also manifest himself in that mathematical order. Moreover, he acknowledges that the argument from the contingency of the world to a necessary cause is plausible only if the ontological argument is valid. But existence is not an attribute that could be added to the other attributes of the perfect being, in order thereby to infer from the concept of God the existence of God. In the first *Critique*, this becomes the plausible distinction between imagined and real thalers. But Kant did not settle the discussion about the ontological argument; for the latter in no way posits that existence is an attribute like others. There are coherent reconstructions in the framework of modern modal logic, which certainly constantly presuppose the possibility of God: that remains, as Leibniz understood, the problematic premise. However that may be, Kant rejected the proof as early as 1763; but he still believed he had an alternative argument, "the only possible" one. It is a variant of the ontological argument, since it does not presuppose the existence of the world, but rather proceeds *a priori*: the inner possibility of things presupposes a necessary being. But Kant doubts the compelling nature of this proof, which he soon abandoned, and with that he reached the position of the first *Critique*. In the latter, the main objection to the ontological proof is not logical but rather epistemological in nature: our cognitive apparatus depends on the senses to move from possibility to reality. But it speaks for Kant's continuing reflection that in the third *Critique* he recognizes that the onto-logical proof could absolutely be valid for a divine intellect.

Kant expressed his increasing doubts about the validity of metaphysics most trenchantly in *Träume eines Geistersehers, erläutert durch Träume der Metaphysik* ("Dreams of a Spirit Seer, Explained by the Dreams of Metaphysics," 1766). This satirical work is directed against Emanuel Swedenborg, who had reported experiencing parapsychic phenomena. As so often happens, Kant's aggression is only a transfer of self-aggression, in this case of self-doubt; the spirit seers are compared to metaphysicians who build castles in the air. For those familiar with the later works, it is striking how much there is in them that is anticipated in Kant's earlier thought. It is almost as if he had been led to his mature position by an unconscious instinct (one might say: dreaming it in advance). According to Kant, the possibility of immaterial sub-stances beyond space and time (i.e., the later *noumena*) and their mutual influence can theoretically be neither refuted nor proven; seeing spirits could proceed from them, but it could just as well be the result of neurological processes. For Kant, the question is undecidable. Experience alone is the criterion that persuades me that the movement of my arm by my will, unlike that of the moon by my will, is real, even if it is no less enigmatic. Therefore metaphysics is understood as the "science of the limits of human reason." For Kant, however, practical reasons lead us to reject the idea that everything ends with death, no matter how wrong it is to want to be moral only for the sake of a reward in the afterlife. A far-reaching empiricism, the undecidability of certain metaphys-ical questions, for which one can argue both sides, the decisive power of practical reasons that cannot be reduced to self-interest: the development of all of these ideas takes place in the three cri-tiques. In *De mundi sensibilis atque intelligibilis forma et principiis* (*On the Form and Principles of the Sensible and the Intelligible World*, 1770), Kant finally makes a sharp distinction between conceptual and sensual knowledge, which for him are in no way distinguished only gradually, as Leibniz had thought.

All three of the critiques are divided into a long doctrine of elements and a relatively short doctrine of method; the former is further divided into an analytic and a dialectic, and the dialectic discusses an illusion that inevitably imposes itself. However, in the first *Critique* a transcendental aesthetics as a theory of space and time precedes the transcendental logic, which divides into analytic and dialectic. The *Critique of Pure Reason* proposes a middle road between empiricism and rationalism. More consistently than the English empiricists Locke and Berkeley, in whose philosophy God certainly had a place, Kant rejects metaphysical speculations detached from experience—not as false, but rather—and almost as radically as did Logical Positivism—as meaningless. According to him, there can be no demonstrable knowledge without reference to possible experience. But at the same time he maintains that experience is possible only because it is guided by principles that are synthetic *a priori* and are valid for every experience, though not for things-in-themselves. (In his book *The Bounds of Sense*, published in 1966, Peter F. Strawson set forth a masterful reconstruction of Kant's ideas that foregoes the theory of things-in-themselves.) Kant's residual rationalism consists in reflection on the conditions of the possibility of experience, which is eliminated in positivism. Kant develops a significant constructive imagination, even if he himself considered all his constructions as justified only insofar as they make experience possible. In general, experience arises from an interplay between sensibility (intuition) and concept: without concepts, intuitions are blind, concepts without intuition are empty. Intuition is oriented toward individual things or processes, but these must be subsumed under a concept if knowledge is to be achieved.

In addition to empirical intuition Kant also assumes that all experience is preceded by a pure intuition of space and time through the external and internal sense, respectively, within which all experience is played out. The experience of one's own self takes place in the framework of the inner sense, and is thus subject only to time, even though the identity problem can be resolved only by reference to one's own body. According to Kant, both forms of intuition make possible the synthetic *a priori* knowledge of geometry and arithmetic. Kant correctly understands that geometrical propositions are not analytical; the *a priori* nature of (Euclidean) geometry, to which he holds fast, is grounded precisely in this pure intuition of space. Kant's philosophy of mathematics is not, like that of the Neoplatonists, concerned with the peculiar status and multiplicity of mathematical entities; what is central for him is the question as to how it is that geometry can be applied to physical objects. His answer is that our empirical intuition can take place only within the framework of the preceding pure intuition; physical objects can therefore not appear in any way other than as embedded in a (Euclidean) space. Kant can explain the *a priori* nature of mathematical knowledge only by arguing that the forms of intuition belong to our cognitive apparatus, and only to it; space and time are therefore forms not of things-in-themselves, but rather of appearances. This is intended to be a synthesis of Newton's and Leibniz's theories. We note that Kant presupposes the validity of Euclidean geometry, even and precisely for physical space. The physics of the twentieth century did not follow him in this; and many earlier philosophical critics had already understood that Kant's transcendental philosophy takes as its starting point not his own reflection, but external presuppositions, such as experience, whose conditions of possibility he seeks to discover. The first premise of his transcendental arguments—for example: that we have synthetic *a priori* knowledge of physical space—is not immune to doubt, because it presupposes something that is distinct from philosophical reflection (even if in the metaphysical exposition Kant invokes a few arguments for his theory of space). And it is hard to see how Kant's epistemological proposition, according to which only pure intuition and the possibility of experience underlie synthetic *a priori* judgments, can itself be grounded.

Kant's transcendental logic deals with the contribution made by the understanding and by reason (which transcends experience) to the conditions of the possibility of experience. According to Kant, experience is possible only on the basis of twelve pure concepts of understanding, the categories. These he derives arbitrarily from the forms of judgment in the logic of his time, though at the same time offering the seminal hint that the third category in each of the four triads combines the two others. Perhaps the most brilliant part of the first *Critique* is the chapter following this metaphysical deduction, which is entitled "Transzendentale Deduktion der reinen Verstandesbegriffe" ("Transcendental Deduction of the Pure Concepts of the Understanding"), and was extensively revised in the second edition of 1787. (Kant's crucial motive for revising his work was the desire to fend off the suspicion that he was defending a material rather than a purely formal or transcendental idealism, and was thus denying a reality independent of consciousness. Against this Kant emphasizes, even if it is questionable whether he has the right to do so, that in his system the empirically given consciousness is just as phenomenal as the external world). Admittedly, a precise reconstruction of the argument Kant intended is difficult, and there is no consensus as to what is conclusive about it. What is central is the idea that the categories have to mediate between the synthetic unity of apperception of the "I think" and the manifold of sense data, and that only a categorically structured objective world can be related to a self-consciousness understanding itself as unitary, because only in that way can an experience with a claim to validity be distinguished from the mere stream of consciousness. The transcendental deduction is followed by a discussion of the so-called schematism: the categories are made applicable to experience by the fact that they are related to time as forms of intuition. In addition to the categories, Kant justifies the principles of pure understanding as general *a priori* conditions of experience, among which the three analogies of experience are especially important and seek to ground the persistence of substance, succession in accord with the law of causality, and simultaneity in accord with the law of reciprocal influence. The thesis that it is only thanks to causality that a distinction can be drawn between the subjective and the objective temporal orders is crucial to Kant's argument.

The dialectic of the first *Critique* offers a general attack on the rational metaphysics of the academic philosophy of the time, which was divided into psychology, cosmology, and theology. That is why the *Critique of Pure Reason* was the only one of Kant's books that was put on the Catholic Church's *Index librorum prohibitorum*. We have already talked about Kant's criticism of the proofs of God. His rejection of the arguments for the substantiality of the soul was based on the claim that the unity of the "I think," which must be able to accompany all ideas, does not allow an inference to an independent substance; the paralogism involved is based on reinterpreting the unity of experience as the experience of a unity. The cosmological ideas lead to antinomies; equally compelling arguments can be found for and against the theses that the world is limited in space and time, that material objects have ultimately indivisible components, that a causality exists which, unlike the causality of natural laws, can begin freely, and that a necessary being exists within or outside the world. Of course, the arguments for thesis and antithesis are not compelling; Hegel already considered them circular. But for the development of Kant's transcendental idealism they were crucial. We can easily see that basically they provide the only support for Kant's dualism of phenomena and noumena. The mere fact that there is synthetic *a priori* knowledge in no way proves, as Kant claims, that this knowledge concerns phenomena alone; only the identification of contradictions in the assumption that the apparatus of pure understanding can be simply applied to things-in-themselves can justify Kant's position. Kant sees the antinomies as an expression of the fact that the categories and principles function only within the limits of possible experience, and therefore cannot be applied to the world as a whole. Research on nature is in fact infinite, but that does not mean that nature itself is infinite. At the same time Kant attributes a regulative function to the three ideas of reason: the soul, the world, and God. They help us order our knowledge, but unlike the categories, they are not constitutive for our experience. Nonetheless, the inextinguishable inclination of our nature to go beyond experience points toward another possible access to the ideas, an access that is grounded in practical reason, which is not subject to theoretical reason's criterion of significance. Here we are concerned not with knowledge but with belief, which is, however, more than mere opinion.

Kant developed his moral philosophy not only in the *Grundlegung zur Metaphysik der Sitten* (*Groundwork of the Metaphysics of Morals*, 1785), the best introduction to his thought, and the *Kritik der praktischen Vernunft* (*Critique of Practical Reason*, 1788), but also in the *Metaphysik der Sitten* (*Metaphysics of Morals*, 1797); whereas the first two works set forth his revolutionary metaethics, the last work offers his concrete ethics. Only someone who has not read it can claim with a good conscience that Kant broke with the tradition of the ethics of virtue: in it the "doctrine of right" is followed by a second part, the "doctrine of virtue." In truth, Kant wants only to provide a foundation for the traditional virtues. Even if he may not have succeeded in building a bridge between the categorical imperative and concrete norms, because universalizability is a necessary but not sufficient condition for a system of norms, he certainly tried to. His starting point is, as we said, the conception that moral duty is absolute and does not serve an end, even were it the pursuit of happiness. The latter is subject to moral reservation, but is obviously legitimate if it is compatible with morality; indeed, an effort to make others happy is, like self-improvement, a central material duty. In view of the naturalness of our pursuit of happiness, the categorical imperative cannot be based on our sensual nature. Its normativity points to another order, and Kant connects this insight with his distinction between noumena and phenomena. We have already seen that its dualism is untenable; and this is not altered by its being identified with the unavoidable dualism of "is" and "ought." This happens in Kant because for him this dualism guarantees the possibility of a noncompatibilistic freedom; but at the same time the moral law can be binding on us only if it is the expression of freedom. However, freedom in the sense of self-determination is not identical with freedom in the sense of causal indetermination, even if we agree with Kant that the moral law arises from a self-obligation made by practical reason—true freedom consists in following the moral law.

Kant's empiricist theory of knowledge leads to the result that freely self-determining practical reason cannot ground a material ethics but only a formal ethics. In its first formulation, the categorical imperative reads: "I should never act in such a way that I could not also will that my maxim should be a universal law." Kant thus conceptualizes the basic idea of the Enlightenment that reformed, at first gradually, then with the French Revolution ever more rapidly, a legal system marked by countless disparities and the hierarchical social order of the *ancien régime*. Kant expresses the universalist conviction that something is permissible (and analogously obligatory or forbidden) for one person if—*ceteris paribus*—it is also permissible for all others. Furthermore, the universalizability of a moral precept as the condition of its permissibility implies that Kant prohibits certain acts not only categorically but also without exception; lying is not allowed even if it is the only way to save an innocent person. This rigorism follows from the lack of a hierarchy of material goods and the fear that once exceptions are allowed, a justification for everything can easily ensue. It is not without predecessors (Augustine held an analogous view with regard to lying) but it diametrically contradicts Plato's ethics, for example; and it certainly left its mark on German culture. The demand that human beings never use the humanity in themselves or any other person as a mere means, but always also as an end in itself goes beyond formalism. Kant errs when he considers this formulation logically equivalent to the first one; in reality, he arrives at it through the explication of the categorical imperative's character as an end in itself, which is transferred to those for whom it holds, namely all persons. Only rational beings are persons, who may exist in nonhuman forms on other heavenly bodies. Kant can therefore justify the ban on torturing animals only by arguing that doing so also blunts sympathy among humans: the duty with regard to animals is not a duty to animals. According to Kant, it is part of moral action that it is not only in accord with duty, but is done out of duty; the motive must not be the inclination to concrete, ethically required behavior, but rather obedience to duty out of respect for the moral law, which may then be followed by self-approval. However, since we do not know our true selves and Kant does not even have a worked-out theory of the experience of other phenomenal selves, we cannot be certain that even a single action was ever performed out of duty.

In the dialectic of the second *Critique* Kant comes to grips chiefly with the relationship between morality and religion. Even if it is simply unacceptable to make the desire for happiness the moving cause of virtue, the converse also seems impossible: worthiness of being happy still does not guarantee happiness, because human beings' sensual nature and their practical reason are heterogeneous in origin. However, a correspondence between the two is the whole and perfect good, and pure reason has a practical interest in believing in this possibility. This leads to the immortality of the soul and God as postulates of practical reason (freedom has a somewhat different status, because for Kant it is given directly with the moral law, even though it, too, is not positively grounded in theoretical reason). Kant's argument for the immortality of the soul is not, however, that we are due a reward for moral behavior, but rather that there can never be an end to the arduous labor of adapting our will to the moral law: Leibniz's eternal progress is reversed from the intellectual into the moral. In simple terms we can say that Kant replaces Paradise with eternal Purgatory as the final condition. The belief in God is justified in an analogous way, since without a common principle for the moral law and for nature, hope in the attainability of the perfect good is vain. According to Kant, the postulates of practical reason do not have the status of knowledge; but insofar as they are compatible with theoretical reason, one may believe in them with a good conscience.

Ethicotheology, the development of a theology on the basis of the experience of the moral law, is Kant's true contribution to the philosophy of religion. Rational ethicotheology is the standard for evaluating actually existing religions, including Christianity, to which Kant's relationship is ambivalent. Naïve Christian piety was foreign to the mature Kant, and he found religious violence, superstition, enthusiasm, and hierarchical arbitrariness abhorrent. In fact, Kant saw in the notion that God stands over the moral law and can demand an immoral action (such as ordering Abraham to sacrifice Isaac) something repellent that undermined morality. But a religious interpretation of reality as the expression of a moral principle he considered legitimate, indeed, morally obligatory. *Die Religion innerhalb der Grenzen der bloßen Vernunft* (*Religion within the Boundaries of Mere Reason*, 1793) subjects Christianity in particular to a test of its compatibility with the religion of reason, which had become so important to the early Enlightenment. Kant reinterprets Christianity: the doctrine of original sin is replaced by that of radical evil, which emphasizes the free human decision to subordinate the moral law to inclination. Analogously, the doctrine of Christ's vicarious atonement is replaced by the notion that human beings can justify themselves through a moral revolution that is guided by the ethical law; Christ is a (not really necessary) model that provides an example of life in accord with the moral law. Miracles, grace, and revelation are integrated into the thoroughly causal nexus of the phenomenal world. The generality of natural laws corresponds to the universality of the moral law. Kant's work, which is close to Pelagianism and Socinianism and as distant from Lutheran orthodoxy as can be imagined, triggered a response on the part of the Prussian censors; Kant had to promise the bigoted King Frederick William II never to publish on religious questions again—a promise that he kept, but only until the king died in 1797. In 1798 he defended, in *Der Streit der Fakultäten* (*The Contest of Faculties*), the sovereign right of philosophy to judge even regarding juristic and theological questions. The typically Kantian combination of an Enlightenment-style commitment to reason with a religiousness fed by moral certainties did not exist in England or Italy; Rousseau came closest to it, but he had a much more negative view of reason and science than did Kant.

Since Kant's central ethical thought consists, as it were, in the adoption of the modern form of juridical thought, it cannot be surprising that he offers a moral legitimation of law. Kant thus continues a thousand-year-old tradition of natural law that he now detaches from all theological and cosmological presuppositions and seeks to ground solely in the categorical imperative. Every human being has an original right to freedom—but that means that he also has to respect other persons' right to freedom. Just law, which is characterized by its authority to coerce, is defined as "the aggregate of those conditions under which the will of one person can be conjoined with the will of another in accordance with a universal law of freedom." Law concerns only external acts, not inner attitudes; legality, not morality; and it is oriented toward the regulation of freedom, not toward the satisfaction of needs; therefore Kant does not justify a welfare state. However, according to Kant one also has a legal obligation to oneself; one's own person is inalienable. His doctrine of right deals with both private and public law. The former is concerned primarily with the justification of private property and contractual principles. His views on marital law were criticized early on; their unworldliness may have something to do with Kant's life as a bachelor and his misogyny. On the other hand, a few of his ideas in this domain, such as that a spouse has a legal claim to sexual intercourse, were until recently also valid in Western European legal systems. In public law Kant favored the principle of the separation of powers as well as republican ideas (even if he still did not advocate universal suffrage). His ideas on international law, as he worked them out in *Zum ewigen Frieden* (*Perpetual Peace*, 1795) are particularly forward-looking. Kant is one of the most severe moral critics of the institution of war: "Now, morally practical reason in us pronounces in us its irresistible veto: *there is to be no war.*" It is true that according to Kant there is such a thing as a morally legitimate war, but not only must strict moral norms underlie the *casus belli* and the conduct of the war, there is also a duty to establish a kind of league of nations that is not a world state but nonetheless will limit the outbreak of wars. In fact, Kant also advocates a general cosmopolitan right that would enable people, not to settle anywhere they wished, but to visit every country; he believes that economic and cultural exchange will erode the human inclination toward war. Since the greatest explosion of intra-European violence since 1648 occurred during the last years of Kant's life, and no serious work on his idea of an international league began until 1945, on reading his work we can be seized by melancholy in view of the rapid evaporation, in the age of nationalism, of Enlightenment cosmopolitism, and on the other hand feel confidence that people ultimately return to reasonable ideas.

However, two ideas in Kant's theory of public law are rather chilling. These do not include his defense of a retributive theory of justice, according to which punishment is demanded by justice regardless of the goals that it might attain, but rather his specific defense of the indispensability of capital punishment in the case of murder. Intellectually, Kant is immensely superior to Cesare Beccaria, who in 1764 published his criticism of capital punishment, by which a few states were timidly influenced still in the eighteenth century; but this does not mean that Kant was right about this question, even if for a long time he made it possible for advocates of capital punishment to preserve a good conscience, indeed even guaranteed them a moral feeling. Furthermore, Kant rejects any right to resist. This is partly a result of his fundamental inability to legitimate exceptions to *prima facie* norms. There is no doubt that there is a *prima facie* norm requiring obedience to the state, if one wants to avoid anarchy. Thomas Hobbes had made particularly powerful use of this argument with regard to the English Civil War. But paradoxically, for precisely that reason his theory of resistance is less dangerous than Kant's, because it rests on a much poorer ethical foundation. Hobbes recognizes only hypothetical imperatives that are subordinate to the individual's drive to self-preservation, and therefore if the state no longer performs its function of providing protection, the duty to obey ceases to apply. Kant is nobler, and for that very reason the duty to obey continues to exist even if it collides with one's own interests. Kant's theory is in part an expression of his Lutheranism; we have already referred to the latter's bondage to the government, which became even greater as Prussia rose to the status of a European great power. However, Kant's theory cuts both ways: He opposes revolutions, but when they have proven successful, he opposes counterrevolutions just as much. His analysis of the French Revolution is not only inspired by his sympathy with its political ideas, but also emphasizes that the revolutionary government must be respected. Nonetheless it remains true that, unlike the Anglo-American world, Germany was not provided by its greatest philosophers with a positive and at the same time moderate theory of resistance such as that of John Locke.

Kant not only teaches that political practice must be adapted to the demands of moral theory, but also assumes, in "Idee zu einer allgemeinen Geschichte in weltbürgerlicher Absicht" ("Idea for a Universal History with a Cosmpolitan Purpose," 1784), that there is a slow movement, based on morally questionable motives, toward the morally required political institutions. Kant shares with various eighteenth-century thinkers the recognition that human action produces a system of unintended consequences, even if with the theory of human nature's unsocial sociability he gave this idea a special emphasis. This recognition can be connected with a belief in divine Providence. In the *Idea*, human action was already embedded in a teleological natural nexus; but Kant discussed this problem much more fundamentally in the "Methodology of Teleological Judgment," a long final section of the *Critique of Judgment* (1790). The rehabilitation of teleology proceeds from the adherence to a normative point of reference and the insight that it can be achieved only through the mediation of natural causes.

The third *Critique* thus deviates from its two predecessors in that it consists of two parts constructed in parallel that are, at least on first inspection, independent of each other: the critique of aesthetic judgment and the critique of teleological judgment, which deal with natural beauty and with natural ends, respectively. They are both forms of reflective judgment which, unlike determinative judgment, ascends from a given particular to the universal. And yet the inner duality of the *Critique of Judgment* cannot conceal the fact that Kant, who for the most part uses dichotomic divisions, now chooses a tripartite division for the structure of his system on the most general level. The third Critique's central task is to bridge the dualism between nature and freedom, understanding and reason; Kant positions the feeling of pleasure and displeasure as mediating between the faculty of cognition and the faculty of desire. (These three faculties are

also made the basis of the descriptive *Anthropologie in pragma-
tischer Hinsicht abgefaßt* [*"Anthropology From a Pragmatic Point
of View,"* 1798].) Kant remains true to the starting point of the
first *Critique* insofar as he attributes to teleological judgments
only a regulative, not a constitutive role. But the explicit discussion of the organic on the one hand, and the place of human
beings in nature on the other hand, goes far beyond the first *Critique* thematically. With regard to the first theme, Kant seeks a
middle way between the vitalistic view that it will never be possible to explain life mechanically, so that there can be no Newton of the blade of grass, and the opposite view, which may be
open to a more complex understanding than our own, for which
the mechanical and the teleological explanations coincide. Kant
grasps precisely inner purposefulness, metabolism, and reproduction as the essential marks of the organic, and sympathizes with
the idea of trans-specific evolution. The organic points beyond
the understanding, toward reason; in the idea of life, the noumenal is immanent, as it were—a thesis which, like Kant's reference
to an archetypal understanding of a nature different from ours,
anticipates German idealism and most convincingly disproves
the anthropologistic interpretation of the *Critiques* that was
widespread before the advent of neo-Kantianism. Kant extends
the teleological reflection on organisms to nature as a whole,
which is interpreted as if it were oriented toward the possibility
of the moral. For Kant, only morality is an ultimate goal; without
this final point of reference, the purposefulness of organisms is
without value. A religion based on it alone is a demonology that
is to be superseded by an ethicotheology.

Herder was deeply disappointed by Kant's aesthetics because
of its formalism. In fact, Kant's experience of art was very limited; moreover, the emergence of a new kind of "human sciences"
(*Geisteswissenschaft,* a development that will be examined in the
next chapter) had left no mark on the old Kant, for whom natural beauty was more important than artistic beauty. Nonetheless modern art, which has largely detached itself from contents,
experiences Kant's formalism as liberating, and his aesthetic theory undoubtedly remains one of the most original and influential
in the history of philosophy. Even if Kant develops his aesthetics
only in the framework of a theory of judgment, for him its function as a bridge is central; he is not the first author of an aesthetics,

but he is the first to maintain that a philosophical system cannot be complete without reflections on aesthetics. Though his ideas do not exclude the aesthetics of the artwork and especially production aesthetics, Kant's point of departure is of a reception aesthetics nature, namely the judgment of taste. Unlike the pleasant and the good, the beautiful necessarily elicits a disinterested enjoyment that is represented as general. The generality of the judgment of taste distinguishes the beautiful from the pleasant, purely subjective; at the same time, the judgment of taste is less general than moral judgment, because it is not based on concepts: therefore it can only "require" agreement from everyone. Kant treads a middle path between the emotive and the rationalist aesthetics of the Enlightenment: a feeling of pleasure is undeniably part of aesthetic experience, but it follows a cognitive phenomenon, namely the free play of the imagination and the understanding (that is the crucial point of Kant's deduction of the generality of judgments of taste, which does not suffice, however, to guarantee agreement in comparative judgments). The pure judgment of taste is concerned exclusively with formal purposefulness, and with neither charm nor perfection; it is directed toward free beauty, like that of flowers, whereas the adherent beauty of, for example, a building, which presupposes a concept of purpose, strays from the purity of that judgment. Since there are no objective rules of taste, the genius has the task of giving art rules; but taste must control genius. In this connection Kant develops the concept of aesthetic ideas, which corresponds to that of the ideas of reason; indeed, despite his formalism, Kant does not hesitate to see beauty as a symbol of morality. The sublime especially, which Kant ranks alongside the beautiful, has the peculiarity of addressing itself both to the imagination and to reason (not to the understanding), and of moving the mind in such a way that it becomes, confronting enormous masses or forces of nature, aware of its own inner sublimity. Thus Kant permanently influenced both German tragic drama, especially from the mature Schiller on, and German theory of tragedy, which with Schiller's pertinent essays (for instance, "Über den Grund des Vergnügens an tragischen Gegenständen" ["Of the Cause of the Pleasure We Derive from Tragic Objects," 1792]) began to free itself from the Aristotelian conception, which put the plot, not the hero, in the center.

๙ 6 ๛

The Human Sciences as a Religious Duty: Lessing, Hamann, Herder, Schiller, the Early Romantics, and Wilhelm von Humboldt

Sometimes the limits of great minds are no less instructive than their achievements. Kant did more to ground modern natural science and morals than almost anyone else, but he did not set forth a critique of interpretive reason (*verstehende Vernunft*). He lacked a sense for the specific nature of the human sciences; indeed, like other idealists, in the first Critique he avoided solipsism only because he did not really raise the problem. This is all the more astounding because in addition to Kant's philosophy the greatest achievement of the German eighteenth century was the development of a new human science. But although in 1805 Goethe coedited *Winckelmann und sein Jahrhundert* (*Winckelmann and his Century*), and thus named the eighteenth century after Winckelmann, Kant's books mention neither Winckelmann nor Goethe (this though Goethe highly valued the connection of nature with art in the third *Critique*). What was the origin of the German human science? It is well known that its creators often came from Lutheran parsonages and/or had themselves studied Lutheran theology, a course of study that included excellent philological training in Greek and Latin, and sometimes also Hebrew. However, it was precisely this education that threw the intellectually best and morally most upright representatives of Lutheranism into a peculiar crisis: in 1799 Novalis complained about the "hectic influence" of philology on theology. For example, philology taught Hermann Samuel Reimarus (1694–1768) to reconstruct the actually intended meaning of the Scriptures; this made apparent the contradictions between particular biblical texts that premodern exegetes had papered over—even and especially authors such as Meister Eckhart. Modern historiographic methods identified secondary causes of religious ideas, and these were not always edifying. Most significant, in the eighteenth century confidence in the historical reliability of biblical narratives collapsed, for instance in the chronological information they provide, while at the same time the universalism of the Enlightenment saw the limitation of salvation history to the Jews and Christians as a narrow-mindedness incompatible with the new ethics. Whereas the Catholic and also the Anglican Churches still did not really accept the challenge of modern biblical criticism, Hume and Gibbon invented a distinctive style of detached irony with which they recounted the natural history of religion in general and Christianity in particular from the vantage point of agnosticism or deism. This form of irony, which is quite different from Voltaire's malicious glee and the world-weariness of the German Romantics, is nonetheless incompatible with the Lutheran pathos of sincerity. Nietzsche's aggressive atheism is Lutheran in its sincerity; but the transformation of Lutheranism that took place in Germany's intellectual elites at the end of the eighteenth century is more complex and consists in the retention of the religious motivation of philology, which was, however, now extended to universal history and philosophically grounded. We can speak of a trinity of theology, philosophy, and philology. The word of God, which was still studied fervently, was no longer limited to the Bible, but manifested itself in the whole history of the human spirit. Understanding it as a unity is not only a valid scholarly interest; it is a religious duty, and presumably it is only by fulfilling such a duty that one has a chance to do something really lasting. No work of Goethe's expressed this view more splendidly than his fragment "Die Geheimnisse" (The mysteries), with its description of a universal religion of humanity, a description that owes much to a suggestion made by Johannes Valentinus Andreae (1586–1654), who was the author of the *Chymische Hochzeit Christiani Rosencreutz* [*The Chymical Wedding of Christian Rosencreutz*], 1616).

No one so energetically pursued the breakdown of the old Lutheran orthodoxy, (and did so with religious arguments that he adapted according to his changing conversation partners) as did Gotthold Ephraim Lessing (1729–1781). Perhaps his most momentous text is *Über den Beweis des Geistes und der Kraft* (*On the Proof of the Spirit and of Power*, 1777), in which he teaches, just as Kant does a little later, that contingent historical truths cannot provide the foundation for necessary rational truths. It would therefore be a mistake, for example, to try to justify Christological dogmas on the basis of biblical accounts of miracles, even if one could persuade oneself of their historical veracity, which is not easy in an age without miracles. (On the other hand, in "Das Christentum der Vernunft" ["The Christianity of Reason"] the young Lessing defends the doctrine of the immanent Trinity on the basis of the idea of God's thinking of himself.) Yet it would be false to attribute to Lessing a farewell to Christianity, with regard to which the defenders of the religion of reason, which is sometimes called "Deism," adopted entirely different positions. Although it decouples the Christian command to love from traditional doctrines of faith, "Das Testament Johannis" ("The Testament of St. John"), which is despite its brevity one of the most moving dialogues in the German language, defends it resolutely. Lessing's most important work in the area of the philosophy of religion, *Die Erziehung des Menschengeschlechts* (*The Education of the Human Race*, 1780), acknowledges the necessity of positive divine revelation at the beginning of the process of education, but argues that the latter seeks to promote reason, which in the end requires neither worldly nor other-worldly sanctions. Autonomy and theonomy once again coincide, but factual history of religion can and should be conceived as rational. Lessing's sympathy with a religion of reason made it easier for him to be friends with Moses Mendelssohn (1729–1796), with whom Jewish thought begins to have an important place in German-language philosophy. Rejecting Johann Kaspar Lavater's unabashed demand that he convert to Christianity, Mendelssohn clung to his religion, which he nonetheless interpreted rationalistically; with his contribution to the Haskalah he paved the way for the emancipation of the Jews. In the eponymous hero of *Nathan der Weise* (*Nathan the Wise*), which is a manifesto directed against the subordination of morality to an irrational God and against ecclesiastical arbitrariness, as well as an apology for a religion freeing itself from external rites, Lessing erected a monument to his friend, who after Lessing's death defended him against Friedrich Heinrich Jacobi's (1743–1819) accusation, in *Über die Lehre des Spinoza* (On Spinoza's doctrine, 1785), that he was a Spinozist. The controversy over pantheism that was connected with this had two consequences that Jacobi had not intended. First, it led to an increased interest in Spinoza; and in 1811 he repeated the accusation of pantheism against Schelling. Second, Mendelssohn rightly pointed out that Lessing's pantheism was much more subtle than Spinoza's, and hardly deviated from a theism like Leibniz's. There can be no doubt that Lessing is a moral realist and defends a teleological interpretation of reality—and this corresponds to Leibniz, not to Spinoza. The fascination with Spinoza in the German culture of the time was determined by his language, which was uncompromising compared to Leibniz's; it was nonetheless, as also in Herder, a Spinozism transformed by Leibniz. That was to change only with Nietzsche. However, Jacobi's philosophical achievement consists in having emphasized the importance of unmediated evidence (of belief and feeling, and later of an immediately intuitive reason) for the theory of knowledge. He held that in it alone a personal God was given.

Lessing might seldom be first-rate as a poet (because he too often says too clearly what matters to him); but as a literary critic and aesthetician he is always first-rate. To be sure, around 1750 German culture had already produced, with Johann Martin Chladenius (1710–1759) and Alexander Gottlieb Baumgarten (1714–1762), important works on hermeneutics and aesthetics, but Lessing represents something entirely new. His *Laocoon* (1766) deals with the "limits of painting and poetry," and is thus an attempt to differentiate aesthetic norms (for example, the role of the ugly) for the different arts. That presupposes the general concept of the fine arts, which first appears in the modern age. What makes Lessing's treatise so magnificent is the combination of a comprehensive knowledge of Antiquity, a great familiarity also with modern literature, and a construction of new categories characterized by precision. He can be accused of having given aesthetics too strong a psychological bias, and of having committed a few philological errors; but in the combination of classical philology and general aesthetics the work is just as trailblazing as

Johann Joachim Winckelmann's *Geschichte der Kunst des Alter-tums* (*History of Ancient Art*, 1764). There had already been antiquarian archeology, but Winckelmann's contrast between Greek and Oriental art, the discovery of a law of development for ancient art in the third part of his fourth chapter, his glorification of Greek civilization on the basis of a religion of art, and finally his way of describing art, which is an art in itself, guarantee his work's epochal standing. It is again the fusion of detailed knowledge and general categories that made it such a success—even Heinrich Wölfflin's *Kunstgeschichtliche Grundbegriffe* (*Principles of Art History,* 1915), with its paradigmatic opposition of Renaissance and Baroque, would be inconceivable without Winckelmann. And the philhellenic idea produced a new form of humanism that, unlike the first humanism, detached itself from Christian dogma, though in its universalistic ethics it owes far more to Christianity than to Antiquity.

Lessing's writings on the philosophy of religion and aesthetics are largely independent of one another. Johann Gottfried Herder's (1744–1802) achievement consists in having developed a theology of the human sciences, so to speak: in his work, the elucidation of the intellectual world, and in particular of the poetic art of peoples, becomes a kind of religious duty. Since Herder interprets the Bible purely immanently, like other texts, and thereby helped found German Oriental studies, he seems to follow Reimarus; but since in decoding all the great texts he senses in them the spirit of God, as it were, we can just as well say that he universalized traditional biblical interpretation. In this regard Herder was influenced by the "Magus of the North," Johann Georg Hamann (1730–1788), in whom uneasiness with the rationalism of the Enlightenment found a hermetic expression: there are few German-language works that are so hard to understand as the short and obscure writings—sparkling with wit and Bible quotations, and deliberately unsystematic-associative—of this Laurence Sterne of philosophy. Hamann's starting point is a religious experience, namely his personal relationship to Jesus and to the Bible as the word of God; to this aspect of his thought only his admirer Søren Kierkegaard remained faithful, not Herder, who followed Lessing in Christology. But Herder was able to achieve a synthesis of Lessing and Hamann only because the latter used a basically old-fashioned form of theology to discover, even in the pagan world, resonances of Biblical salvation history. In his first work, *Sokratische Denkwürdigkeiten* (*Socratic Memorabilia*, 1759), which is directed against Kant's critique of Hamann's way of life, he presents Socrates as a predecessor of his own existential conception of philosophy; the bodily aspects of philosophizing, such as Socrates's homoeroticism, are emphasized. At the same time, Socrates is an equivalent of the Jewish prophets; indeed, the whole of human history has to be interpreted as mythology, that is, as a type of biblical events: "a riddle that cannot be solved, unless we plow with a calf other than our reason." According to Hamann, and his friend Jacobi, belief can and should not be justified, "because *belief* takes place as little through reasons as do *tasting* and *seeing*"; feeling is irreducible to concepts. Hamann's *Aesthetica in nuce* (Aesthetics in a nutshell) emphasizes the pre-rational origin of human culture in poetry, song, and similes; in the modern world, which has lost its connection with the divine, the creature becomes alternately a sacrificial victim and an idol. Hamann's biblical piety leads him to a metaphysics of language. In his *Metakritik über den Purismum der Vernunft* (Metacritique of the purism of reason) he cites as one of his main objections to Kant's ideas his neglect of the linguistic nature of our reason. He refers thereby to a central theme of later philosophy, even though his philosophical style is so little commensurable with Kant's rigorous analyses. The later opposition between hermeneutic and analytic philosophy is preshaped in the debate between Hamann/Herder and Kant.

Herder is central in the history of German culture for three reasons. First, he gave German philosophy a new focus in the disciplines of philosophical anthropology, the philosophy of language and history, and aesthetics and hermeneutics. Second, through his poetics, which broke with French classicism and rehabilitated popular poetry and Shakespeare, through his own highly expressive style, and also due to his personal meeting with Goethe in Strasbourg in 1770/71, he helped found the "Storm and Stress" (*Sturm und Drang*) movement, which represents, as it were, the spring awakening of German poetry. Third, through his career as its general superintendent, he introduced the new philosophical religiousness into the Evangelical Church. However, his philosophy is less rigorous methodologically than that of Kant, who wrote a sharply critical review of Herder's main work, *Ideen zur Philosophie der Geschichte der Menschheit* (*Ideas toward a Philosophy of the History of Man*, 1784–1792); and even if Kant did not do justice to its importance, the mediation between Herder's substantial insights and a formally more rigorous philosophy remained a task that only the German idealists proved capable of performing—with regard to anthropology, Fichte, and to the remaining disciplines, Hegel. Herder's prize-winning *Abhandlung über den Ursprung der Sprache* (*Treatise on the Origin of Language*, 1772) is directed, on the one hand, against Johann Peter Süssmilch's theory of the divine origin of language, and on the other against Condillac's theory of the animal origin of language. Herder's assumption of a purely human origin reflects a deeper religiousness, precisely because it avoids using elaborate stage machinery and anthropomorphizing God, while at the same time attributing creative powers to human beings, precisely *qua* creatures of God: "The origin of language thus becomes divine in a worthy manner only insofar as it is human." The possibility and necessity of language emerged from the specific nature of human beings, who differ from other animals through their lack of instincts: a thesis that deeply influenced Gehlen. Precisely because man's senses are less acute, he can relate to the whole world; and this relationship to the world is not something that is imposed on an animal basis, but instead changes the nature of animal functions: "The most sensual condition of humankind was still human." The decisive mark of the human being is language, which according to Herder must develop even in an isolated human; in his work, language's communicative function plays a smaller role than its expressive and representative function. In the context of a complex philosophy of the senses, Herder justifies the special status of the intermediate sense of hearing. Thinking manifests itself in speech and underlies it; thus the development of the mind can be inferred from that of language. Poetry precedes prose; abstract concepts are acquired late.

Herder's work *Auch eine Philosophie der Geschichte zur Bildung der Menschheit* (*Yet Another Philosophy of History for the Education of Humanity*, 1774) is even more important; it is directed against Voltaire's *Philosophie de l'histoire* (*Philosophy of History*). Since the publication of Herder's book there has been a specifically German philosophy of history; Hegel's lectures on the philosophy of history simply carry out Herder's program. The true turning point in the history of the philosophy of history occurs in the eighteenth century, when the ancient cyclical model—to which the greatest Italian philosopher, Giambattista Vico (1668–1744), still clung—is superseded by the idea of progress. Although Vico and Herder share similar interests (it was, significantly, in one of Hamann's letters to Herder that Vico was mentioned almost for the first time in the German-speaking world) and both of them took a particular interest in the prerational phases of human culture (which in no way makes them opponents of Enlightenment), Herder's philosophy of history, like Voltaire's, approves of progress: the development from the world of the patriarchs of the Orient through Egypt, Phoenicia, Greece, Rome, and medieval Christianity down to the modern age is compared with the ages of human life. But unlike Voltaire, and entirely like Vico, Herder insists that the individual epochs have their distinctive logics which have to be grasped as such: even Winckelmann is reproached for having unjustly subjected Egyptian art to Greek standards. It is a mistake to attribute relativism to Herder, or even to celebrate him, as did the National Socialists, as a predecessor of an antiuniversalistic nationalism: Herder is concerned only to recognize without prejudice the values that are possible at a specific stage of development and that are sometimes incompatible with later ones; virtues and vices are therefore often interwoven. Seeing more than mere barbarism in pre-Enlightenment cultures is for Herder a religious duty, because thereby Providence is recognized in history; fundamentally, it is the expression of a universalistic ethics, to which he adheres and which he sees as prepared by Christianity's supersession of the ancient ethnic religions. The advancement of humanity always remains Herder's goal. To be sure, he grants each culture a right to its own specificity. He criticizes the moral atrophy and hypocrisy of the Enlightenment (for example, European colonialism), but he knows that this latter period, too, has its necessary place in the history of humankind. In his main work, the history of humankind is integrated into the history of nature, within which the special status of humans is worked out in a way that remains valid today.

Herder was helpful to Goethe's poetic genius, because he drew his attention to the vitality of original folk poetry and offered him a universal-history perspective on all the creations of the human spirit. Thus a unique mixture of natural freshness and philosophical subtlety was produced that characterizes German culture around 1800 and distinguishes it as much from the artificiality of the Rococo as from the ultimate hostility to the intellect that characterized the Rousseauist revolt directed against it, from the naïveté of Anglican orthodoxy as well as from the condescending winks of the Scottish Enlightenment thinkers. The German concept of *Kultur*, in contrast to the French *civilisation*, has its origin here, and in it compensation plays a role: the resort to Germany's own folklore was possible and necessary, because Germany did not enjoy the same intellectual prestige as did France. Lessing's twofold talent as a poet and a philosopher was not granted to many; but his model sensitized German poets to philosophical questions and oriented German philosophers toward aesthetics. Goethe himself gave perfect poetic expression to the complex worldview that was now formed, and, with the *Bildungsroman*, created a new and typically German (because intellectual) subgenre, even if he himself was not a professional philosopher, or even an original aesthetician (only his concrete interpretations of artworks, in the plastic arts even more than in poetry, are pathbreaking).

In contrast, Friedrich Schiller (1759–1805) has a permanent place in the history of aesthetics; indeed, he gave it a central role in the conclusion of the system of philosophy that is only envisaged in Kant. In "Über Anmut und Würde" ("On Grace and Dignity," 1793), Schiller already thoroughly criticized Kant's moral rigorism on the grounds that although subjection to the moral law is needful, with grace, a harmony of inclination and duty is possible. Thus a traditional aesthetic category is given a moral function. The letters "Über die ästhetische Erziehung des Menschen" ("On the Aesthetic Education of Man, 1795) attribute in a more general way a central role to beauty in mediating between nature and morals; without it, morality easily becomes coercion. Certainly Schiller's valorization of the sense of beauty also pursues a political goal; aesthetic education is conceived as an alternative to revolution, which is according to Schiller a misguided path to the realization of moral ideas. Presumably he thereby furthered the ideal of an apolitical aesthete that distinguishes the German culture of the nineteenth century from English or French culture, in which intellectuals were often involved in the government or acted as its challengers. And yet the hope of restoring, through aesthetic sensitization, the ancient unity of all spheres of life and thereby preparing the way for a more moral society is a noble one; and the theory of the play drive, which mediates between the sensuous and the formal drive, gave pedagogy a new twist. "Über naive und sentimentalische Dichtung" ("On Naïve and Sentimental Poetry," 1795) attempts to distinguish two basic types of poetry that also reflect the opposition between Goethe and Schiller themselves, but belong to a philosophy-of-history perspective. The opposition between ancient and modern poetry, which had been agitating European poetics since the Quarrel between the Ancients and the Moderns, was thereby raised to a new conceptual level; in particular, Schiller recognized that the longing for nature is not itself a natural feeling, and emerges late.

This linkage between aesthetics and the philosophy of history constitutes an essential characteristic of the early Romantic reorientation. Since it was also strongly influenced by Fichte, it should actually be dealt with in the next chapter, but will be discussed now because of its aesthetic focus. The importance of August Wilhelm Schlegel (1767–1845) and Friedrich Schlegel (1772–1829)—who, along with the Humboldts, Grimms, and Manns, are among the most significant pair of brothers in German intellectual history—consists in the fact that they were the first to command an exhaustive knowledge of the whole of world literature; with them was born a canon of world literature. To the new ideal of the autonomy of art, which is manifested in the theory and in the reality of absolute music, consummately described by Carl Dahlhaus, as well as in the triumph of poetics over rhetoric, corresponds criticism's sense of its mission as a middle term between philosophy and history. August Wilhelm Schlegel's lectures "Über dramatische Kunst und Literatur" ("On Dramatic Art and Literature," 1809–1811) not only lay out a panorama of unprecedented breadth, but they also adhere to the principle that different norms underlie classical and Romantic drama: despite their differences, Sophocles and Shakespeare are equally important. The special status of Greek poetry consists not only in the quality of its masterpieces, but also in the paradigmatic nature of its development. The Schlegels were not only equally competent in ancient and modern literature, but also had begun to explore literature outside Europe. They founded German Indology, which in the nineteenth and twentieth centuries enjoyed a leading role worldwide. Friedrich Schlegel was less disciplined than his brother, but he used new literary forms for literary criticism. In addition to the treatise, he was master of the aphorism and of the dialogue as well; his "Gespräch über die Poesie" ("Dialogue on Poetry," 1800) mirrors the Romantics' culture of conversation, in which for the first time women also had a place, even if limited to providing inspiration, and which itself represents a poetical poetics. Philosophy was to be poetic, and poetry was to become philosophical. The fragments published in the periodical *Athenäum*, which appeared only from 1798 to 1800, also express the early Romantics' common philosophizing. The commonality remained as short-lived as that of the "Storm and Stress" writers, and yet the ideal of philosophical friendship among young people remains so beautiful and is so typical of German culture, that we cannot smile at it but only elegiacally invoke it. Schlegel's fragments anticipate many ideas that Hegel was to elaborate, though they are expressed in a deliberately paradoxical, antisystematic form that at the same time yearns for system: "It is just as lethal for the spirit to have a system as not to have one. It will therefore have to resolve to combine the two." One cannot live with such paradoxes; in the long run the sense of ultimate forlornness that arises when one is faced with an infinite abundance of important intellectual works produces an inner emptiness against which even the Romantic theory of irony is of only a little comfort. Schlegel finally converted, along with his wife, Moses Mendelssohn's daughter Dorothea, to Catholicism, which however only slowly became the starting point for innovative German intellectuals.

One of the most original contributors to *Athenäum* was Georg Friedrich von Hardenberg (1772–1801), who called himself Novalis. His "Hymnen an die Nacht" ("Hymns to the Night") provided a dark counter-accent to the Enlightenment's metaphor of light, justified a longing for death (which never became aggressive, however), and nostalgically invoked pagan and Christian religious history. His essay "Die Christenheit oder Europa" (Christianity or Europe) glorifies, even if it ironically refracts them, the Catholic Middle Ages and criticizes both the Reformation and the main trends of the Enlightenment, which in his view undermine any enthusiasm. At the same time, Novalis had great hopes for German culture, which was in the van of "a slow but sure movement ahead of the other European countries"; Goethe is said to believe that "the intellectual barycenter lies under the German people." To be sure, Novalis was a convinced European; for him, Germanness was in principle a universal ideal. But he emphatically defended the Prussian monarchy, which was not yet constitutional; a genuine royal couple is more important to him than a constitution, as we read in his "Glauben und Liebe oder der König und die Königin" ("Faith and Love, or the King and the Queen"), which rhapsodizes on Queen Louise. Given Novalis's endearing disposition, it is not easy to criticize him; but it is nonetheless true that political Romanticism, which was given eloquent expression especially by Adam Heinrich Müller (1779–1829) and to which Friedrich Wilhelm IV, for example, adhered, made more difficult Germany's transition to a parliamentary monarchy on the British model. The reader will evaluate more positively Müller's astute discernment of the moral and religious presuppositions that underlie economic processes (factors that had less interest for contemporary British economic science), which motivated him to grant the state a more important role in the economy.

To art's new autonomy corresponded the autonomy of religion, which Friedrich Schlegel's Reformed friend Friedrich Schleiermacher (1768–1834) elaborated in *Über die Religion. Reden an die Gebildeten unter ihren Verächtern* (*On Religion: Speeches to its Cultured Despisers,* 1799). According to Schleiermacher, religion is to be reduced neither to metaphysics nor to morality, but is instead a "sense and taste for the infinite." Thus religion became accessible once again to people who had detached themselves from the old dogmas. Schleiermacher's theology of feeling has roots in the Enlightenment and in Pietism, even if it represents something entirely new and is probably the greatest caesura in the history of theology since Thomas Aquinas. Scholarly theology was now to be based on subjective seriousness and modern standards of rationality rather than on the authority of tradition. Thus even in his later theological writings Schleiermacher continues to adhere to a modern hermeneutics which he decouples from any consideration for dogma: we are not allowed to read later dogmas into the Bible. *His Hermeneutik und Kritik* (*Hermeneutics and Criticism,* 1838) is perhaps the classical work of the discipline, in part because Schleiermacher was, among other things, a first-rate classical philologist. His translation of Plato remains unsurpassed because, like other great German translations of the time, it remains close to the language of the original, rather than following the model of Dryden's translation of Vergil or Pope's translation of Homer, which make their authors sound like elegant Englishmen; and his study of Plato's philosophy deeply influenced his own philosophical writings. However, in his work, in contrast to Hegel's, dialectic is understood as an art of conversation, not a method for producing concepts. Whereas the eighteenth century had studied primarily Hellenistic philosophy, a shift to classical Greek philosophy now took place that ultimately can be explained only by the fact that German idealism is the most original reincarnation of Platonism. The idea that it is up to the Germans to receive the Greek heritage motivates the German fine arts, poetry, and philosophy of the time; it could be argued that only a culture that had developed slowly had the ability to understand the Greeks.

Wilhelm von Humboldt (1767–1835) in particular articulated the neohumanist conviction that no other nation could understand the Greeks as well as Germany, for Germany was essentially related to them "in its language, the many-sidedness of its strivings, the simplicity of its sense, its federalist constitution, and its latest fortunes." This he wrote in his *Geschichte des Verfalls und Unterganges der griechischen Freistaaten* (*The History of the Decline and Fall of the Greek Republics*), which was never completed, and which, in contrast to Edward Gibbon's history, is devoted not to Rome, but to Greece. Humboldt's importance lies in part in his creation of institutions in which the project of a new human science could be permanently established. In 1809–1810, as director of the section for ecclesiastical affairs and public education within the Prussian Ministry of the Interior, he was instrumental in founding the University of Berlin, which, in contrast to most contemporary universities in Europe, was conceived as a research center. Its research would, however, be inspired by teaching students who would participate in the research. In addition, Humboldt bequeathed to Germany a legacy of educational and cultural policies that encouraged instruction in music and drawing and the organization of libraries and museums, introduced state examinations for certifying teachers, and ended the prohibition on visiting foreign universities. Not all of his ideas were realized—for example, alternatives to the humanist *Gymnasium* were created, though the latter's great prestige is owed to Humboldt, who in his school plan for Lithuania wanted even carpenters to know Greek. Humboldt was part of a broader movement that concentrated on inner regeneration after Prussia's defeat by Napoleon; but he had few allies who shared his enthusiasm for reaching this goal through the use of culture, embodied in a comprehensive concept of education (*Bildung*). Disciplines were to be pursued only with a view to the whole and to shaping the self, and they were to be understood in their historical development; that was, in his view, what distinguished education from the mere accumulation of knowledge. Therefore Humboldt rejected the partitioning of the Academy of Sciences into divisions. His concrete political decisions continued to be shaped by his early *Ideen zu einem Versuch, die Grenzen der Wirksamkeit des Staats zu bestimmen* (Ideas for an attempt to determine the limits of state action, 1792), which exercised a lasting influence on John Stuart Mill and sought to limit the state's tasks in a way quite foreign to Germany. Certainly, Humboldt neglected the state's economic and social obligations; but his insight that the nation suffers when the state undertakes too much remains correct: if the state distributes goods, abilities atrophy. The autonomy of scientific institutions remained a central concern even for this Prussian official; the state had to know that science "would go infinitely better without it." As a diplomat, Humboldt advocated classic liberal principles and feared that a united Germany would endanger the European balance of powers and might wage wars of conquest, which would hardly be conducive to its spiritual education. More important than the essay "Über die Aufgabe des Geschichtsschreibers" ("On the Historian's Task," 1821), in which Humboldt emphasizes that the grasping of facts must always be guided by ideas, are his linguistic works, especially "Über die Verschiedenheit des menschlichen Sprachbaues und ihren Einfluß auf die geistige Entwicklung des Menschengeschlechts" ("On the Diversity of Human Language Construction and Its Influence on the Mental Development of the Human Species," 1836), the posthumously published introduction to his work on the Indonesian Kawi language. Before Humboldt, hardly anyone had mastered so many languages; his linguistic typology, which was partly anticipated by the Schlegels, is still influential today. But the truly philosophical aspect of his work, which guarantees linguistics an intrinsic value and legitimates, for instance, the interest in dialects, lies in his analysis of the relationship between language and thought. To be sure, Humboldt focuses on the influence of language on thought; what interests him more than the classification of the world that takes place in vocabulary is the basic grammatical structure of language. He overestimates the influence that inflection exercises on thought, for example in Sanskrit, which he contrasts to the isolating linguistic structure of Chinese, even though he is certainly aware of the reduction of inflection over time in Indo-European languages. But Humboldt's thesis that there is no standpoint outside language differs from the views of later linguistic relativists in that he interprets language itself as an—unconscious—work of the mind. He emphasizes that a universal linguistic competence underlies every individual language, and that it is this principle that makes mutual understanding possible, even if, because of the holistic nature of language, the connotations of words corresponding to each other in different languages are in no way the same. Every language can express an infinite number of ideas by further modifying a finite number of elements; in particular, poetry and philosophy expand language.

᠉ 7 ᠉

The Longing for a System:
German Idealism

Only one philosophical school of thought has retained the epithet "German"—German idealism. Why? On the one hand, because it was the most intellectually ambitious philosophy that Germany has produced; on the other, because it succeeded in integrating almost all the innovative achievements of earlier German philosophy in the shape of a system, the most complex form of philosophical thought. The religious motivation of the three main figures within this movement, all of whom had studied theology, contributed to the emergence of a kind of philosophical religiousness that was new in world history. This religiousness permanently marked Germany's educated middle class in the nineteenth century—especially its Protestants, but rudimentarily the Catholics as well; indeed its offshoots are still discernible in Thomas Mann, and it had hardly any equivalent in other European countries. It is out of the question to portray in the context of this introduction the history of idealism's development, which has recently been much enriched by studies concentrating on less well-known intermediate figures. (In terms of intellectual history, it is interesting that Karl Leonhard Reinhold [1757–1823], an Austrian Catholic priest who converted to Protestantism, and Salomon Maimon [1753–1800], a Lithuanian Jew, contributed to the transition to Fichte.) The three crucial figures—Johann Gottlieb Fichte (1762–1814), Friedrich Wilhelm Joseph Schelling (1775–1854), and Georg Wilhelm Friedrich Hegel (1770–1831), who at the end of their careers all taught at the University of Berlin, where both Fichte and Hegel were rectors for a time—had so many brilliant ideas that it is impossible to describe even the most important of them here.

Compared with Leibniz and Kant, Fichte is a philosophical dilettante; he had as little understanding of mathematics and the natural sciences as he did of the revolution in the human sciences that had recently taken place; and his exaggerated, even dogmatic sense of mission, which compensated for his inferiority complex arising from his humble social background and humiliating experiences as a private tutor, too often makes reading his work unpleasant. He sought constantly to force his reader to be autonomous, and since he could not achieve that goal, he largely ceased publication toward the end of his life, and in his popular lectures cultivated a German tendency to berate the audience. His unconditional need for freedom explains his enthusiasm for Kant, whom he first read in 1790, and for the French Revolution—he considered 1793 a historical threshold, the "last year of the old darkness." If with his Jacobinism he shows courage, his abstract universalism in *Beitrag zur Berichtigung der Urteile des Publikums über die Französische Revolution* (*Contribution to the Rectification of the Public's Judgments Regarding the French Revolution*, 1793) also went so far as to develop one of the most aggressive anti-Jewish polemics in modern German intellectual history. This polemic, which denied Jews not human rights but civil rights and foresaw a day when they would be forced to go to the Promised Land, arose from the feeling that Jews rejected modern ethical universalism. It was thus no longer religious, but not yet racist. It resulted in Saul Ascher's pamphlet "Eisenmenger der Zweite" ("Eisenmenger the Second," 1794), which alludes to the Protestant theologian Johann Andreas Eisenmenger, whose *Entdecktes Judentum* (*Judaism Unmasked*, 1700) stands at the apex of Christian anti-Judaism.

And yet Fichte is one of the most brilliant thinkers of all time. His weaknesses irritate us, but we remain fascinated by the energy of his character and overwhelmed by the quality of his new foundational ideas, his ability to organize the various philosophical disciplines into a systematic context, and by the existential pathos with which he demands a philosophy developed from one principle. If the French revolutionaries wanted political freedom, Fichte wants more: he wants to avenge the affront that corporality represents for a rational being, by providing insight into its necessity, i.e., by a "deduction." Hegel wished to be buried next to him, with good reason. Fichte's meteoric rise began with the anonymous publication of *Versuch einer Kritik aller Offenbarung* (*Attempt at a Critique of all Revelation*, 1792). It was taken to be Kant's not yet published work on the philosophy of religion, because Fichte had with enormous cleverness thought his way into Kant's approach. Like Kant, he subordinated any alleged revelation to a moral reservation, while at the same time insisting that a revealing God had no need to intervene directly in the causal nexus, but could instead arrange the latter in such a way that his will would be expressed on the basis of immanent secondary causes. Fichte was always of the opinion that his whole philosophy deviated only from the letter of the Kantian theory and remained true to its spirit. Kant disagreed (and soon rejected Fichte's philosophy), but even Fichte's admirers should feel compelled to insist on his originality with respect to Kant. It is still breathtaking that Fichte managed to lay out in just a few years his conception of philosophy, in *Über den Begriff der Wissenschaftslehre oder der sogenannten Philosophie* (*Concerning the Concept of the Wissenschaftslehre*, 1794), his theoretical philosophy in *Grundlage der gesamten Wissenschaftslehre* (*Foundations of the Entire Science of Knowledge*, 1794–95), and his practical philosophy, in both *Grundlage des Naturrechts* (*Foundations of Natural Right*, 1796/97, and thus even before Kant's *Doctrine of Right*) and in *System der Sittenlehre* (*The System of Ethics*, 1798). And alongside his scientific compositions, he wrote numerous popular works. 1798 was the crucial turning-point in Fichte's career. The publication of his essay "Über den Grund unseres Glaubens an eine göttliche Weltregierung" ("On the Ground of our Belief in a Divine World-Governance"), which ends, characteristically, with quotations from Goethe's conversation on religion in *Faust* and from Schiller's "Die Worte des Glaubens" ("The Words of Faith"), led to charges of atheism and to the loss of his professorship in Jena. The conditions of his fall were, however, more lenient conditions than those to which Wolff was subjected in his own time. In his "Appellation an das Publikum" ("Appeal to the Public," 1801) Fichte put his case before the public, arguing for a kind of freedom of opinion and scientific investigation that was not then recognized in either positive or natural law. It is a distinctive characteristic of German culture, in contrast to French, that in the eighteenth century there was no materialistic atheism; what was vilified as atheism in Fichte's work was instead the identification of God with the moral order of the world, which according to Fichte is necessary in order to believe in good faith that a radically intentionalist ethics contributes to the good in the world. Jacobi's soon-published letter to Fichte (1799) probably contributed to the crucial turn in Fichte's philosophy; for as much as Jacobi celebrates Fichte as the "Messiah of speculative reason," he insists equally that Fichte's extremely coherent philosophy leads to "nihilism" (the word is a neologism coined by Jacobi), because it dissolves everything in thought. Therefore in matters of religion Jacobi favored belief, not-knowing as opposed to knowing.

What are Fichte's enduring philosophical achievements? First, in his programmatic text of 1794 he presents with unsurpassable clarity an extremely ambitious concept of philosophy. Philosophy's task, he says, is to justify the principles of the individual sciences, as well as the logic in accord with which theorems are derived from these principles; in addition, it must demonstrate the inner unity of the system of the sciences. At the same time, this science of science or theory of science must itself be a science; it therefore requires its own principle, which grounds itself through a special unity of form and content. The interest in the self-grounding of philosophical theory makes Fichte's approach into a reflexive transcendental philosophy, whereas Kant's philosophy was largely irreflexive; however, in striving for a systematic organization of all human knowledge, Fichte follows many a hint in the third *Critique*. The first principle in his main theoretical work is "I am because I am." According to Fichte, this undeniable proposition underlies the logical principle of identity; and although Fichte's knowledge of even the formal logic of his own time was limited, his idea that formal logic has to be grounded in a transcendental logic is his second enduring contribution. Third, Fichte seeks to put the faculties of the mind that were grasped by Kant empirically in a relationship of derivation; ultimately he wants to show that they are presuppositions for self-consciousness. In particular, he seeks, like other critics of Kant before him, to eliminate the things-in-themselves from transcendental philosophy. He in no way denies that, in knowing, the I is determined through objects, that is, the "non-I" (*Nicht-Ich*);

whereas, in action, the "I" shapes the non-I; but it is always the I that opposes in the I a divisible non-I to the divisible I. Self-consciousness is not reducible to anything else, and a materialistic explanation of consciousness is excluded. Fourth, in Fichte's concept construction we recognize an approach to dialectical method: out of a concept and its counter-concept a mediating concept is formed.

Fifth, Fichte's philosophy is philosophy in the first person, which is doubtless a legitimate alternative to the realism that forgets that it is always the I that in actions raising a claim of validity mediates itself with a non-I. However, the danger of any such philosophy is solipsism; and it remains an enormous achievement of Fichte's to have sought for the first time to produce, in view of this danger, a deduction (though an unsatisfactory one) of inter-subjectivity in § 3 of the *Foundations of Natural Right*. Sixth, this work presents a new way of thinking about natural law that differs from ancient-medieval as well as early modern natural law theories, such as Locke's, through its will to systematization, its attempt to deduce anthropological facts that were before simply empirically grasped, such as the corporality of rational beings, and its inexorable rigor in the separation of natural law and morals. According to Fichte, law consists in the mutual recognition of rational beings and their spheres of freedom; its essence is that it can be enforced by means of coercion. Civil, penal, constitutional, and international law are put in a plausible foundational order. The starting point is, as in Hobbes, the individual's selfishness and distrust, but for Fichte the symmetry of the legal relationship is an obligation that is independent of factual power relationships. It remains a mystery how this distrust can be overcome in the process of founding the state. Fichte rejects the retributive penal theory of Kant and Hegel, and he is, therefore, one of the few German thinkers of his time to reject capital punishment. Indeed, in accord with his radical limitation of the tasks of the law, he declares the punishment of numerous criminal offenses of the time to be contrary to natural law, anticipating in this certain penal law reforms of the late twentieth century. But in this he also goes disturbingly far: declaring, for example, that since only beings with actual self-consciousness have rights, even the exposure of infants does not really violate natural law. At the same time, Fichte defends, even more resolutely in the late

Rechtslehre (*The Science of Right*) of 1812, the state's duties in the areas of social welfare and education.

Seventh, for Fichte law is only a deficient prefiguration of true morality, which is not based on the principle of self-interest. The highest moral duty consists in being an autonomous I. His *System of Ethics* breaks, unlike Kant's, with the tradition of the doctrine of virtues; for it, there are no supererogatory or morally neutral acts. Fichte rejects duties toward nature, unlike those toward fellow humans, though the latter are not presupposed by ethics. He urges asceticism in eating only for the sake of the autonomy of the I. It is astounding how Fichte manages to maintain traditional moral norms (for instance, belonging to a Church) while reinterpreting them in the context of his demand for autonomy. He emphatically adheres to Kant's intentionalism and his doctrine, for example, that lying is forbidden under any circumstances, regardless of the consequences.

The atheism controversy led to a revision of Fichte's basic position, even though his conviction that he had early on gained infallible insights prevented him from acknowledging his own development. Jacobi's accusation of nihilism hit the mark; and in Fichte's most perfect work from a literary point of view, *Die Bestimmung des Menschen* (*The Vocation of Man*, 1800), subjective idealism is celebrated as a liberation from the threat of naturalistic determinism, as the latter was represented by the modern natural sciences. The price to be paid for this new position is declared to be high, however, since it transforms everything, ultimately even the I, into images. Only practical belief can save us from the abyss of this knowledge, since only the command to do our duty, and no theoretical argument, guarantees the objectivity of reality. The later versions of his theory of science assume a concept of the absolute as transcending both being and thinking, approachable only in the mode of negative theology, and manifesting itself in the empirical world. In "Die Anweisung zum seligen Leben" ("The Way Towards the Blessed Life," 1806), Fichte recognizes Plato and the Gospel according to John as precursors of his own philosophy; had he had more historical training, he would have also been able to name Plotinus and, especially, Meister Eckhart. According to the mature Fichte there are five worldviews: the realistic everyday view, a legal view, a moral view, a religious view, and a view from the perspective of philosophical consciousness.

Instead of the moral striving for autonomy, religion recognizes "that this Holy, Good, and Beautiful is by no means a product of our own, . . . but that it is immediately the manifestation in us, as the light, of the inward Divine Nature"; indeed, even the worldviews are grounded in God. Like Meister Eckhart, Fichte also teaches that genuine religion is active, and not only contemplative; and the rational penetration of religion from the point of view of science (that is how Fichte, and Hegel still, always designate philosophy) is the last and highest standpoint, because seeing is more than mere believing. Fichte repudiates a belief in God that is based on external assurance as "a superstition through which at most a defective constabulary is supplemented, [though] humans remain inwardly as bad as they were before." A heteronomous God should be abandoned. God manifests himself within the world, for example, as beauty, as a just state, as science. The truly religious person gives up his self, no longer has any genuine sense of freedom, and even remorse is alien to him, because he considers his earlier life to be nonexistent. In one of his sonnets Fichte wrote: "The shroud rises up quite clear before you, / It is your I: what is destructible shall perish, / And henceforth only God lives in your striving. / Penetrate with your glance what survives this death, / Thus the shroud becomes visible as shroud; / And you see divine life without a veil."

Fichte was aware that his philosophy contradicted the spirit of the time, which he interpreted in *Die Grundzüge des gegenwärtigen Zeitalters* (*The Characteristics of the Present Age*, 1806) as the expression of a state of complete sinfulness. In his conception of the philosophy of history the present is the third of five stages: disgust with the bustling activity of the Enlightenment is thus combined with the hope that a theoretical change can prepare the final stage, in which humanity will autonomously shape itself into the image of reason. In the *Reden an die deutsche Nation* (*Addresses to the German Nation*, 1808), which were delivered by the former admirer of France in a Berlin occupied by the French, Fichte tried to become directly practical: like other German intellectuals, he hastened to the aid of Prussia in its darkest hour, after the defeats at Jena and Auerstedt in 1806. Indeed, Prussia would scarcely have recovered without the reforms that were then introduced by intellectual politicians. The speeches, which appealed to a nation beyond the individual German states

and tribes, showed courage and helped shape a German nationalism. In Fichte we can find an exemplary case of both nationalism's
achievements and its hubris. Only the feeling of constituting a
community could justify, for example, Fichte's demand, inspired
by the pedagogue Johann Heinrich Pestalozzi (1746–1827), that
a comprehensive national education program be established for
both men and women. At the same time, this feeling itself had to
be justified by the conviction that a special role was intended for
the German people.

Of course, German nationalism was also a reaction to French
power politics, and Fichte was certainly far too subtle to make use
of clichés: he expressly disputes the notion of a German ancestral
purity, noting for instance that they had mixed with Slavs, praises
Germany because it has not been guilty of engaging in colonialism (in "Der geschlossene Handelsstaat" ["The Closed Commercial State"] of 1800, he already rejects global trade), emphasizes
the complementarity of the various nations, wants Germans to
be citizens of the world, and sees in Germanness an original spirituality that will ultimately be accessible to all. At the same time,
he wants to distinguish the Germans, not from Scandinavians,
but from other nations of Germanic descent, through the originality of their language; having one's own language founds the
right to have one's own state. Unlike the French, Germans have
not only intellect, but also soul; the educated classes remain connected to the people; instead of affectation, naturalness prevails.
Luther he considers the central figure in the formation of the
German nation, seriousness and concern for a blessed life being
in Fichte's view the distinctive characteristics of Germans. He
rightly observes that the opposition between religion and philosophy was less marked in Germany because the struggle for autonomy had religious roots; belief in the supersensible was never
abandoned, but was instead reoriented by reason. It is surely this
philosophical spirit that for Fichte augured "world dominion."
But it coalesces in a dangerous way with the real circumstances
of the German nation; for in the context of the *Addresses* Fichte
attempts to prepare the German nation to defend itself against
the French; indeed, he polemicizes—just like Machiavelli,
whom he enthusiastically praises in an article—against what he
sees as the Christian enervation of the will to fight and, indeed,
against the traditional policy of limited cabinet wars. We must

not criticize Fichte from the vantage point of our twenty-first-century knowledge; and especially we must not forget that it was the French revolutionary armies that swept away cabinet wars and which could not be stopped by the ideas that inspired the cabinet wars. But even if he does so in the context of competition with France, when Fichte promises his potential freedom fighters that the years of salvation will be counted anew from the date of their deeds, he crosses a boundary that Leibniz and Kant would not have dared approach.

The peculiarity of Schelling is most aptly indicated by noting that the most productive phase of his thinking ended when he was twenty-five years old; he published his last important book at thirty-four. He nonetheless continued to give important lectures until he died, and although volatile changes in his interests and in his position—from a youthful pantheism to a form of Christianity that comes closer to traditional Christology than Fichte's and Hegel's forms—caused people to call him Proteus, we are able to see more and more continuities in his development: as a teenager, he was already fascinated by myth, and his late philosophy seeks only to complete, not to replace, the early outlines of his system; throughout his life, freedom remained a major theme. Probably no other philosopher published so many original works so early in his life, and even if awareness of his genius often led him to adopt the superior tone in philosophy that the old Kant had warned was an enemy to clear argumentation, the rapidity of his intellectual development is nonetheless astonishing. In his schooldays he could already read Hebrew and Arabic, and at the age of fifteen he was accepted in the Tübinger Stift, where he shared a room with two collegemates who were his elders by five years, Hegel and Friedrich Hölderlin (1770–1843). Their ideas so influenced one another that the so-called "oldest systematic program of German idealism" (probably dating from 1797, but first published in 1917 by Franz Rosenzweig) could be attributed singly to each one of the three or to the collaboration of two of them. And yet these three thinkers, without whom classical German philosophy could hardly have emerged, were extremely different intellectually: Hölderlin expressed in enormously complex poems, some written even after the outbreak of his mental disorder, the suffering modernity caused him; and he interpreted human history as alienation from the divine, in opposition to the Enlightenment's historical optimism. The *dioscuri*, Schelling and Hegel, both pursued a related project; but modern objective (or absolute) idealism was created by Schelling, in whose work most of Hegel's later ideas can be found. Schelling, however, was not able to elaborate them into a coherent whole, for his brilliance was not combined with the tenacious endurance that characterized Hegel. The latter was the most important of Schelling's many pupils, a few of whom contributed, through the awkwardness of their ideas and language, to the isolation of German philosophy that Schelling himself complained of in 1834: "Germans had so long philosophized only among themselves that they gradually moved farther and farther away in thoughts and words from the *generally* . . . comprehensible." Hegel might also be obscure, but it was through him that Schelling's program first fascinated the whole of Europe. His achievement remains his success in the lonely, detailed work of constructing from his old friend's brilliant ideas a system far more cohesive than any that the sociable Schelling could ever have devised. After he had lost his youthful friendships, Schelling lost also the joy he had taken in creation. In fact it was the belated, but then meteoric rise of Hegel, who was initially clearly his inferior, that produced resentment in Schelling, whose early fame (which is not always a blessing) had awakened expectations in him and in others that he was no longer able to meet. In a letter to Victor Cousin written in 1828, he compares Hegel to an insect who has taken possession of his ideas as if they were the leaf of a plant; in 1841 he declared that without him, neither Hegel nor Hegelians would exist. The unexpected encounter between the former friends in Karlsbad in 1829 is worthy of a literary representation on the model of Thomas Mann's novel *Lotte in Weimar*. But no matter how circumspectly one tries to evaluate this complex relationship, it remains objectively true that only Hegel's unique sense of systematicity, the judicious selection he made from among Schelling's effervescing and not always tenable ideas, and his superiority in the philosophy of law and the state was able to fulfill the promise of German idealism.

One of Schelling's limitations was his relative lack of interest in law and politics, along with his lack of mathematical talent, which Kant certainly had, even though he was not a creative mathematician like Leibniz. Schelling compensated for this lack through an approach to nature that was partly intuitive, partly conceptual, and that allowed him to perceive in it aspects that escape modern natural science. This fascinated Goethe, who in 1798 called him to the University of Jena. No less remarkable is his exceptional sense for aesthetic phenomena, which was developed thanks to his friendship with the early Romantics (August Wilhelm Schlegel's wife Caroline left her husband and ultimately married Schelling, who was twelve years her junior). Schelling began his career as a Fichtean: his first philosophical work, *Über die Möglichkeit einer Form der Philosophie überhaupt* (On the possibility of a form for all philosophy), may confuse the modern reader with the logic it adopts from Kant, but it will overwhelm him as a congenial version of the idea of philosophy set forth in Fichte's *Über den Begriff der Wissenschaftslehre*, especially since it is the work of a nineteen-year-old. At first, as in *Vom Ich als Prinzip der Philosophie* (On the I as the principle of philosophy, 1795) Schelling sought to situate his new material insights in a Fichtean framework. However, we can already discern in his *Philosophische Briefe über Dogmatizismus und Kritizismus* (Philosophical letters on dogmatism and criticism, 1795) the independence of his mind: although, like Kant and Fichte, he defends critical philosophy because it alone makes it possible to conceive freedom of the will, at the same time he is fascinated by Spinoza and rejects contemporary theology's cooption of Kant's moral proof of God, and this partly on aesthetic grounds. Only the immoral person needs a punitive God. Kant's question about synthetic judgments is transformed into a metaphysical one: how can the absolute proceed from itself? As in Hölderlin's contemporaneous text "Urtheil und Seyn" ("Judgment and Being"), it is emphasized that an absolute unity must precede the synthesis; this model is opposed to that of the mature Hegel, for whom the highest principle is achieved only in the synthesis at the end. No less deviant from the mature Hegel is the early Romantic idea that there is necessarily a plurality of philosophical systems in which individuality is expressed; for a complete system would destroy freedom. The view that a system is grounded not through knowledge but through action is Fichtean. The idea that complete realism is at the same time idealism anticipates the later development.

What soon distinguished Schelling from Fichte was his interest in the substantial richness of the world. While for Fichte nature was only the non-I, Schelling—in his writings on natural philosophy, from *Ideen zu einer Philosophie der Natur* (*Ideas for a Philosophy of Nature*, 1797) to the dialogue *Bruno* (1802), which vies with Plato—seeks to understand nature's articulation in various forms or "powers" (*Potenzen*); that is, as a hierarchical order. At first he interprets these in a very Fichtean way, as solidified results of the I's cognitive activity; they are supposed to replace the chimeras of things-in-themselves. "We regard the system of our ideas not in its being, but rather in its becoming. Philosophy becomes genetic. . . . The system of nature is at the same time the system of our mind." What are the most important powers? It is obvious that the inorganic and the organic are different forms of nature; but since the end of the eighteenth century, with "galvanism" (electrophysiology) an intermediate element had become a subject of discussion, fascinating in particular on account of its polar structure. Such an element still played no role in Leibniz and Kant, but it underlies Goethe's *Die Wahlverwandtschaften* (*Elective Affinities*). Schelling not only reacted to contemporary discoveries, but also inspired concrete research in the natural sciences, for example that of Johann Wilhelm Ritter, one of the founders of electrochemistry. A particularly important role in Schelling's natural philosophy is played by the special status of light as the counter-principle to gravity—that connects a millennial tradition of the metaphysics of light with contemporary scientific discussions: because for modern science as well, it remains indisputable that only fools like the Schildbürger put light in bags. What is crucial is that according to Schelling, polarity appears not only within a phenomenon such as electricity, but is the very metaphysical principle according to which the whole of reality is constructed. For him, light is the *ideal* principle in nature, while gravity is its *real* principle. We cannot resist connecting Schelling's construction of the whole of reality on the basis of this polar structure with the variation on themes, usually two, in the contemporary sonata form; polarity was as remote from Leibniz's monadology as from Bach's "Art of the Fugue." Only with the integration of duality into a harmonic whole did the German spirit reach the culmination of its creativity.

Schelling's natural philosophy breaks not only with the old physico-theology but also with Fichte's idealistic reformulation of it, in which light is "not a bursting out of the divine principle in nature, not a symbol of the eternal, original knowledge instilled into nature," but instead exists only so that humans can see. Opposing this view, Schelling rejects, in *Über das Verhältnis der Naturphilosophie zur Philosophie überhaupt* (On the relationship of natural philosophy to philosophy in general, 1802), an ethical functionalization of nature: for him, observation of nature as an end in itself is more religious than Kant's and Fichte's anthropocentrism, according to which God is merely a postulate. Even if Schelling's natural philosophy was soon discredited because, as "speculative physics," it repeatedly took positions on questions that could be answered only by thorough experimentation and the construction of mathematical models, his instrumentalist caveat regarding the "fictions" of physics is legitimate, especially since he does not deny that these fictions are "absolutely necessary for the further progress of investigation and observation." On the other hand, his concern to understand why there are precisely these basic forms in nature, which natural science merely enumerates, is indispensable. This question is hard to answer, but it is justified—indeed, from an idealistic and a religious point of view, it is ineluctable—if nature is not a *brutum factum*, but rather the expression of reason. Schelling's goal is to interpret the basic structures of reality as developments of a polar opposition between the real and the ideal—which is articulated on the abstract level in the opposition between nature and spirit and is then further differentiated within each discipline. In this way, and only in this way, can principles be grasped: "This place in the system is the only explanation of them that there is."

Analogously, Schelling's *System des transzendentalen Idealismus* (*System of Transcendental Idealism*, 1800) attempts to situate the basic structures of the mind "as an uninterrupted history of self-consciousness" in an orderly arrangement, keeping in mind a "parallelism of nature with intelligence." In an especially important and substantial complement to Fichte's work, Schelling, after discussing theoretical and practical philosophy, turns to the philosophy of art. The latter's inclusion in the philosophy of mind explains why Schelling, unlike Kant, is interested only in the beauty of art, and not the beauty of nature. He emphasizes all the more strongly the naturalness of the artist's production. The artist is governed "by a power which separates him from all other men, and compels him to say or depict things which he does not fully understand himself, and whose meaning is infinite." Starting out from contradictions, he strives to achieve infinite harmony. The high status of art corresponds to early Romantic sensibility. Art and science pursue the same task, which however remains infinite for the latter; art, by contrast, is already where science is ultimately to arrive. Only art registers what philosophy cannot represent, namely the unconscious element in production, and lays bare the unity that underlies nature and history. "What we speak of as nature is a poem lying pent in a mysterious and wonderful script. Yet the riddle could reveal itself, were we to recognize in it the odyssey of the spirit."

In the course of his increasingly exacerbated correspondence with Fichte, Schelling understood that the lack of a philosophy of nature and an aesthetics in Fichte pointed not simply to gaps that remained to be filled, but instead required a fundamentally different systematic structure. In the important appendices to the second edition of the *Ideas* published in 1803, Schelling described his new position as "absolute idealism," as opposed to the relative idealism of Fichte and of his own early work. Absolute idealism is at the same time a realism, because it no longer reduces nature to finite consciousness, but rather, like Spinoza, grasps both as manifestations of the Absolute. Concepts are not something that we force on things; instead, *they* grasp their true being. In its title, the *Darstellung meines Systems der Philosophie* (*Presentation of My System of Philosophy*, 1801) already alludes to the break with Fichte and seeks to develop the notion of absolute identity that he considers the foundation of the philosophy of nature as well as of transcendental philosophy. Schelling's intuitions are powerful, but his specific arguments are hard to reconstruct. On the basis of his new insights, however, Schelling lectured on the philosophy of art in Jena in 1802–1803, and in Würzburg in 1804–1805; here we find for the first time an attempt to deduce *a priori* a system of the arts along with a systematic development of central aesthetic categories such as "the naïve" and "the sentimental," and a philosophical penetration of literary criticism's discovery of the differences between ancient and modern poetry. The method of concept construction still wavers between two- and three-part classifications; it continues the procedure of the earlier philosophies of nature, but with more enduring results, since the revolutionizing of the empirical natural sciences in the nineteenth and twentieth centuries was far more profound than that of the human sciences. The central organ of the new philosophical program was the *Kritisches Journal der Philosophie* (1802–1803), which was coedited by Hegel. The introductory article "Über das Wesen der philosophischen Kritik überhaupt" (On the essence of philosophical criticism generally) reflects ideas common to both friends; the crucial task of contemporary philosophy is said to be overcoming the dualism prevalent since Descartes. Connected with this are religious hopes for the "true Gospel's time of the reconciliation of the world with God," while "the temporary and merely external forms of Christianity crumble"; the required intellectual work is simultaneously understood as an ethical task—just as it is in most ancient philosophies. One may smile at this, but it ought not to be forgotten that those who completely disconnect philosophy from morality and religion deprive the former of its special status among the sciences. However, the early Schelling's religiousness is rationalistic, like that of Kant and Hegel; in "Philosophie und Religion" (Philosophy and religion, 1804), he rejects the notion that philosophy needs to be complemented by faith, because beyond the absolute conceived by philosophy there is still a God. He strongly emphasizes that taking the absolute as the point of departure is the mark of true philosophy. He explains the finite's origin (*Abkunft*) by a free lapse that does not take place in time; egoity represents the greatest distance from the absolute and at the same the return to it; human history is to be conceived analogously. The lapse is thus the means of God's complete revelation. Moral commandments and rewards for virtue exist only at a lower stage; eternity already begins in this life.

Schelling's return to a more traditional Christianity was influenced by, among others, the Catholic Franz von Baader (1765–1841), who had read Jakob Böhme with great care, and whom Schelling met in Munich, where he went to live in 1806. His *Philosophische Untersuchungen über das Wesen der menschlichen Freiheit und die damit zusammenhängenden Gegenstände* ("Philosophical investigations into the essence of human freedom and matters connected therewith," 1809) defends an incompatibilist conception of freedom, but sees objective-idealistically the possibility of evil in the universe as a whole—"hence the veil of dejection that is spread over all nature, the deep indestructible melancholy of all life"—and rejects the age-old theory of evil as privation, represented by Augustine and Aquinas, for example. According to Schelling, evil is not mere imperfection but rather finiteness that tears itself away from the universal will and is raised to selfhood. The work's true concern is to distinguish between the ground of God's existence and God himself; only this discrepancy, which God sublates within Himself and which thus does not establish any kind of dualism, makes evil possible outside God. God is not a "mere logical *abstractum*" from which everything necessarily follows; for such a God would be only the highest law without any personality. However, according to Schelling, God is "not a system, but a life." At the same time, Schelling endorses Leibniz's rejection of the claim that God could have created a better world. This text is symptomatic of Schelling's desperate attempt to avoid a retreat to a naïve belief in revelation and at the same time to escape the consequences of a rationalistic conception of God (significantly, the will plays an increasingly decisive role in his thought), although it was precisely his early philosophy that made Leibniz's program concretely feasible, by presenting, instead of a merely formal metaphysics, an attempt to grasp the real world in its concrete structures. Schelling was never able to elaborate into a book the alternative philosophical theology that now danced before his eyes—which, in view of his brilliance, shows that it was not a project that could be easily carried out.

The late lectures on the "Philosophie der Mythologie" (Philosophy of mythology) and the "Philosophie der Offenbarung" (Philosophy of revelation) declare programmatically that a purely rationalistic interpretation of reality is a negative philosophy that has to be complemented by a positive philosophy. In these lectures delivered in Berlin, where Mikhail Bakunin, Friedrich Engels, Alexander von Humboldt, Søren Kierkegaard and Leopold von Ranke were sometimes in the audience, Schelling interweaves metaphysical reflections with an interpretation of human myths and of the Christian revelation sharply distinguished from them. Behind this connection stands the thought that God makes his existence known in the historical development of religions, whereas the negative philosophy has to do only with the *what*, and not with concrete reality. What is crucial is that Schelling now rejects the ontological proof on which the rationalistic transition from concept to reality depends. In the chapter on Hegel in his lectures *Zur Geschichte der neueren Philosophie* (*On the History of Modern Philosophy*, 1827), Schelling already emphasizes that God is more than a concept. However, he did not see that Hegel recognizes, in addition to the psychological concept, a logical concept that constitutes the essence of reality, the divine thought, as it were; Hegel is much more of a Platonist than is Schelling, who never recognized an autonomous sphere of the logical alongside nature and spirit. Schelling insists that conceptual structures are necessary, not sufficient conditions of reality. "The whole world lies, so to speak, in the nets of the understanding or reason, but the question is *how* exactly it got into these nets, since there is obviously something other and something *more* than mere reason in the world." Even a reader who does not consider Schelling's critique of Hegel compelling and who repeatedly finds his interpretation of Christianity incompatible with modern Bible criticism nonetheless remains overwhelmed by the richness of his philosophical interpretation of myths, in which a theogonic, i.e., God-producing, process goes on in the human mind. Not things, but rather powers arising within consciousness move people. The true God keeps a tight rein on people through their ideas of God, which have an entirely different power than poetic ideas, as is shown for example by sacrifice. Schelling distinguishes his approach to myth from those approaches that deny myths any truth, seeing them as merely poetically intended or even meaningless, as well as from those that view myths as deliberately veiling historical or physical truths, or distorting scientific or religious truths. In his view, there is truth in mythology as such. The determination to find meaning in the apparently meaningless makes Schelling's last work a highlight of German idealism's hermeneutics; and we can easily see that his late writing continues the concerns of his natural philosophy: while the latter sought to find a hidden meaning in what does not think, the former looks for reason in what seems explicitly to contravene reason.

It fell to Hegel to complete the systematic program shared during the Jena period. The fact that he remained true to it until the end and that he was not tormented by the doubts that disturbed its restless creator, who anticipated the anti-idealistic revolts (which differed from one another) of Kierkegaard and Marx, might be interpreted as sluggishness. But it can also be explained by pointing out that Hegel, whose *Phenomology of*

Spirit, natural philosophy, and aesthetics are coherent elaborations of Schelling's ideas, established absolute idealism better than Schelling was ever able to do. In fact, the latter acknowledged the "uncommonly clever" methodological ideas in the *Science of Logic*, Hegel's most original work, to which Schelling's earlier studies had made hardly any contribution. In addition to having greater formal intelligence, including mathematical intelligence, Hegel—the son of a government official, not of a theologian—understood the nature of political problems in a much more concrete way than did Schelling. In his early theological writings (which were published in their complete form only in 1907), he made, with ruthless clarity, the collapse of traditional Christology in the face of the new Bible hermeneutics the starting point for any intellectually honest defense of Christianity. His *Das Leben Jesu (The Life of Jesus)* eliminates, as did for instance that of his near-contemporary Thomas Jefferson, all of Jesus's miracles including the Resurrection. Naturally, Hegel did not publish this himself, for in 1835 *Das Leben Jesu kritisch bearbeitet (The Life of Jesus, Critically Examined)* of his pupil David Friedrich Strauß (1808–1874) still earned its author painful negative sanctions. At the same time, *Der Geist des Christentums und sein Schicksal (The Spirit of Christianity and its Fate)* defends a Christianity inspired by the Gospel according to John as superior even to Kant's legalistic morals—however much the disciples misunderstood Jesus's message. God the Holy Spirit, not God the Son, inspired Hegel's philosophical transformation of Christianity from the start, and even though we immediately sense that Hegel's Christianity lacks an eschatological dimension, we should not deny his enormous religious seriousness, which bids farewell to the postulate of personal immortality only because the truly moral person needs no prospect of a reward. The slow dying out of the traditional belief in individual immortality began among the German elites at this time; think of Schiller's "Resignation" (1786). The letter of condolence Hegel sent to the Prussian minister of Culture, Karl vom Stein zum Altenstein, after the death of the latter's sister in 1830 is a masterful example of the new sensibility, which did not make it easier to express sympathy.

Differenz des Fichteschen und Schellingschen Systems der Philosophie (The Difference Between Fichte's and Schelling's Systems of Philosophy, 1801) is Hegel's first book, in which he proves himself a loyal follower of Schelling. His critique of Fichte's individualistic theory of law is particularly innovative: "The community of the person with others must therefore be seen essentially not as a limitation of the individual's true freedom, but rather as a broadening of the same." In *Glauben und Wissen* (*Faith and Knowledge*), the new philosophical program is opposed to "the reflective philosophy of subjectivity" ascribed to Kant, Jacobi, and Fichte, and Hegel's last article in the *Kritisches Journal*, "Über die wissenschaftlichen Behandlungsarten des Naturrechts" ("On the Scientific Ways of Treating Natural Law"), develops, in opposition to Kant's formalistic universalism, a new concept of ethical life through an analysis of Greek tragedy, among other things. His turn away from the cosmopolitanism of the Enlightenment is unfortunate, but Hegel rightly understands that moral conduct is possible only within the framework of social institutions, whose inner logic he tries to reconstruct in the posthumously published *System der Sittlichkeit* (*System of Ethical Life*): he wants to reconstruct, as if he were a Schelling of the social world, the social world's powers. Hegel's main work from the Jena period is the *Phänomenologie des Geistes* (*Phenomenology of Spirit*, 1807), which he presented as the "First Part" of the *System of Science*. It may be doubted whether the system later laid out in the *Enzyklopädie der philosophischen Wissenschaften im Grundrisse* (*Encyclopedia of the Philosophical Sciences in Outline*, 1817; of which a third, heavily revised edition was published in 1830) really needs the *Phenomenology* from the point of view of the theory of validity—especially since most of its chapters are found in the later work, sometimes in a different order. But in it Hegel seeks to make clear the rise to absolute knowledge, which will then develop the Encyclopedia's *a priori* system of categories with confidence that it is grasping the true nature of reality. The "preface" outlines in a grandiose, obscure language the Hegelian program, especially his holism expressed as "the true is the totality," and the early stages of his rejection of Schelling's theory of identity: the absolute is essentially a result. Hegel develops a kaleidoscope of forms of consciousness, from the simplest kind of sense-certainty to absolute knowledge, moving, in the categories of the mature system, from the subjective through the objective to absolute spirit, and thus from a philosophical psychology through a social doctrine to the philosophy of religion. His ability to capture in a few strokes the essence of a world view, for instance Greek ethical life or Kantian moral philosophy, is stunning; and his subtle distinction between what is the case *for* one form of consciousness and what occurs only *in itself or for us* as observers is fascinating. The goal of the work is a coincidence of the two perspectives, that of the subject and that of the object, but also that of the I and that of the We. The *Phenomenology* assigns more space to the theme of intersubjectivity than the *Encylopedia* does; and the chapter on "Lordship and Bondage" in particular deeply influenced later developments from Marx to Sartre.

Hegel's *magnum opus*, the *Encyclopedia*, is telegraphically concise, especially if we ignore the oral supplements added to the first complete edition of his works, which were taken from students' notes on his lectures. Fortunately, Hegel was able to elaborate on the first part and on the second section of the third part in separate works, the *Wissenschaft der Logik* (*Science of Logic*, 1812–1816) and the *Grundlinien der Philosophie des Rechts* (Elements of the Philosophy of Right, 1821). After his death his lectures on the philosophy of history, aesthetics, the philosophy of religion (including the proofs of God), and the history of philosophy, were published on the basis of his manuscripts and of transcripts—not in a form that meets current philological standards, but that nonetheless reflects Hegel's abundance of ideas. Because of their colloquial tone, the lectures are easier to read than the books Hegel published. In particular, his philosophy of history was read by a wide audience in the nineteenth century, to which it communicated the plain view of an optimistic philosopher of history emphasizing progress, whereas the complexity of the foundational structures of his metaphysics were grasped by only a few. In addition, his school's split into right-wing and left-wing Hegelians was possible only because Hegel's subtle panentheism was missed by most of his students. Hegel most certainly assumes that the manifestation of the absolute in nature and in spirit is part of its essence, which contradicts many a traditional interpretation of Christianity. But he is no less convinced that the spirit is *not* the first sphere of the system: it develops out of nature, which itself presupposes a self-constitutive ideal structure that Hegel does not hesitate to designate as God's essence before the Creation. It is this threefold structure of logic, nature, and spirit that characterizes Hegel's mature system and distinguishes it from Schelling's, which has no elaborated logic.

What makes Hegel's system so attractive? What explains why there have been repeated Hegel renaissances, and why no important philosopher can avoid coming to terms with him? One may reject Hegel, but anyone who ignores him will miss the chance to glimpse a certain level of philosophizing without which it is impossible to achieve philosophical greatness. (This does not exclude—in fact it rather implies— that merely parroting Hegelian formulas is extremely detrimental to the acquisition of technical skills in philosophy.) First of all, Hegel is the greatest systematic thinker in the history of philosophy. There is no other thinker who has comparably enriched all the disciplines of philosophy, but also (Kant only dreamed of this) brought these disciplines into a coherent, orderly connection into which many later insights can easily be integrated—most of these later insights appearing to have been present in embryo in his work. Specialization is the fate of all disciplines, but one can remain true to the idea of philosophy only if one develops antidotes to specialization, and the study of Hegel's system arguably remains the most potent of these. The philosophical disciplines are interconnected, so that one cannot do ethics, for example, without knowing about the philosophy of biology, since all the moral beings (that we know of) are also organisms. Anyone who studies a partial domain of reality will almost always tend to consider it fundamental; reductionisms are the natural outcome of a refusal to look at the whole. "Philosophizing *without a system* cannot be scientific." Unlike Auguste Comte, Hegel does not simply adopt the relationships of presupposition that exist among the empirical sciences; he wants an *a priori* explanation of the inner architectonics of the sciences. Hegel is interested not so much in synthetic *a priori* judgments, as in an *a priori* system of concepts; basically, the *Encyclopedia* is an elaboration of the cosmos of ideas that Plato and Plotinus had in mind. Whatever objections might be raised against the details of Hegel's order, which was slowly articulated in Jena, Nuremberg, Heidelberg, and Berlin, we should not deny that our access to reality is inevitably guided by concepts and that fruitful criticism of a conceptual system can only consist in proposing a better one—not, for instance, in exiting the sphere of conceptuality. Concepts are not something we impose on reality; reality itself is conceptually structured, even if the concepts are not acquired by abstraction from experience. "To say that understanding and reason are in the world is to say what the expression 'objective thought' contains." Objective (or absolute) idealism is the conjunction of the insight that conceptual empiricism is untenable, and that fundamental concepts thus proceed from an *a priori* process of construction, with the realistic conviction that we are on the pulse of reality—not despite, but rather because of our concepts. This sounds paradoxical, but it is definitely in agreement with the religious belief that the world is the expression of divine thoughts, even if Hegel has a confidence alien to naïve faith that the right method will allow him to apprehend these thoughts.

But what, then—secondly—is Hegel's specific method, his dialectic? He handled it with greater virtuosity than he himself was able to make clear; indeed, sometimes we find misleading statements that seem to suggest that Hegel considers contradictory propositions true, especially when he opposes understanding and reason to one another. In truth, any rational reconstruction of the Hegelian dialectic presupposes the law of noncontradiction; Hegel himself states that contradictions in theories and institutions prove that they are not true. But he teaches that contradictory theories and institutions exist; and he thinks that concepts are contradictory when they are one-sided, do not recognize the relative legitimacy of their counter-concepts, and do not catch up with their own presuppositions: those are the marks of dogmatic understanding. According to Hegel, the concept of pure being, with which the *Science of Logic* begins, is self-contradictory, because it signifies indeterminacy but is itself determined by this signification; therefore the concept of determinate being as something determined is progress. The concept of the finite does not do justice to the stability that it must have *qua* concept, but the concept of "bad infinity" which is opposed to it opposes the infinite to the finite and thus transforms it into something finite (because what has a limit is finite); only the concept of the true infinite including the finite, which underlies Hegel's panentheism, is adequate. As in Böhme, what is crucial is the inclusion of the negative in the absolute. The last category in the *Logic*, the "absolute idea," is the principle that underlies the tripartite structure of Hegel's concepts; a positive concept is followed by a negative concept, and finally by a completing synthetic concept. The reason that forms synthetic concepts Hegel calls not "dialectical" but rather "speculative." To be sure, we can see something mechanical in Hegel's triads (which are sometimes replaced by groups of four); however, according to Hegel, they guarantee the unity of reality and at the same time make its differentiation possible. Even if Hegel was not unhappy to see in his triads echoes of the Christian doctrine of the Trinity, he argued rationally for his general principle of articulation. Such a principle seems especially natural if we reject conceptual empiricism and wish at the same time to avoid arbitrariness in concept formation. And a three-part division allows differentiation without falling into a dualism, because the third category provides mediation. Even someone who repeatedly rejects Hegel's specific concept formations should recognize that no other thinker can tell us as much about plausible subdivisions of concepts.

The most comprehensive triad in the system is the subdivision into logic, nature, and spirit: logic deals with essential concepts that instantiate themselves—the concept of being *is*, while that of space, the first in natural philosophy, is not itself spatial. Therefore Hegel calls nature the idea's being-outside-itself (*Außersichsein*); but it is designed toward an increasing internalization that culminates in the organic's special mode of being, in which the parts exist for the sake of the whole and in which something like feeling finally develops. Finally, although spirit derives from nature, it at the same time transcends nature by returning to logic. Thereby Hegel does justice to the twofold nature of human beings (who on the one hand belong to the real world, and on the other hand make normative claims to validity), but without for that reason continuing Kant's dualism. Spirit results from the development of nature, which is, however, so conceived at the outset that first, it participates in conceptual structures, and second, it *has to* produce a natural being that understands these structures. The final form of spirit is philosophy; it makes explicit what was implicitly happening from the outset in the unfolding of the system. Thus the system ends up subsuming itself—an elegant alternative to the transcendental philosophy that is unable to conceive its own constitutive achievement as being at the same time an element of reality.

In an exciting way and unlike modern formal logic, the *Science of Logic* combines first, the tasks of a general metaphysics that deals with the categories that underlie all existents before the distinction between nature and spirit; second, a transcendental philosophy that reflects on the conditions of the possibility of any theory construction, and therefore also includes a logic; and third, a rational theology with the ontological proof of God as its foundation. Hegel's God is not transcendent but rather transcendental; he is grasped by going back to what makes thinking possible in the first place. Since there cannot be two *absoluta*, this identification is plausible. The true achievement of the work is to use the self-movement of the concept to bring into an ordered relationship of increasing complexity the categories that Kant had extracted from the forms of judgment—the polar categories from the doctrine of essence, such as form and content, have more content than simpler categories from the doctrine of being, such as quality and quantity; and the logic of the notion explicates the level of conceptuality that is inherently presupposed from the outset, but was not yet thematized. Hegel repeatedly attacks problems in contemporary science; for example, the structures of measure in the third part of the doctrine of being. Particularly astounding are his mathematical insights, for instance, into the defects in contemporary infinitesimal calculus (which was not rigorously founded until the work of Cauchy and Weierstraß), or the impossibility of deducing mathematically Euclid's parallel postulate. The logical categories anticipate the structures of reality, whose development roughly corresponds to that of the logical sphere, for instance space to being, the absolute spirit to the absolute idea.

In the framework of his *Logic* Hegel also comes to terms with classical positions in the history of philosophy, since he defends the—false—notion that there is a precise correspondence between categorial development in logic and the advance of the history of philosophy. However, this theory allowed Hegel to attribute a systematic meaning to the history of philosophy that no earlier philosopher had recognized. His lectures on this topic remain one of the best introductions to the whole of the history of philosophy, because they see it as an organically developing whole. Hegel's knowledge of medieval philosophy was very modest, but his insights into ancient and early modern philosophy, for example into the essence of the Hellenistic schools, are impressive, and one of the numerous achievements of the Hegelian school is to have elaborated a scientific history of philosophy. Yet it would be absurd to interpret Hegel's *Logic* historicistically; it seeks to describe timeless structures whose genesis no more takes place in time than does the construction of a pentadodecahedron, even if they underlie everything, including even historical developments. Although Hegel also outlines a theory of the absolute that because of its triadic structure and its self-thinking inherits many of the traits of the Christian God, his theory is naturally fallible; the constant corrections he made in the various editions of his works show how critically he saw, not the basic ideas of his system, but the way it was carried out.

Hegel's *Philosophy of Nature*, which with the *Philosophy of Spirit* represents the philosophy of the real world (*Realphilosophie*), is weak at the point where he tries to conceptualize phenomena that the natural science of his time had not yet penetrated; and his defense of Goethe's theory of colors (whose new insights belong to physiology, not to optics) against Newton is even more embarrassing than his vain attempt to present Kepler's astronomy as superior to Newton's much more general theory. But—thirdly—Hegel's conception of nature is one of the most fascinating in the tradition, because he argues for a partial *a priori* knowledge of nature without betraying, as Kant does, our realistic intuitions, and because he recognizes in the abundance of the forms of nature manifestations of the absolute, but without for that reason denying a teleological orientation toward spirit. The third part of the work, "Organics" is the most important philosophy of the living since Aristotle, splendid in its detailed analysis of the essential characteristics of the organism (shape, assimilation, reproduction) and of the distinctions between plants and animals. Hegel's reflections on the special status of light have been seen by one of the leading experts on the *Philosophy of Nature* and one of the shrewdest interpreters of his dialectic, Dieter Wandschneider, as anticipating in part the special theory of relativity; we can also recognize in Hegel's notion that the principle of inertia is not valid independent of gravitation an intuition pointing toward the general theory of relativity. According to Hegel, nature rises to forms that ever more subtly overcome the separation of space: gravitation, chemical process, and sexual intercourse are the concluding categories of the three parts of the work. Kant's and Hegel's *apriorism* probably led German natural science to grant a greater role to thought experiments and theoretical reflections on general principles than, for example, its British counterpart. At the same time, we must insist on the fact that Hegel, unlike Leibniz, is not a "panlogist": he assumes that there are irreducible contingencies in the world of the real; and according to him it does go without saying that in the philosophy of the real world, unlike in logic, it is necessary to relate a certain experiential content to a conceptual structure. In the course of doing so, however, errors may occur that do not necessarily put the deduction of the conceptual structure in question.

Hegel's natural philosophy is not crucial solely because of the abundance of its insights; anyone who ignores it, as many Hegel interpreters do, and concentrates instead on the *Phenomenology* and the third part of the *Encyclopedia*, usually misses the objective-idealistic overall structure of the system, which is misinterpreted as subjectivist-constructivist or even historicist. However, it remains correct that the *Philosophy of Spirit* that completes the system is Hegel's most brilliant work. He accomplished nothing less than the integration of all the insights that were achieved by the Enlightenment and by classical and early Romantic thinkers into a system whose complexity is without peer from the point of view of the theory of foundation. It is Hegel's fourth great achievement—the creation of a theory of spirit without which the magnificent development of the German human sciences up to 1933 would not have been possible. This remains true even if the disconnection from Hegel's metaphysical assumptions began immediately after his death and if, for example, Dilthey's attempt at a new *Introduction to the Human Sciences* is as far from Hegel's assumptions as can be imagined. But the aporias in which Dilthey's project soon became entangled clearly show that the enormous drive of the German spirit in the human sciences was owed to a more solid foundation—the classical philologist Bruno Snell's *Die Entdeckung des Geistes* (*The Discovery of the Mind*, 1946) still feeds on Hegel's substance. More significant than the doctrine of subjective spirit, in which Hegel sketches a broad panorama of theoretical and practical activities ranging from unconscious mental processes to complex intellectual operations, are his theories of objective and absolute spirit. What is important about the philosophy of subjective spirit is that it once again deals with the *concept*, this time as a subjective correlate of the metaphysical core of reality. Thus Hegel does not deny that the human spirit creates concepts; but concepts can grasp reality in principle only because the latter is structured conceptually and is intelligible only thereby. According to Hegel, a thing-in-itself that is not conceptualizable is nothing but a self-contradictory conceptual construct. And not only can being be grasped conceptually, it can also be articulated in language, because in language the spirit reproduces the conceptual structure of the world.

Hegel's most fully elaborated text is the *Grundlinien der Philosophie des Rechts* (*Elements of the Philosophy of Right*), the most important work of German philosophy of law and the state. Hegel could write it only because from his youth on he was a perceptive observer of political events. We see this already in his early description of the inwardly moribund constitution of the German Empire, and it appears clearly in his commentary on the "Verhandlungen in der Versammlung der Landstände des Königreichs Württemberg im Jahr 1815 und 1816" ("Proceedings of the Estates Assembly in the Kingdom of Württemberg in the Years 1815 and "1816," 1817), in which he sides with the party of the king, which wanted to give the country a modern constitution, and opposes the narrow-mindedness of the corporatist society of Württemberg (which Hegel, not unlike Karl Kraus, unmasks simply by quoting it). Finally, there is "Über die englische Reformbill" ("On the English Reform Bill," 1831), which competently and carefully discusses the battle over nineteenth-century Britain's greatest constitutional upheaval (before its peaceful resolution). Indeed, Hegel registers the political changes of his time like a seismograph. His youthful enthusiasm for the French Revolution and the promise he made Hölderlin in the poem "Eleusis," "Peace with the statute / That regulates opinion and feeling / Never, never to accept,"— were only apparently abandoned by the Prussian state philosopher. In truth Hegel could well believe that important ideas of the French Revolution, especially equality before the law, had really been implemented in Prussia after the Stein-Hardenberg reforms. Hegel, unlike Fichte and just like the other greatest German mind, Goethe, viewed German nationalism with unconcealed antipathy; he never considered common nationality as a necessary or even sufficient element in a state. The realization of the idea of law, on the other hand, is crucial for a legitimate state; and Hegel's completion of the natural law tradition, which he defended against the historical school of law, consists in the elaboration of a material theory of justice in the first part of the *Elements,* "Abstract Right." In few parts of his system is the conceptual development as persuasive; and even if consistency and conceptual differentiation remain indispensable elements of any jurisprudence, Hegel's philosophy of law is not simply conceptual jurisprudence, because in the second part of his work, "Morality," there is, in addition to a critique of Kant's ethics, also a justification of concern for one's own welfare and that of others; that is, for interests. However, the idea of law cannot be reduced to interests because, according to Hegel, property (for instance) has an intrinsic worth as a sign of the sovereign right of the spirit over nature that is completely independent of its importance for the satisfaction of needs. Hegel also offers for the first time approaches to a theory of strict liability, which did not exist at that time—Fichte, for instance, justifies only culpable liability.

The main problem of the *Elements* is that it does not represent simply a normative theory like Kant's and Fichte's theories of law, but rather, at the same time, a political sociology in the wake of Montesquieu. This becomes particularly clear in the third part, "Ethical Life," which discusses the family, civil society, and the state. The combination of a normative and a descriptive dimension proceeds from Hegel's basic approach—for him, social institutions and intersubjectively shared ways of life have, like natural powers, an intrinsic value. Nonetheless, it remains indispensable to distinguish between forms of ethical life that are morally acceptable and those that are not. Statehood is in itself an achievement, but that does not prevent certain state structures from justifying resistance—though Hegel nowhere discusses that. At the same time, the concrete state that Hegel defends is an absolutely classical liberal state, and therefore it is a mistake to see his political thought as part of the prehistory of totalitarianism, as Karl Popper does. Hegel's state recognizes a natural law that precedes the state—and it is not easy to see what could set stricter limits to the state. Moreover, Hegel emphatically defends an autonomous civil society—he is the first German to make it an object of discussion. Unlike Fichte, Hegel had read the British economists, and he knew about the market's self-regulating powers. But these can operate only if, on the level of the state, there is rational concern for the common good, whereas the family is based on particular altruism, and civil society is based on universal selfishness. Without state oversight, civil society necessarily produces a polarization into rich and poor, and the so-called rabble.

Hegel's ethical justification of the state shaped the rigorous ethos of German officialdom. He himself was for the most part baffled by the social questions that he relentlessly brought to light, but a welfare state program that made the state responsible for solving social problems was nonetheless sketched on the basis of his ideas, for example by Lorenz von Stein (1815–1890), an important expert on administrative law. In this model, the state is largely disconnected from society and rules "from above"—in 1882 Stein told Ito Hirobumi, who sought him out in Vienna and was later to be the first Japanese prime minister, to avoid a democracy based on political parties and universal suffrage. Elements of democratic theory are also only rudimentarily present in Hegel, for instance in the demand for jury trials. His central constitutional demand regarded the separation of powers—for him, state power should be manifested in a cooperation between the Crown and the upper and lower houses of the legislature. The precise limits of the monarch's power remain unclear; in oral supplements, Hegel seems to reduce the monarch's role to putting the dot on the "i," and in view of the Carlsbad Decrees of 1819 it is very possible that the printed text of the book contains adjustments intended to ward off the censors. The most problematic part of Hegel's work is the conclusion. No matter how acute his description of international relations may be, his brusque rejection of Kant's hope that the institution of war could be overcome by institutions on the model of a league of nations is disappointing. Hegel's philosophy of history is an appendage to the philosophy of objective spirit; it sees the progress of the consciousness of freedom as the true meaning of history, even if Hegel also teaches that the greatest historical breakthroughs occurred not through conscious planning, but rather through a "ruse of reason." This explains why Hegel assigns to his own philosophy no power to shape the future but only a power to conceptualize what has already happened. "The owl of Minerva spreads its wings only with the falling of the dusk." He regards the post-revolutionary modern state as the *telos* of a complex development in which the Reformation plays an essential role; however, he doubts that its blessings could ever benefit the Oriental world. But nothing is further from Hegel than the relativistic historicism according to which all cultures are equally valuable.

In Hegel, absolute spirit is the human attempt to make certain of the absolute principle of the world; it articulates itself in art, religion, and philosophy. Hegel's aesthetics is distinguished from Kant's, because it is an aesthetics of content; and that is connected with the fact that in his system it is closely connected with religion. It is not merely a matter of the free play of the understanding and imagination, but rather of "the sensible appearing of the idea." Contemporary artists usually find Kant's formalism more in accord with their activity; but this may be a result of the fact that the ambition of the great art of the nineteenth century, which was to represent the greatest human questions, had withered away. Hegel could certainly hold fast to his normative conception of art and exclaim, with regard to different present-day tendencies, "So much the worse for the facts." His interest in the various contents of art (whose formally appropriate—that is, organic—structuring naturally remains the artist's task) explains his detailed study of the historical development of art, which remained alien to Kant. Indeed, Hegel adds to the classical and Romantic (medieval-modern) forms of art the symbolic form of art, under which he subsumes all forms of Oriental art, whose peculiar logic he seeks to determine, despite all his criticism of it. The triad symbolic-classical-Romantic is unusual insofar as the perfect element is the second one, not the third. For Hegel, Greek art is the most perfect, because it strikes a unique balance between objectivity and subjectivity, whereas in symbolic art the former is predominant, and in Romantic art the latter. Hegel develops his system of the five main arts in awkward correspondence with the forms of art: architecture corresponds to the symbolic form, sculpture to the classical, and painting, music, and poetry to the Romantic form. Primacy should therefore be attributed to sculpture, but Hegel prefers poetry, and within it, the drama, as a synthetic genre following epic and lyric. His theory of tragedy has been particularly influential; he sees its essence in the conflict between two equally justified, similarly one-sided principles. Thus the tragic is transformed from a purely aesthetic into an ethical concept, and though several tragedies brilliantly exemplify Hegel's conception, it does not hold for all of them. There are hardly any detailed interpretations of artworks in Hegel, but with his resolute focus not on the producer or the recipient, but rather on the artwork itself, he prepared the way for such interpretations. In coming to terms with him nineteenth-century Germany produced an abundance of aesthetic systems and theories; especially important are the *Ästhetik des Häßlichen* (*Aesthetics of Ugliness*, 1853) by Karl Rosenkranz (1805–1879) and *Vom Musikalisch-Schönen* (*On the Beautiful in Music*, 1854), a study belonging to the aesthetics of form by Eduard Hanslick (1825–1904).

The term "philosophy of religion" is used to refer to two different disciplines—a philosophical theology (Hegel discusses it in his lectures on the proofs of God's existence, which Goethe considered no longer timely) and a philosophy of the human phenomenon of religion. On the basis of its position in the system, Hegel can consider only the latter in his philosophy of religion; however, according to him the divine proves itself in a particularly intensive way in human attempts to return to God, even if not so clearly in religion as in philosophy. Hegel discusses an abundance of historical religions and guarantees Christianity a special status as the absolute religion, since in it the concept of religion has found its adequate form. Even if, unlike the young Hegel, the mature Hegel allots a large place to Trinitarian and Christological dogmas, it is crucial that he does so only in the framework of a reconstruction of the inner logic of Christian belief; he does not teach these dogmas himself *intentione recta*. Hegel's God does not suffer, but it is part of his plan for the world that humans should go through sufferings and in the figure of Christ divinize, as it were, the inevitability of suffering and its overcoming; indeed, even the modern feeling that God himself is dead, the "speculative Good Friday" in Hegel's *Faith and Knowledge*, is for him a necessary moment of transition. Hegel's own philosophical equivalent of the doctrine of the Trinity is found in the chapter on the absolute idea of the Logic; the *belief* in God's incarnation as a man fascinates him because through it the human being can achieve a proximity to God that would otherwise be denied him. In Hegel, pneumatology absorbed Christology; Jesus had to die so that the disciples could acquire an autonomous relationship to God in the religious community. Whereas the young Hegel saw the real history of Christianity negatively, the Berlin Hegel discerned the true realization of Christianity in the philosophical penetration of the Christian dogmas, originally given in the medium of representation, as well as in the construction of the modern constitutional state.

Can Hegel still be called a Christian? That depends entirely on the how "Christianity" is understood. Hegel is doubtless a rational theologian, even a radical Trinitarian (unlike the unitarian rationalists), and in the framework of his rational theology he attributes an exceptional importance to Christianity. The crisis of naïve Christian religiousness that he observed in his time deeply disturbed him; Nietzsche correctly writes that Hegel was the thinker who most delayed the victory of atheism. But he could not base Christianity on traditional stories of miracles. As a Lutheran, he was too sincere, and as probably the last person to retain a comprehensive grasp on almost all the knowledge of his time, not least the methods of modern source criticism, he was too intelligent. That he did not take up the problem of a personal appropriation of Jesus's moral revolution and the moral arguments for an eschatological dimension explains why first Søren Kierkegaard, and then the dialectical theologians of the twentieth century revolted, especially since cultural Protestantism, against which they turned, had trivialized Hegel and Schleiermacher by depriving them of a metaphysical foundation, and thus transformed religion into a mere cultural phenomenon, and sometimes even into an edifying support for German nationalism. But anyone who believes that he owes God consistency in his thinking, is urgently advised to study in depth, not only Leibniz's and Kant's, but also Hegel's philosophical doctrine of God.

❧ 8 ❧

The Revolt against Christian Dogmatics: Schopenhauer's Discovery of the Indian World

Opinions about Arthur Schopenhauer (1788–1860) vary more than those about almost any other philosopher. He is doubtless one of the greatest German prose stylists: whereas Hegel is only powerful in his language, Schopenhauer is unsurpassably clear and elegant. His essay "Über Schriftstellerei und Stil" ("On Authorship and Style") should be read by anyone who ventures to write in German. We sense that as a child this polyglot son of a merchant had already learned French and English; he was repelled by the kind of obscurity that claims to be deep, and thus by the German culture of his time, to which he preferred "the most reasonable and most intellectual of all European nations," Great Britain, even though its stubborn adherence to Christianity enraged him. His phenomenological insight is penetrating, his many interests are almost as encyclopedic as Hegel's, and his architectonic system-building talent is considerable. His hard-edged, brusque personality—like Luther, he had "character"—made this first European Buddhist say things that were still taboo in his time, which is never a guarantee of truth, but increases the likelihood of grasping new truths. In fact, Schopenhauer's originality is enormous; it was he who radically challenged the philosophy of the *logos* that had existed since the Greeks, and he did so without falling into the alternative of materialism, which is flat (and has been commonplace since Antiquity). Without

Schopenhauer, Nietzsche and his descendants would not have been possible; and his influence extends to the whole of subsequent German, indeed European intellectual history. Richard Wagner and Thomas Mann owe important debts to him; indeed, even fictional figures like Thomas Buddenbrook could not escape his influence. Whereas Schelling achieved fame in his early years, Schopenhauer, despite his acquaintance with Goethe, was never given a professorship; his lectures in Berlin, which he had, with excessive self-confidence, scheduled for the same hours as those of Hegel, were a fiasco, and his magnum opus, *Die Welt als Wille und Vorstellung* (*The World as Will and Representation*, 1818 and, greatly expanded, 1844), was hardly noticed; even *Über die Freiheit des menschlichen Willens* (*On the Freedom of the Will*), which was given a prize by the Norwegian Society of Sciences, and *Über das Fundament der Moral* (*On the Basis of Morality*, 1841) were not very successful. Not until the publication of his essay collection *Parerga und Paralipomena* (1851) did he gain widespread attention, and even then mainly through a review and an essay by the British dramatist John Oxenford, "Iconoclasm in German Philosophy" (promptly translated into German), in which Schopenhauer was credited with subverting the dominant German philosophy. Schopenhauer lived to see not only the publication of a third edition of his magnum opus (in 1859), but also the beginning of his worldwide fame—for instance, he received a visit from Friedrich Hebbel, who had begun his dramatic career as a Hegelian. But the preceding long period of neglect increased the bluster of his criticism—in Fichte (whose lectures he had attended) and Hegel (who was present at his postdoctoral qualifying examination, the *Habilitation*) he saw charlatans; for the Christianity of his time and for academic philosophy adapted to the church and the state he felt nothing but contempt. "On the whole, the feed shoveled out to professors in stables is best suited to ruminants. On the other hand, those who receive their own pickings from the hands of nature feel better being free." All this makes reading him a rare pleasure. His "Aphorismen zur Lebensweisheit" ("Aphorisms on the Wisdom of Life) in the *Parerga* remains a masterpiece not of moral philosophy but of the art of living; for instance, the description and mockery of the various forms of honor is timeless. Schopenhauer had studied, among other authors, the great Spanish moral theologian Baltasar

Gracián, whom he congenially translated into German. In psychology as well, for example in the systematization of parapsychic phenomena, Schopenhauer remains a trailblazer.

And yet the objections to Schopenhauer are no less important than his attractions. Politically, he was extremely conservative, for he lived on inherited wealth; the political changes of his time did not interest him because he rejected any philosophy of history based on progress. If he was an heir to the Enlightenment, then only in religious, not social matters. He defended capital punishment as energetically as Kant and Hegel did, even if he rejected their absolute theories of punishment (according to him, punishment serves as a deterrent). His attitude toward democracy was decidedly hostile; he not unjustly emphasized the contradictions in American slave-holding democracy and defended hereditary monarchy because the right of birth is related to property rights, insofar as the latter are inherited. His misogyny, which is most clearly expressed in the essay "Über die Weiber" ("On Women") is pathological, even if it was relatively widely shared among nineteenth-century philosophers with literary ambitions. The breakdown of traditional gender roles deeply unsettled many men of the period—think of Kierkegaard and Nietzsche, not to mention Otto Weininger (1880–1903), who belongs to general cultural history, not the history of philosophy. But whereas Kierkegaard was sexually inhibited in general and Nietzsche was probably homosexual, Schopenhauer hated women because he was so strongly attracted to them sexually—they endangered his striving for asceticism. It is appropriate to wonder whether this is really a good reason for hating women, even if it must be admitted that a strong sex drive accompanied by an inability to love— and Schopenhauer was not capable of more than compassion—is painful. No less disturbing is the fact that Schopenhauer rejected Christianity especially on account of its Jewish heritage: the later doctrine of the Aryan Jesus is foreshadowed in him. Like Fichte, he did not deny Jews human rights, but he did deny them civil rights; he considered the Jewish religion the lowest of the religions of high cultures.

But the decisive objection to Schopenhauer is philosophical in nature: the clarity of his language does not alter the fact that his arguments are bad and his theses often ludicrously exaggerated. Elementary reflections on the nature of justifications are foreign to him; indeed, the combination of revolutionary metaphysics with traditional ethics and aesthetics was shown to be unstable as early as Nietzsche. His reversal of Leibniz's thesis is famous: according to Schopenhauer, we live in the worst of all possible worlds. But Leibniz knew that his thesis could not be grounded empirically; in his work it follows from the ontological proof of God. Schopenhauer, however, has no functional equivalent at his disposal to justify his counter-thesis; he can ground it only inductively. In general, he defends—unlike Kant, Schelling, and Hegel, but like many a less well-known nineteenth-century thinker, for instance Eduard von Hartmann (1842–1906), who was influenced both by him and by Hegel—an inductive metaphysics that does not proceed *a priori* but rather takes basic experiences as its starting point. But it is not hard to imagine considerably more suffering than one can actually experience. Schopenhauer cannot argue, in symmetry with Leibniz, that such an increase in suffering would be conceivable only by assuming absurdly complicated natural laws, because for Leibniz the simplicity of natural laws is a good, and while perhaps it is value-free, it is hardly an evil, as Schopenhauer would have to maintain in order to claim that our world is worse than all alternatives. Schopenhauer's claim is thus objectively absurd, so why does he make it? His fame rests on the fact that he forcefully expresses a sense of life, namely, the world-weariness first deeply felt in the Romantic period. This pessimism, as Nietzsche rightly notes, was not developed in a particularly dreadful time, but rather at a time when people had lost the ability to endure suffering as a normal part of life. Schopenhauer's protest against theism and pantheism finds its moral justification in the overly sensitive perception of animal and human suffering. For him, given these pains which the optimist witnesses without experiencing them himself, as if in a peep show, philosophies like those of Leibniz and Hegel are downright nefarious. If Leibniz tamed the theodicy problem logically, Schopenhauer declares its existential insolubility; and after the failure of the German revolution of 1848, the country was ready to agree emotionally with Schopenhauer. His sense of life was shared by others in the nineteenth century; in particular, by the Italian poet Giacomo Leopardi, whom he loved, and by the American writer Herman Melville. But in the optimistic USA, Melville was not recognized as a classic until the twentieth century; and Leopardi, who never gave up his politically progressive ideas, was not a systematic philosopher. Europe's hangover after the gradual flickering out of Christianity was expressed by no one more eloquently and with greater philosophical depth than by Schopenhauer, who concluded the first edition of his magnum opus (before the appendix titled "Critique of the Kantian Philosophy") with the word "nothing" (*Nichts*). It would be better, he declared, had the Earth produced no more life than the moon. This is a new and far more dangerous conception of German nihilism than the one Jacobi diagnosed in Fichte.

Schopenhauer could develop his alternative worldview with all the more authority because he was convinced that it coincided with the heart of Buddhism. Since Schopenhauer, Western intellectuals have been able to draw on Asian worldviews as superior sources of wisdom—an enormous change in terms of the history of consciousness, which undermined, for example, the justification of colonialism, against which Schopenhauer railed (a position presumably easier in a state without colonies). Since Friedrich Schlegel's *Über die Sprache und Weisheit der Inder* (*On the Language and Wisdom of the Indians*, 1808) a first-class German Indology has been developed that is to this day not inferior to the British achievement. The first of so far only three German winners of the Kyoto Prize (given since 1985) was, significantly, an Indologist, the outstanding Paul Thieme. Schlegel had not only been one of the first Germans to learn Sanskrit. His book fascinates readers by its linguistic methodology, but it is no less remarkable for its attempt to discover fundamental ways of thinking that he found exemplified, for example, by Zoroaster's dualism and by the Vedanta's pantheism. Whereas in the eighteenth century the Chinese had been the Asian culture that most fascinated European intellectuals, India and Zoroaster's Iran now replaced it, at least in Germany.

There are three reasons for this: first, Indian and Avestan texts had been translated into European languages only at the end of the eighteenth century. The Avestan texts were translated by Abraham Hyacinthe Anquetil Du Perron, but it was a German theologian, Johann Friedrich Kleuker, who defended Du Perron against the accusation that he had been deceived by a forgery. Second, the linguistic kinship between Sanskrit, Avestan, and most European languages was recognized (definitively with Franz Bopp); at first, Friedrich Schlegel even considered it possible that Sanskrit was the original language of the whole family, and that by exploring it one might approach the origin of the human race (Europe's chronological ideas had broadened somewhat in the course of the eighteenth century, but they were still far from ours). Third, Indian mysticism fascinated people; this in contrast to the soberness of the Chinese, whose lack of myths had pleased Enlightenment thinkers; it was precisely the Romantics who were seized by "Indomania," to use Schelling's expression. Schopenhauer's concrete knowledge of India was, however, modest. He never learned Sanskrit, as had the Schlegels, Wilhelm von Humboldt, and Karl Christian Friedrich Krause (1781–1832), a student of Fichte and Schelling whose panentheism and progress-oriented philosophy of law exercised, in the form of *krausismo* (Krausism), an immense influence on the Spanish-speaking world; Schopenhauer even resided for a time in the building in Dresden where Krause lived. Indeed, he did not even have the broad knowledge of Indian culture that Schelling and especially Hegel had. He read the Upanishads only in Anquetil Du Perron's Latin retranslation of a Persian translation. But Schopenhauer nonetheless owed to his encounter with India his discovery of the possibility of a religiousness entirely different from Judeo-Christian theism and from rationalism, and of an ethics of compassion that includes animals and detaches itself from Kant's imperativist ethics. He saw also the possibility of a revival of ascetic ideals such as were steadily losing ground in Christian Europe, especially in the wake of the industrial revolution's promise of prosperity. However, his use of the "tat tvam asi" ("that art thou") of the *Chandogya Upanishad* to allegedly ground ethics is entirely of his own devising.

In addition to the *Upanishads* and Buddhism (which he studied only later on), Schopenhauer saw in Plato and Kant the most important sources of his philosophy. His philosophy clearly reacted to Kant, and he shared the German idealists' wish to bring the thing-in-itself to light. But, on the one hand, Schopenhauer remained very much in the grip of Kant's subjectivism, which he needed because it was, he thought, the only possible way of ultimately avoiding the determinism that absolutely rules the phenomenal world. (At the same time, Schopenhauer rejects the "vertical" dimension of the principle of sufficient reason, which in Leibniz leads to the proofs of God.) The world, as it appears to us, is our representation: space, time, and causality (the only category that he recognizes) are only our subjective constructions, and even, on the basis of a theory of identity that anthropologically flattens out Kant's transcendental philosophy, functions of our brain. Naturally one wonders how space could be reduced to something spatial like the brain. On the other hand, according to Schopenhauer the ultimate ground of reality is not an unknowable thing-in-itself; instead, it is familiar to us from our inside view. However, it is neither reason nor the concept, but rather the will to live; hence his interest and his extraordinary competence in biology—environmental biology goes back to him. For Schopenhauer, anyone who observes the world without prejudice sees organisms that battle with one another and that are forced by the sexual drive to preserve a life that, though profoundly senseless, is undeniably characterized by teleology. What appears to be reason, "a winged angel's head without a body," is in reality nothing more than a symptom of the will to live; human knowing stands in a continuity with animal knowing, and it must be interpreted pragmatically as serving vital interests. Influenced by Kant and anticipating Freud, Schopenhauer points to the unconscious as the true original ground of our fully conscious thinking: "If we compare our knowledge with a body of water of some depth, then the clearly conscious thoughts are merely the surface; most of them are unclear, feelings . . . mixed with the genuine voice of our will, which is the core of our being." The greatest intensification of the will occurs in the act of procreation, which "may never and nowhere be explicitly mentioned, but, as the main issue, is always and everywhere taken for granted and is therefore present in everyone's thoughts." "But that is the spice and the fun in life, that humans' main concern is pursued secretly and is ignored outwardly as much as possible. In fact, however, we see this concern as the true and hereditary lord of the world . . . sitting on the ancestral throne and from that vantage point laughing scornfully at the institutions that humans have set up to control, to imprison, or at least to limit it. . . ." Thus Schopenhauer proves to be, even before Marx, Nietzsche, and Freud, a master of a "hermeneutics of suspicion" (to adopt Paul Ricœur's expression). According to him, every great person turns out to be ultimately small; no hero is a hero to his chamber servant. (In contrast, Hegel limited this result specifically to the chamber servant's perspective.)

However, adopting in a remarkable way the basic idea of objective idealism, Schopenhauer interprets reality as a series of objectivizations of the will, which he calls "ideas"—and which range from the inorganic via organisms to human individuality. These are the themes of the second part of his system, which develops a metaphysically grounded theory of nature, whereas the first part was concerned with epistemology. Schopenhauer emphasizes the priority of intuition over the concept; in the twentieth century, his radicalized Kantianism in the philosophy of mathematics found an important successor in the intuitionism of the great Dutch mathematician Luitzen Egbertus Jan Brouwer. Though Schopenhauer may have vastly underestimated the importance of logical deduction in mathematics, his criticism of, for example, the congruence "proofs" at the beginning of Euclid's *Elements* (an analogue of which is also found in Hegel) is extremely clever; a specific congruence axiom is rightly found in Hilbert's work. The third part of the system concerns aesthetics, and the fourth part ethics, which Schopenhauer, who is in this at least a Kantian, sees as the most important part of philosophy. Taking pleasure in art, behaving morally, and asceticism, the highpoint of ethics, are for him the three forms in which a negation of the will takes place. Naturally one wonders, first, how this denial is possible, and second, how it is legitimate; unlike the Hegelian system, where the spirit returns to the absolute idea as the principle of the world, Schopenhauer's system does not close but instead ends with a revolt against its own metaphysical principle, which is barely concealed by occasionally using the term "will" (*Wille*) to refer homonymically to the moral order of the world. Moreover, Schopenhauer's ethics is purely descriptive; it starts by asking which power transcends egoism, and finds it in compassion. But why altruistic behavior is moral is not explained. The metaphysical reference to the monistic source of reality is, of course, no answer; if there is a single thing-in-itself, Schopenhauer's adoption of the Kantian theory that transcendental freedom is present in different individuals is absurd; and his doctrine of eternal justice, according to which the executioner and the victim are basically the same, is a grotesque parody of the traditional ideas of theodicy.

Schopenhauer's aesthetics is one of his most important achievements. We can count his theory that laughter is the perception of an incongruity between the abstract and the intuitively given (discussed in the first part of his system) as a part of his aesthetics. Certainly, his theory does insist too one-sidedly on the priority of intuition, but it is indisputable that the ridiculous is essentially connected with incongruity. Apart from the countless concrete remarks on genres and individual artworks, most of which show excellent taste, Schopenhauer teaches, first, that the artist captures (Platonic) ideas—and in this he is entirely in agreement with Schelling and Hegel. It is in this orientation toward something that transcends one's own needs that the happiness of self-abnegation consists. What is new in Schopenhauer's high estimate of art is that it appears as an escape from suffering; art in his scheme could become almost a substitute for religion for those who were not created for asceticism. Second, the genius possesses this capacity for contemplation in a heightened form. Schopenhauer's description of the psychology of the genius, his achievements as well as the dangers that threaten him, is impressive. But it has a disturbing side as well, which stems not so much from the Romantic glorification of the connection between genius and madness as from the condescension with which people who are not geniuses are dismissed as "nature's manufactured items." Third, Schopenhauer's rank ordering of the arts shows the greatest originality. According to him, the highest art is music, because it is not simply an image of ideas, but rather an image of the will itself. Its power over the emotions, along with the impossibility of translating it into concepts, guarantees its unique status.

It is hardly surprising that a brilliant composer who conceived himself in terms of a religion of art reacted to Schopenhauer's work with fascination. In 1854 Richard Wagner sent Schopenhauer *Der Ring des Nibelungen*, which was truly a *Gesamtkunstwerk* in accord with the principles of Wagner's aesthetics. Schopenhauer, who (like Hegel) loved Rossini, did not react positively; but Wagner's stage festival play (*Bühnenfestspiel*) certainly expressed Schopenhauerian (as well as Feuerbachian) ideas. It is mentioned briefly here because this work created a specifically German myth that was very opportune on the eve of Germany's political unification. In "The Perfect Wagnerite" (1898), George Bernard Shaw showed brilliantly how *Das Rheingold* presented, in the garb of archaic German mythology, an allegory of the rise and fall of modern capitalism. The hope that the will to power (which, unlike in Schopenhauer, is seen as more threatening than the sexual drive) could be abjured is Schopenhauerian, and in particular the twilight of the gods at the end of the opera, with its restoration of the daughters of the Rhine, corresponds to a vision of the extinction of suffering that is inherent in all culture. But what is new in Wagner is that the downfall is set in motion by violence, which the poet-composer affirms, whereas the moralist Schopenhauer could hardly take pleasure in the naïve brutality of a Siegfried. Violence, however, fascinated Schopenhauer's most intelligent pupil, who began to revolutionize ethics on the basis of his master's metaphysics. And unfortunately it was not only Nietzsche who was inspired by the *Ring*. After 1918 a humiliated people identified with Siegmund's sufferings and waited for its own Siegfried. He arrived in 1933 and, entirely according to plan, set in motion the twilight of the gods and turned Wagner's anti-Semitic fantasies into bloody realities.

The Revolt against the Bourgeois World:
Ludwig Feuerbach and Karl Marx

However, before that occurred, nineteenth-century philosophers had been concerned with freeing the world. It is beyond doubt that it was through the ideas of Karl Marx (1818–1883) that German philosophy became the most directly powerful in historical terms. Marx's position in communist states far surpassed that of the Church Fathers in Catholicism, because he had to share his fame only with his loyal friend Friedrich Engels (1820–1895). The latter was clearly inferior to him intellectually, but Marx wrote several works together with him, and Engels completed Marxism's worldview in his book *Herrn Eugen Dührings Umwälzung der Wissenschaft* (*Herr Eugen Dühring's Revolution in Science*, the so-called *Anti-Dühring*) of 1887, though it was obviously the work of a philosophical dilettante.

Since 1989, with the final collapse of the bloody social experiment that invoked Marx and Engels, it has been generally recognized that their influence was in fact very strong, but also much more short-lived than that of, say, Augustine, and that seeing in it the culmination of German, or indeed world philosophy, was a grotesque error not only of the moral sense, but also of the intellect. On epistemological and metaphysical questions, such as the mind-body problem that torments everyone with a philosophical bent, they not only had nothing original to say; they did not even understand them. Whereas Schopenhauer suffered from his atheism, Marx treated atheism as an intellectual matter of course, whose final achievement could only advance humanity. His

sometimes apt critique of religion is based on a complete ignorance of philosophical religiousness in the manner of Leibniz or
Kant and on a naïve ignorance of the potential danger of misus-
ing an atheistic will to power. Even the true foundational problem of ethics remained foreign to him. He made a contribution to
normative political theory only in his early work, while ignoring
liberalism's lasting insights on the necessity of the separation of
powers, indeed sweeping them aside as ideological—and to that
extent he at least favored, through an enormous sin of omission,
the rise of totalitarianism.

And yet Marx is underestimated today. It is not simply that anyone who wants to understand the period between 1848 and 1989
has to study him, and that many of his absolutely original ideas
have changed forever the shape not only of numerous academic
disciplines, but also of literature (think only of Bertolt Brecht).
His often journalistic style has captivated readers through its
witty, pointed emphasis and polemics, and the range of his culture is striking in the age of specialists with one-track minds. His
typical combination of cold, sometimes cynical description of the
social world (including that of proletarians) with the hot flame
of his moral outrage has kept generations spellbound. In addition
to all that, today the emotion with which he assigns a historical
task to philosophy has something moving, even downright melancholic about it, precisely because the threat connected with it
has disappeared. The dogmatism with which Marx offered simple solutions to difficult problems sprang from a will not only
to personal power, but also and especially to social change, and
underlying the latter was an understandable indignation at the
moral condition of the bourgeoisie—the class from which, however, both he and Engels came. Not remaining indifferent to
undeserved and conquerable suffering definitely ennobles philosophers. And understanding that capitalism is more than a
kind of economy, that it undermines in subtle ways traditional
virtues because it turns everything—virtue, love, knowledge, and
conscience—into commodities, remains a considerable achievement, precisely because we have every reason to brace ourselves
for a long duration of this system and to defend the timeless superiority of the market economy over a centrally-planned economy.

A sense for the exceptional subtlety of the Hegelian system
and at the same time an immanent critique of it by alternative

conceptualizations were for the most part more highly developed among conservative right-wing Hegelians, but it was nonetheless the left-wing Hegelians who were decisive for the history of European consciousness. Being the pupil of a great thinker is never easy, and sometimes it is a curse; because having understood the master's greatness does not mean that one shares it, or even that one has truly understood the arguments that underlie his insights. And if "autonomy" is one of the master's watchwords, splinter movements that do not necessarily lead to superior insights are preprogrammed. The feeling that Hegel had completed philosophy fed the need to criticize reality in accord with the demands of the new thinking, indeed, to transform reality. And since this was a violation of the "Owl of Minerva" adage, it led some to think that they had surpassed the master, and even that they were called upon to conceive entirely different philosophical ideas. The oppressive political situation in the *Vormärz* period, and the Christianity that had been interwoven with the Restoration and was no longer felt to be suited to the time, invited the sharpest criticism. Among the works of the left-wing Hegelians (the mature Marx was no longer one of them) the most influential was *Das Wesen des Christentums* (*The Essence of Christianity*), by Ludwig Feuerbach (1804–1872). It first appeared in 1841; two further editions were published in the same decade, and French and English translations soon followed, the latter by Mary Ann Evans, who also translated David Friedrich Strauß and under her pseudonym George Eliot is one of the great authors in world literature. Today, the study of this book is still strongly recommended to every intellectual Christian. It is more timeless than Strauß's *Life of Jesus*, because it does not go into specific exegetical questions, even though it includes in its argumentation manifest but disturbing findings, such as Jesus' imminent expectation, i.e., his belief that he would soon return, and evidence of the nonhistorical nature of the Gospel according to John.

The son of Paul Johann Anselm Ritter von Feuerbach, an important penologist, Ludwig Feuerbach first studied theology with great seriousness, but then turned, under Hegel's influence, to philosophy, and finally acquired some knowledge of the natural sciences. His anonymously published book *Gedanken über Tod und Unsterblichkeit* (*Thoughts on Death and Immortality*, 1830), posed the explicit challenge to personal immortality that was only implicit in Hegel, and provoked a scandal. It was banned by the censors and led him to give up teaching in Erlangen, where he was a *Privatdozent*; later on, he also failed to gain a professorship in Heidelberg, where students invited him to lecture in 1848, and where he had a great influence on Gottfried Keller, among others. Nonetheless, a referee recognized that Feuerbach was the only person (Schelling excepted) who deserved such a professorship—if only his philosophy were not so subversive. As Feuerbach wrote in 1843, the police were still the barrier between truth and academic science.

Feuerbach's magnum opus consists, like Kant's *Critiques*, of two parts, an analytics and a dialectics (along with an appendix that demonstrates astonishing knowledge of the history of theology; in addition to Luther, with whom he was very familiar, Feuerbach had also read the Church Fathers and Thomas Aquinas). In the first part, Feuerbach seeks to find meaning in religion by revealing its true—that is, its anthropological—essence. In the second, he attacks its untrue—that is, its theological—essence, by trying to uncover contradictions in Christian dogma. Whereas Hegel's philosophy of religion detaches itself from many historical Christian ideas and replaces them by a speculative metaphysics, Feuerbach knows Christianity in detail, including the "wildest excesses of the religious consciousness"; and his goal is to explain how it arrived at its specific ideas. Such an explanation cannot rely on extraworldly factors, for only human factors underlie religion. Feuerbach thus counts as the father of "religious studies" (as distinct from "theology") even though he does not proceed, as the modern discipline of religious studies does, in a value-neutral way, but is instead driven by an anti-theological affect: "Theology will be discussed neither as a mystical *pragmatology*, as it is by Christian mythology, nor as an *ontology*, as it is by speculative philosophy of religion, but rather as a psychic *pathology*." Like Epicurus, he pursues a therapeutic goal; that is, he seeks to free humans from religious "alienation" by helping them to rid themselves of self-contradictory ideas, which are also incompatible with the age of modern railways and steam-powered vehicles, and especially of a morality hostile to the body, which Protestantism had already conquered. Feuerbach sees his own sensualist humanism as a continuation of Protestantism, which in its ethics leaves Catholicism far behind—but precisely because of that it has lost

the coherence that characterizes Catholicism. Despite his rejection of early Christianity, Feuerbach sees in it a greatness that he
denies to the compromise-Christianity of his own time with an
aggressiveness that reminds us of Kierkegaard.

If no divine revelation underpins religious ideas, what then are
they based on? According to Feuerbach, religion is "the dream
of the human mind," "the childlike condition of humanity." In
France at the same period, we find religion banished to a primitive stage of development in the work of Auguste Comte, and this
banishment underlies all theories of secularization—to which,
however, religion has opposed an astoundingly powerful resistance. Presumably it will outlive all such theories. What is specific
to Feuerbach's theory is its background in Hegel's philosophy of
consciousness and his theory of the speculative sentence according to which the subject has no meaning independent of its predicates. In Feuerbach's work, religion is a way in which humans
behave toward themselves, or more precisely toward their essence
as another essence. In religion, humans objectify as external
powers the properties of their own spirit that they experience as
particularly valuable: "The consciousness of the infinite is nothing other than the consciousness of *the infinity of consciousness*."
Hence for Feuerbach, religious history is a central indicator of
the evolution of the human spirit. He does not deny the divinity
of the predicates religion transforms into a subject, namely God;
and for that reason, he does not describe himself as an atheist:
"What holds for atheism today holds for religion tomorrow." His
proposition that a property is not divine just because God has it,
but instead God has it because it is divine, is the argument of a
good Platonist; the intelligent Christian tradition has taught that
God does not *have*, but rather *is* his properties. No less justified
is Feuerbach's harsh critique of religious voluntarism (including
the notion that election for grace is a "mysticism of accident"),
because it undermines any moral sense.

In particular, Feuerbach wants to show how human understanding or moral experience are hypostatized as God. And
among all religions Christianity comes closest to revealing this
secret, because it identifies God and humans in the doctrine of
Incarnation; for that reason it is "absolute religion." However,
it is human beings divine in themselves who create a God who
becomes a human being. Christ's sufferings are an apotheosis of

the readiness to suffer for others, the Trinitarian doctrine of the I-Thou relationship; the veneration of the saint in an image is a veneration of the image as something sacred; the power of miracles manifests the power of the imagination (and is detrimental to unbiased research on nature). In reflections on the personhood of God, humans speculate on themselves "in the deluded belief that they are exploring the secrets of another being." In particular, Jehovah is "the personified selfishness of the Israelite people." All the same, Feuerbach sees in religion also a compensation for what is lacking in real life—in Protestantism, Mary's significance as an ideal spouse decreases the moment celibacy is abolished.

It is true that the mechanisms described by Feuerbach explain in part the emergence of religious ideas. But an objective description of the secondary causes of religion is compatible with a theological interpretation of the religious, such as we find, for example, in Rudolf Otto's classic *Das Heilige* (*The Idea of the Holy*) and, in literary form, in Thomas Mann's *Joseph* novels. For even if there are psychological causes of religion, it is still not impossible that a divine plan is realized through them. Feuerbach seems to have sensed this objection, and therefore wrote the second part of his book, which looks for contradictions in Christianity. Chapter 21, however, is directed against the proofs of God, indeed the existence of God in general. The centrality of the ontological proof is recognized, but the proof is repudiated, with Kant and against Hegel. The contradiction in the existence of God is said to consist in the fact that it is neither sensible nor mental (in the sense of a purely subjective thought-content). But the underlying alternative is rather modest; mathematical objects, for instance, do not fall under it, indeed not even the general concepts that Feuerbach himself presupposes when he identifies God with the essence of humanity. No less erroneous is his argument that the belief in God robs virtue of its intrinsic value. That is not the case if moral ideas constitute the core of God. More fundamental is his critique of the belief in revelation—tradition masquerading as revelation simply reveals the nature of humans, and declaring that insights that are merely historically valid are absolute leads one inevitably to superstition, or into the caprices of exegesis in order to cover up contradictions in the Bible. It is true that Christian theology is at the center of Feuerbach's critique, but he also repudiates the speculative doctrine of God defended by Hegel and the right-wing Hegelians, whose distinction between understanding and reason is suitable "for the justification of any nonsense." For Feuerbach, the Trinity is the contradiction of monotheism and polytheism, the two-natures doctrine of Christology is hopelessly inconsistent, and the doctrine of the sacraments promotes superstition and immorality. But the worst contradiction is between faith and love—the former excludes, the latter unites. Persecution of heretics results from faith, and the pride taken in being something special because of one's own faith, even though it is concealed behind humility, is an evil principle that sweetens one's pleasure with the idea that Hell awaits others. "The flames of hell are only the flashings of the exterminating, vindictive glance which faith casts on unbelievers."

Despite the harshness of his critique, which he himself sees as screening, not negation, it would be wrong to describe Feuerbach as an enemy of Christianity: that title should be reserved for Nietzsche. For Feuerbach writes, "God is love. This is Christianity's loftiest proposition." It is crucial to connect love with reason rather than with faith, to ground it through itself. For Feuerbach, love is the rule of Christ's life, not the other way around. "Thus anyone who loves humans for humans' sake . . . is Christian, is Christ himself." Certainly, Feuerbach assails the supernatural as a euphemism for the contranatural, which is immediately followed by hypocrisy; he wants to derive religious meaning from life as such. But this latter idea is not un-Christian; the "Amen" at the end of his book is therefore not insincere. What is un-Christian is only the naïveté with which he tries to trace ethics back to the phrase "Homo homini Deus" ("man is a god to man"); and after the experiences of the twentieth century, it becomes almost ludicrous when this thought is presented as the "turning point in world history." And it is unphilosophical that he nowhere explains the metaphysical, epistemological, and ethical presuppositions of his own worldview, unless it is through a generic reference to sensualism, whose untenability as an epistemology Kant had already perceived. Why some human properties, which are not all admirable, are supposed to be more valid than others, Feuerbach never explains, nor does he even conceive of it as something in need of justification. Compared to the metaphysical and metaethical subtleties of Leibniz and Kant, Feuerbach is primitive; but that primitivism contributed to his book's best-seller status. However little his work supersedes Kant's *Critiques* or Hegel's *Encyclopedia*, he can nonetheless claim to have opened up for philosophy, with for instance the I-Thou relationship in his *Grundsätze der Philosophie der Zukunft* (*Principles of the Philosophy of the Future*, 1843), an alternative to German idealism's subject-object model.

Although Feuerbach joined the Social-Democratic Workers' Party in 1869, he was no political agitator. Marx and Engels, on the other hand, wanted not only to interpret the world differently, but to change it—as we read in the eleventh of Marx's "Thesen über Feuerbach" ("Theses on Feuerbach," 1845). With this as their goal, they left the domain of philosophy's tasks behind them. One of the points of Marxism, however, is that certain kinds of knowledge can be acquired only through practice, not through mere sense perception. The second criticism that Marxism directs at Feuerbach is that his materialism is not historical. Religion, for instance, he derives from "human nature," rather than from changing historical conditions. Both ideas are certainly worth discussing. Anyone who reads, for instance, the *Federalist Papers* or John Stuart Mill's political writings, finds them saturated with a concreteness that could only arise from political practice. But a standard of evaluation that transcends factual practice remains indispensable; and this standard is inevitably theoretical. Even if there is also great historical variation in the phenomenon of religion (which the later Feuerbach certainly tried to grasp), something can count as a variation on religion rather than on art only because there is a suprahistorical concept of religion; the historian cannot dispense with a basic form of essentialism insofar as he wants to set boundaries to his domain. Marx's historicism has repeatedly led him to believe that certain regularities in the economy are limited to only one period and thus could be overridden in the future. That is true; a few basic conditions of the economy are relative to a period—but by no means all of them. The historical school of national economics (of which Marx was not the only member and which had its center in Germany) proved methodologically incapable of distinguishing between conditions that are relative and those that are not; the return to a more deductive procedure in the later history of economic doctrine was therefore right, on the whole, even if some of the insights of the historical school were lost in the process.

The left-wing Hegelian who influenced the young Marx most was his teacher Bruno Bauer (1809–1882). Although Strauß originally described Bauer as a right-wing Hegelian, his critique of the New Testament ultimately went beyond Strauß and led to the loss of his position at the University of Bonn. Marx's break with Bauer was triggered by the pompousness of the left-wing Hegelians, who attributed to their theological debates an importance that in his view was infinitely surpassed by real contemporary events. In 1843 Marx already wrote his *Kritik des Hegelschen Staatsrechts* ("Critique of Hegel's Constitutional Law"), in which he reproached Hegel, as Aristotle had Plato, for having neglected true reality by starting from the idea. In addition to his nostalgic invocation of the ancient republics and his interest in parallels between theological and political concept formation (an interest that anticipates Carl Schmitt's), his criticism of modern bureaucracy ("a course no one can get out of") and his commitment to democracy as "the solved riddle of all constitutions" are of special importance. In 1844, he published only one part of it, "Zur Kritik der Hegelschen Rechtsphilosophie. Einleitung" ("Contribution to a Critique of Hegel's Philosophy of Right: An Introduction"), in which the proletariat was associated with messianic hopes. Germany, Marx claims, has fallen behind, and because of its very marked tendency to thoroughness it has to be revolutionized from the ground up. His book *Die heilige Familie, oder Kritik der kritischen Kritik. Gegen Bruno Bauer & Consorten* (*The Holy Family, or a Critique of Critical Criticism: Against Bruno Bauer & Company*), published in 1845 under the names of Marx and Engels (though the latter contributed little to it), testifies by the merciless harshness of its criticism to a depressing lack of human loyalty; but it remains, for instance in its parody of religious language, one of the wittiest polemics of all time. The emptiness of pure criticism's self-referentiality, which dedicates itself to the serenity of knowledge, renounces all passion and love, and as spirit condescendingly looks down on the masses, is opposed to the solidarity with the proletariat. It is the being of the proletariat, not its ideas, that wants changing. Ideas alone cannot do anything. Marx protests against "metaphysics," which turns the world on its head, and which he distinguishes from philosophy—an opposition (which still influenced Habermas) between what was traditionally seen as first philosophy and what was now considered genuine philosophy. With enormous naïveté, communism was thereby presented as the natural result of materialism, despite the fact that the latter actually supported just as well—indeed, far better—a form of Social Darwinism (consider Marx's British contemporary, Herbert Spencer, who remained, however, a deist). Woven into the work is a debate with Eugène Sue's serial novel *Les mystères de Paris* (*The Mysteries of Paris*, 1842–43), which brilliantly understood both the essence of modern formula fiction (as an ersatz satisfaction, through fantasies of wealth and revenge) and the unappetizing nature of the bourgeois moralism that is deeply moved when it encounters occasional noble actions of its own.

Die deutsche Ideologie (*The German Ideology*), written in 1845–46 by the two friends, but first published in the Soviet Union in 1932, continues the critique of the left-wing Hegelians. In addition, in the first chapter on Feuerbach it lays out the fundamental principles of historical materialism. Even if the title is not original, the polemic against the idealism of the Germans, who are considered inferior to the French and English, against "these sheep who take themselves . . . for wolves," is a central concern of the work. To the belief in the power of religion and concepts is programmatically opposed a historiography that does not describe "the political actions of princes and states," but rather understands people in relation to their natural bases, and especially their economic activities. The various relations of production—for example, property relationships—depend on the development of productive forces; the intellectual "superstructure" (*Superstruktur*; later on, Marx called it the *Überbau*) is said to be a function of the economic base. "In direct contrast to German philosophy, which descends from heaven to earth, here we ascend from earth to heaven. . . . Morality, religion, metaphysics, all the rest of ideology and their corresponding forms of consciousness thus no longer retain the semblance of independence." They must be explained externally, not understood in their own terms, yet German history "takes every period at its word, what it says and imagines about itself." As something communicated in language, consciousness is always a social product. The construction of classes is central; class conflicts spring from the contradiction between productive forces and the form of commerce (which took shape in property relationships), and are the driving force in history. The modern state is nothing other than a function of the ruling classes of bourgeois society, whose ideas are the ruling ideas of a period. The impotence of the modern state is sarcastically described: "[I]ts existence in the fall and rise of government bonds on the stock market has become completely dependent on commercial credit." Modern large industry is a turning point: "It destroyed as far as possible ideology, religion, morality, etc., and where it could not do this, made them into a palpable lie. It produced world history for the first time, insofar as it made all civilized nations and every individual member of them dependent for the satisfaction of their wants on the whole world. . . . It made natural science subservient to capital. . . ." However, the present was determined by the impoverishment of the proletariat and the alienation resulting from capitalism's high degree of the division of labor. As an alternative, Marx envisages the idea of a "communist society where nobody has one exclusive sphere of activity but each can become accomplished in any branch he wishes, society regulates the general production and thus makes it possible for me to do one thing today and another tomorrow. . . ." How is humanity to achieve such a society? The suffering of alienation must become intolerable, especially through the contradiction between poverty on the side of the proletariat and wealth and culture on the side of the bourgeois; at the same time, the proletariat must be internationalized, which is possible thanks to the emergence of a global market, and the pressure of suffering must drive it not to criticism, but to revolution. This revolution is welcomed, because with it human beings become active subjects of history. Marx and Engels imagined that by identifying a real causal mechanism they had transformed communism from an ideal into a genuine movement, and this is connected with their claim that they had overcome utopian socialism by means of "scientific" socialism.

The transition from the early to the mature Marx, who is more an economist than a philosopher, is quite continuous, even if around 1968 this was disputed by neo-Marxists who wanted to rescue Marx from Soviet co-option. The shift to the study of economy began in the "Misère de la philosophie" ("The Poverty of Philosophy," 1847), which was directed against Pierre-Joseph Proudhon. Here Marx articulates the theory of value that he maintained right to the end: that the value of a product is proportional to the minimal labor time (that is, because of competition, the average labor time over the long run) required to produce it. The importance of demand for the constitution of value is generally downplayed. Marx engages in polemics both against the Englishman David Ricardo, who transformed men into hats, and against the German Hegel, who transformed hats into ideas. He rightly accuses the contemporary national economics of failing to clarify the institutional parameters within which economic activity takes place. He erroneously concludes that these are always historical and ephemeral, and that the principles and laws of the economy do not precede the people's action, and are changeable depending on the development of the productive forces. He mercilessly describes the exploitation of children and the human machines that industrial capitalism produces. Contemporary economics is divided into the fatalistic, the Romantic—in which the former's naïve indifference becomes coquetry—and the humanitarian-philanthropic, which wants to make every person a bourgeois. His own communist economics, Marx declares, is no longer doctrinaire, but rather revolutionary—which means, of course, that any criticism of it is counterrevolutionary.

The work by Marx and Engels that is most widely read is *Das Manifest der kommunistischen Partei* (*Manifesto of the Communist Party*, 1848), which is more a political pamphlet than a text presenting a coherent argument. The magniloquent language with which the historical and worldwide achievement and the moral atrophy of the bourgeoisie are depicted is splendid, and repeatedly hits the nail on the head:

> [The bourgeoisie] has pitilessly torn asunder the motley feudal ties . . . and has left remaining no other nexus between man and man than naked self-interest, than callous "cash payment." . . . It has resolved personal worth into exchange value . . . for exploitation, veiled by religious and political illusions, it has substituted naked, shameless, direct, brutal exploitation.

Whereas the members of earlier classes could work their way up, it is the fate of today's proletarians to sink ever deeper if they do not unite and join the Communist Party. The bourgeois' fear of losing higher education in communism is hypocritical, because for most people today education consists in being trained to be

machines, and the fear of the destruction of marriage is also hypocritical because the bourgeois seduce not only the wives and
daughters of proletarians but also each other's wives. It is a question of overcoming the position of women as instruments of production as well as a nationalism from which the hostile attitude
of nations to one another proceeds. Marx's own approach is also
distinguished from deficient forms of socialism, such as those
that want to achieve their goals by peaceful means.

Among Marx's numerous occasional writings on politics, the
most brilliant, and possibly also his best book in general, is *Der
achtzehnte Brumaire des Louis Bonaparte* (*The Eighteenth Brumaire of Louis Bonaparte*, 1852), which describes Bonaparte's
1851 coup d'état. (A present-day counterpart analyzing Berlus-
coni's perversion of Italian democracy would be a desirable sign
that Marx's form of analysis is not yet dead.) The categorial differentiation of his political sociology here reaches an apex, and with
its mixture of satire and tragic outcry the work is also stylistically
first rate. Marx neither demonizes the little Bonaparte nor justifies him by suggesting that he represents greater interests; instead,
he shows in detail which class interests support Bonaparte—
contrary to what one might expect, those of the peasants and the
Lumpenproletariat—and why the bourgeois parties were incapable of opposing his seizure of power. There is a masterly description of the empty pathos that imitation of a greater predecessor
entails—Marx contrasts it with the lack of predecessors for the
communist revolution (which has the unfortunate consequence
that the latter cannot be imagined concretely in any way). The
foolishness of putting one's trust in a new constitution that is
neither particularly good nor enjoys social recognition is rightly
mocked, since force without phrases must win out over the force
of phrases—but a general contempt for law is bound up with this
and has been one of Marxism's greatest moral weaknesses. We
also have to grant Marx that a republic without, or even with,
universal suffrage is no guarantee of a just politics, but that does
not mean that there is a better alternative to it.

Marx's numerous economic writings—for instance *Zur Kritik der politischen Ökonomie* (*A Contribution to the Critique of
Political Economy*, 1859), which has an important foreword—
culminate in *Das Kapital* (Capital), whose first volume appeared
in 1867; Engels published the second and third volumes in 1885

and 1894, on the basis of manuscripts. Its categorial development, inspired by Hegel, of the basic economic categories, the
enormous knowledge of the history of economy and its doctrine
that it demonstrates, and caustic remarks on crimes such as colonization and the pauperization of workers that go hand in hand
with the capitalistic transformation, guaranteed the book its status as a classic. And so it remains, even if the underlying labor
theory of value is untenable, with the result that the theory of
surplus value, on which the thesis of the exploitation of workers
is based (a thesis that is certainly not always false), also collapses.
With the refusal to take seriously Malthus's important integration of demography into economics, and the view of labor as
the only factor of production, Marx falls below the level of what
had already been achieved before him; and it was pure dogmatism when, in the twentieth century, Marx's economic theory was
defended against the scientific revolution that neoclassical theory had in the interim brought into being. Nonetheless, Marx
made brilliant use of, for example, the distinction between use
value and exchange value to explain the fetishistic character of
commodities. Exchange value proceeds from social relationships;
and these social relationships disappear in the sensible object of
the commodity, and are, so to speak, objectified. "A commodity
is therefore a mysterious thing, simply because in it the social
character of men's labor appears to them as an objective character stamped upon the product of that labor, as social, natural
properties of these things; because the relation of the producers
to the sum total of their own labor is presented to them as a social
relation, existing not between themselves, but between the products of their labor." The desire for commodities blinds people to
the complex process that produces them, and the social world
is conceived in accord with the model of external objects. It is
"reified," to use the language that has been standard since Georg
Lukács's *Geschichte und Klassenbewußtsein* (*History and Class
Consciousness*, 1923).

Analogously, Marx discusses the magic of money and the
fetish of capital. To be sure, he is right in saying that capitalism
substitutes for the commodity—money—commodity process a
money—commodity—money process: money is not so much a
medium of exchange used to get commodities as commodities are
a means of increasing money. The autonomization of the striving

for profit is what is truly alarming about capitalism, even if it is not clear how its positive consequence, an increase in productivity and innovation, could be achieved without that autonomization. In addition, Marx overlooks the fact that most people find the anonymous power of the market less humiliating than direct dependence on the orders of the staff in command of a planned economy. His expectation that the proletariat would experience increasingly severe impoverishment has fortunately not been fulfilled, and the absurd hope that a dialectical leap would lead directly from pauperization to a classless society has only contributed to the discrediting of the dialectic.

What are we to think of Marxism in general? Marx's work was the first to give social and economic history legitimacy, and his concrete analyses of historical development are frequently brilliant: he is one of the founding fathers of historical sociology. He offers also a splendid analysis of globalization, which in the early twenty-first century is merely continuing a process that began in the nineteenth century but was interrupted between 1914 and 1989 by two world wars and the Cold War. Moreover, there is no doubt that the unmasking of the economic interests concealed behind pretentious ideologies is often convincing, even if in the long run it undermines not only naïveté but also trust in what is good. Indeed, through its economic reductionism it may have led to economic ambitions being asserted without hypocrisy, and that means, above all, without inhibitions. But the philosophical weaknesses of the approach are obvious. First, it is not clear what is empirical in it, and what is grounded *a priori*; a distinction between these two elements of knowledge in the social sciences is nowhere drawn. Marx and Engels did not seek to practice an independent philosophy: they claimed to base themselves on observations. However, their frequently innovative categorization of social reality and its history certainly did not proceed solely from unprejudiced observation (which, as should have been known since Kant, always already presupposes categories). In particular, the polemic against Hegel's idealistic dialectics is off target, first because his theory of concept development does not seek to answer scientific questions of causality and does not imply that human ideas are the moving principle of history. Second, Marx's emphasis on the primacy of the economic is one-sided. Both politics and religion have influenced economic events; they do not merely react to them (as is acknowledged in a few passages); and therefore the hope harbored by someone like Ferdinand Lassalle, that the state could restrain capitalism, is reasonable. If in 1844, following Heinrich Heine, whom he knew, Marx called religion the "opium of the people," that was partly a way of belittling it, since religion can also stimulate violence, and partly a neglect of the foundation of common values that can follow from religion and therefore positively transform history. Indeed, Marx and Engels nowhere see that religion is a recognition—granted, for the most part a naïvely reifying one—of an ideal world to which anyone who makes a claim to validity must refer. How the human mind can be capable of grasping truth if it is only a function of matter and economic interests is not easy to understand; and thus the question naturally arises as to why we should take Marx and Engels's own theory seriously. Carelessness in dealing with the central task of justifying one's own claim to philosophical truth begins with Schopenhauer; Marx and Engels represent the next step, but they will be far surpassed by Nietzsche.

Third, since a legal solution of conflicts minimizes the violence that most brutally robs people of their autonomy, there are moral grounds for avoiding revolutions. Marx and Engels's enthusiastic invocation of the day "whose dawn is the reflection of burning cities in the sky, when . . . the guillotine strikes the beat," by contrast, represents a horrifying break with the Western ethical tradition, even if eschatological ideas owed to Judaism and Christianity continue to operate in Marxism in a secularized form. But to them a solid ethical foundation must be preferred, which Marx and Engels never worked out, since they basically assumed that revolution would take care of everything. From this point of view, the question as to how one grounds ethical claims and cultivates virtues such as generosity and compassion appears obsolete—as does concrete social policy. In addition to his criticism of the labor theory of value, the theory of pauperization, and the instrumentalization of democracy, the "revisionist" social democrat Eduard Bernstein (1850–1932) advocated a return to Kant in order to save what could be saved in Marxism: his motto, "Kant against cant" is famous. If we compare Marxism with the French philosophy that most closely resembles it, that of Auguste Comte, which also offers a purely immanent worldview and makes knowledge of the world culminate in sociology, the Germans' enthusiasm for revolution immediately strikes us, whereas Comte can be seen to connect order with progress and to assign positive value to religion, seeking to use it for his own goals despite his atheism. This is explained by the fact that the high price to be paid for a revolution was much clearer to the Frenchman than to the Germans, who felt a need to compensate for their lack of successful revolutions.

In Marxism, the automatic character of historical development replaces any kind of ethics; an arrangement that would be preposterous even if the triumph of communism were guaranteed. But fourth, the prediction that a communist society would be the final outcome of history does not accord with experience, which teaches that economies tend to stagnate without competition. It is a prophecy grounded in fascination with the industrial revolution and the productive forces it unleashed, which for the first time offered the prospect that poverty might be overcome historically. But why this should be accompanied by the abolition of private property is nowhere explained. It is not inaccurate to say that freedom can be won only by the community, but this is true only if the community is not acting under compulsion. In particular, Marx's radicalization of Adam Smith's and David Ricardo's theory of value was refuted theoretically by the neoclassical revolution in economics, which finally understood, already in the 1870s (or even earlier, thanks to Hermann Heinrich Gossen), the distinction between total utility and marginal utility. Among other things, Marx's theory is not capable of explaining the value of scarce unprocessed resources, and thus is not a good foundation for an environmental economics (even if passages on the destruction of the environment as a result of capitalism are to be found in *Das Kapital*). Marxism's claim to be scientific became increasingly laughable as it proved less and less capable of explaining even real prices, not to mention the impact of its failed prediction that capitalism would collapse. And even if Marx was correct to note that crises are inherent in capitalism, his refusal to work out a normative theory of the distribution of power for the classless society, because in it any form of dominion would be superfluous, became a recipe for appalling abuses. We can console ourselves with the thought that in this process a special dialectic prevails.

The Revolt against Universalistic Morals: Friedrich Nietzsche

I am not a man, I am dynamite. —And with all that there is nothing in me of a founder of a religion—religions are affairs of the rabble. I have need of washing my hands after contact with religious people. —FRIEDRICH NIETZSCHE

Despite his claims to the contrary, a DNA analysis of the mortal remains of Friedrich Nietzsche (1844–1900) would prove that he was a member of the human species. But as a philosopher he is most definitely outside the norm. After perusing his intellectual autobiography, *Ecce Homo*, from which the quotation above is taken, "normal philosophers" may even feel like taking a shower. (In this chapter, I make use of the polemical tone that Nietzsche himself adopted in many of his works.) For consistency is a minimal condition of truth, and there is no other thinker who is less concerned about the consistency of his statements, who indeed wallows in contradictions, and with whose work it is therefore possible to prove anything. Naturalists and radical hermeneuticists, moralists and cynics, opponents of capital punishment and glorifiers of violence, libertarians and Nazis, Romantics and cool psychologists of art all find whatever it is that they are looking for. But logic was not his forte, and even the study of the tradition, which is strongly recommended to every philosopher, was in Nietzsche's case mediated chiefly through the secondary literature of his time (especially the *Geschichte des Materialismus*

[*History of Materialism*] by the neo-Kantian Friedrich Albert Lange [1828–1875]). As a philosopher and as a historian of philosophy, Nietzsche is thus something of dilettante, even if his unique, seductively beautiful style, which he found only in 1878, for the most part conceals his lack of arguments and evidence. His philosophy, moreover, was not improved by the megalomania with which he increasingly compensated for his self-hatred and which must presumably be explained in the end "materialistically," that is, as a symptom of his progressive paralysis, which probably caused the mental derangement that began to afflict him in 1889. It compelled him to return to his mother and sister, from whose tutelage he vainly struggled to free himself throughout his life, a struggle that goes far to explain his polemic against women and especially against their emancipation. (He predicted that the period preceding the successful completion of women's emancipation would be a difficult one for all concerned. And he was right about that, at least.)

Why devote a long chapter to him? Because this man really was dynamite. No other thinker has destroyed as much as this philosophical terrorist, and no other has contributed so much to Germany's estrangement from its classical era. (The only figure of that time whom Nietzsche venerated was Goethe; and he acknowledged Hegel's superior historical instinct.) But it is also true that he could demolish so much only because what he attacked was already rotten. Instead of haughtily ignoring the hollowness of German culture after political unification in 1871, he conceptualized it better than anyone else, even if it was not really his aim to be a "soldier of culture." What is more, his criticism of his time remains relevant because much of what he scourges—for example, the increasing importance of newspapers—continues to spread, while the standards of high culture have grown even weaker. However, Nietzsche's tragedy consists in the fact that the low quality of his philosophical technique, along with his phenomenological power and brilliant style, accelerated the cultural decline. Journalists and intellectuals prefer to read him rather than Leibniz or Kant, and this has not improved the press or the culture industry. His discontent prophetically anticipated that of whole generations which fell under his spell, because he expressed their sensitivities with unsurpassable incisiveness. Good philosophy is considerably more than expressiveness; but like art, it has also has a duty to express; and expressionist philosophers of Nietzsche's rank have never existed before or since. Among the positive changes in the history of consciousness that Nietzsche triggered is a sensitivization with regard to the abyssal depth of the human soul and culture, as well as knowledge of the risk to the spirit and the questionable nature of exceptional moral achievements, both of which were phenomena that he could amply observe in himself. Thomas Mann is the most important, though certainly not the only beneficiary of Nietzsche's insights, and he is so important because he broke with Nietzsche's ethics and integrated his specific insights into a worldview that was far closer to that of German idealism than he himself knew. At the same time Nietzsche bears the main intellectual responsibility for the German adventure of crushing the Christian order of values and the creation of an alternative value system that dripped with the desire to kill, and then for the worldwide spread of a vulgarly pretentious relativism that since 1989 has often paralyzed those who have thrown off Marxism.

But Nietzsche himself was neither murderous nor vulgar, and from the middle of his career he was even a despiser of German nationalism and especially of the anti-Semitism of his time. Most philosophers have been healthy, but Nietzsche was a man who battled numerous diseases and therefore had a enormous sensitivity to the bodily presuppositions of philosophizing that are not likely to occur to a healthy person. His affirmation of life despite the pains he suffered, and despite the absence of any prospect of a life after death, has something heroic about it (and, in his rejection of happiness, also something Kantian); but his psychological insights tell us why he increasingly affirmed others' suffering as well. His physical awkwardness, which manifested itself, for instance, when he volunteered for military service in 1870, was compensated by unusual talents in various domains: he was capable as a philologist, competent as a composer, innovative as a lyricist, and brilliant as a psychologist. In addition, he had a Luther-like sense of an unconditional duty to be sincere, even at the price of complete isolation from his fellow men. Indeed even at the price of destroying a world. His blustering verbal cruelty was balanced by a great compassion and gentleness in dealing with others (even, and especially, with people who lacked compassion). Since he increasingly regarded this as a weakness, he forced himself to be hard, but he directed the hardness mainly against himself. He abolished his youthful Romanticism and suppressed his yearning for friendship. But his hymns to hardness inspired people who were his opposites. In him we can recognize what seems to be a general truth: that aesthetic sensitivity, psychological acuteness, and philological and historical knowledge are more damaging than useful, if they are not accompanied by logical intelligence and a sense for a consistent metaphysics, and that the combination of great virtues with a few weaknesses is often more dangerous than an unadulterated brew of all the vices.

Already appointed professor of classical philology in Basel in 1869, in early 1872 Nietzsche published *Die Geburt der Tragödie aus dem Geiste der Musik* (*The Birth of Tragedy Out of the Spirit of Music*). The book triggered heated controversy—the young Ulrich von Wilamowitz-Moellendorff, who was to become Germany's most important philologist, attacked it in the two parts of his *Zukunftsphilologie!* (*Philology of the Future!*). Richard Wagner, whom Nietzsche had met in Leipzig in 1868, defended Nietzsche, as did his friend Erwin Rohde, who also became one of the greatest German classical philologists of the late nineteenth century; both replied to the first part of Wilamowitz's book. Since this controversy philosophy and classical philology have become strictly separated disciplines; the splendid combination of the two that still existed at the beginning of the nineteenth century (think of Schleiermacher, the Schlegels, and Humboldt) fell apart for good.

Nietzsche's work pursues three different goals: it seeks to provide a philological explanation of the origin of Greek tragedy; following Schopenhauer, whom Nietzsche read as early as 1865 (and who is the only philosopher whom he really knew, except for the pre-Socratics), the book offers a new aesthetic theory based on the categories of the Apollonian and the Dionysian and explains the decline of art by arguing that the vital, amoral power of the Dionysian was destroyed by Socrates's Apollonian rationality; and it makes the case for Wagner's "music drama," which is interpreted as a congenial renaissance of Aeschylean tragedy. Here once again the Germans are the new Greeks. However, Greeks and Germans are no longer united by the philosophy of the *logos*, but on the contrary by their susceptibility to an irrational power—the appeal to Antiquity has become anti-humanistic.

(Later, when he no longer had hope that he might influence contemporary German culture, Nietzsche declared that the French were the new Greeks, and traced the barbarity of the Germans back to Luther, whose peasant revolt against the intellect prevented the dissolution of Christianity that had already begun with the Renaissance papacy.)

His promotion of Wagner and Schopenhauer was couched in an overblown style and with the fervor of an adherent to the religion of art. The expression is chosen advisedly, because Schopenhauer and Wagner had to fill the vacuum that developed in Nietzsche when as a teenager he lost the Lutheran belief of his ancestors (his father was a pastor, his grandfather had been a church superintendent, and he himself initially enrolled at the University of Bonn to study theology), partly as a result of reading David Friedrich Strauß. Nietzsche was one of the first to note the power of the irrational among the Greeks. Although music played a role in Greek tragedy that is central but difficult to reconstruct, the anti-Aristotelian glorification of the origin and the harsh criticism of Euripides are problematic in Nietzsche's book; Euripides's interpretation of reality is wrongly connected with Socratic optimism. On the contrary, Euripides is the most pessimistic of the tragic poets; a fact that Nietzsche does not want to see because in 1872 pessimism, thanks to Schopenhauer, was still a positive value, and because he does not like Euripides' devotion to the audience and to the "little people." A strong distaste for democracy and social thought is one of the few constants in Nietzsche, whose thinking can otherwise be divided into three periods (he himself saw it that way—that he distanced himself from his earlier works is made particularly obvious in his prefaces to their second editions). To simplify, one can say that in the first phase Nietzsche blindly worships his two heroes; in the second, he gives up his faith in them on the basis of a subtler psychology; and in the third he sets himself up as a genius. We would owe a debt of gratitude to anyone who used the style of the second Nietzsche to bring down the monument to himself erected by the third.

The hostile reaction of professional scholars caused Nietzsche to turn away from philology. If philology no longer sought to teach the present anything normative, but only to do research on the dead, then he must become a philosopher, even if he was not trained as one. But external impetuses are more central in philosophy than in any other discipline. The four *Unzeitgemäße Betrachtungen* (*Untimely Meditations*), written from 1873 to 1876, express in their title Nietzsche's increasing isolation. His first patricidal attack was made on David Friedrich Strauß's late work *Der alte und der neue Glaube* (*The Old Faith and the New*, 1872), then a best-seller but in fact one of the most banal works in the history of German philosophy. With his inconsistent mixture of the commonplaces of a time that was no longer Christian, Strauß showed how little he had understood Hegel's philosophy, seeing in Darwin's discoveries a refutation of German idealism, simultaneously advocating a secularized Christian ethics, and concealing under pathetic talk about progress the fact that he no longer had any idea what a rational worldview was. (Needless to say, Hegel's philosophy must *a fortiori* have remained impenetrable to Nietzsche.) More important than the first of these meditations, or the third and fourth, which celebrate Schopenhauer and Wagner (though here, too, patricide was soon to follow), is the second one, "Vom Nutzen und Nachteil der Historie für das Leben" ("On the Use and Abuse of History for Life"). As an experienced philologist Nietzsche understood how the historical observation of reality can lead to a crippling of life and of the will to achieve something timeless. As the end result of the three basic types of history—monumental, antiquarian, and critical (i.e., glorifying, preserving, and destroying)—appears "the man who recognizes greatness but cannot himself do great things," "the antiquary without piety," and "the critic without need." Unfortunately, Nietzsche does not discuss the way in which radical historicism also clouds the ability to think logically because it no longer allows us to see that true propositions are timeless structures. Instead, Nietzsche himself demonstrates this clouding in his later works, which belong to critical history in its most radical form—written in the hope of erecting, through this radicalization, a monument to his own greatness.

Nietzsche's middle period is his most fruitful philosophically. In it he already articulates almost all of his important insights, while still trusting in science and without the aggressiveness that characterized his late works. It is also at this stage that in *Menschliches, Allzumenschliches—Ein Buch für freie Geister* (*Human, All Too Human: A Book for Free Spirits*, 1878–1880), *Morgenröte*

Gedanken über die moralischen Vorurteile (*Dawn: Thoughts on the Prejudices of Morality*, 1881), and *Die fröhliche Wissenschaft* (*The Gay Science*, 1882) he brings the aphorism, a form congenial to him, to a perfection not achieved before or since in German philosophy. The collection of aphorisms is the form opposite to the system, because it expresses pointed, often paradoxical insights and does not need to concern itself over whether these individual insights follow from one another or whether they are even consistent. These brilliant short texts do not bind the author definitively and invite the reader to reflect, and even to object, since "for the author, the point is precisely the objection." Under modern conditions, the allusiveness of the form can be used for moral criticism with special ease, because it wounds less than a diatribe (which is usually counterproductive) and shows more respect for the reader's autonomy. The French moralists of the seventeenth and eighteenth centuries who, as Nietzsche acknowledges, had Christian roots and sought to shine a light on the corruption of human nature, were the first to use this form in a masterful way, but they had only a few imitators in Germany (Lichtenberg, the early Romantics, Goethe, and Schopenhauer are the most important). Nietzsche owes much to the French model, which he supplements, however, insofar as he does not always deny the subjective honesty of moral ideologies, but denies only that something objectively true underlies them. In his view, the moral interpretation of reality will disappear just as did the Pythagoreans' belief that they could hear the harmony of the spheres. Paradoxically, it was the Kantian revolution in moving ethics toward autonomy that ensured the triumph of the aphorism: someone who sees freedom as the highest good will find his new sensibility wounded not only by Aquinas's *Summa theologica* but also by Kant's *Critique of Practical Reason*. This sensibility will be still more deeply satisfied if in addition to avoiding the treatise form, one also exposes the morally questionable motives of the preacher of morals. The paradox of Nietzsche—a moralist who did not believe in objective morals—consists in the fact that in the long run he undermines the moral subtlety that animated the genre and at first animated Nietzsche himself. No doubt Nietzsche perceived, with great pain, the hypocrisy of bourgeois morality and, increasingly, that of the art scene as well. He also practiced stern self-criticism: the Nietzsche of the middle period often talks about himself, even if he does not yet call himself by name. What a great deal of vanity ("the human 'thing-in-itself'"), how great a desire for superiority and a fear of inferiority underlie so-called virtues (for instance, pompously telling the truth because one doesn't trust one's ability to dissemble), how much lurking meanness underlies everyday conversation—no one felt more deeply than this moral rigorist. Reading him is more challenging than making one's severest confession. For no matter how disastrous Nietzsche's battle against the levelers, i.e., universalism, was, he acknowledged that modern formalism is often blind to the wealth of values and virtues possessed by the tradition; and what distinguishes even the late Nietzsche from commonplace atheists and positivists is how seriously he takes moral differentiation, which nothing can breed so readily as religion does.

The first volume of the first of three collections of aphorisms is Nietzsche's best book, because it is the most comprehensive and the least extreme. At the outset, the metaphysical philosophy to be overcome is opposed to a historical philosophy; a "lack of a sense of history" is said to be the hereditary defect of all philosophies. At the same time, Nietzsche's own method is called, in homage to modern natural science, a "chemistry of concepts and feelings." It inevitably proceeds deterministically. In referring to chemistry and historical studies Nietzsche appeals to the positivistic scientific beliefs of his time; but he does not care how the two sciences are related to one another, nor does it occur to him that both of them presuppose a logic and ontological assumptions (for example, regarding natural laws), since for him "metaphysics" refers to the theory of a transcendent order. For Nietzsche, our metaphysical errors are the result of seduction by language and an overestimation of logic, whose presuppositions in no way correspond to reality. However, Nietzsche seems not to notice that with this judgment he undermines the foundations of the sciences. In fact, in his third phase, he harshly opposes the sciences' claim to truth, while at the same time hating skepticism because it provides a basis for the reintroduction of Christianity. The criticism of the false conclusions of the dream-logic in Nietzsche's profound analyses of dreams, which partly anticipate Sigmund Freud's *Die Traumdeutung* (*The Interpretation of Dreams*, 1900), presupposes the ascent to logical rigor as an advance. In all his attacks on metaphysics Nietzsche absolutely acknowledges that, along with the age of metaphysics, incentives to create enduring institutions that will survive oneself are no more. His own era is described as the age of comparison and acceleration. And its essence is instability, indeed barbarity. Life maintains itself, it seems, only through self-deception as to one's own motives, but also those of recognized models: "The beast in us wants to be lied to; morality is a lie that is necessary to prevent it from tearing us apart." Religion is not based solely on hypocrisy, but also on strenuous and successful self-deception. The free spirit, about whose ideal way of life Nietzsche has many intelligent things to say, observes this world without sputtering and thereby arrives at peace of mind—the praise of cool-headed knowledge is a legacy from Schopenhauer, as is the thesis that the will is the intellect's prompter. However, Nietzsche also inherited from Schopenhauer the problem of explaining how the free spirit can know reality if it is, as he claims, in its essence hostile to the mind.

Whereas Nietzsche repudiates the metaphysical significance of morality in Schopenhauer, he is interested in the development of moral ideas and values out of historical processes in which human society is divided into the powerful and the weak. Unlike Marx, Nietzsche opts for the strong. His causal explanation of the genesis of moral ideas out of coercion and violence, and of religion out of magic, is always magniloquent and often plausible; but he does not understand that this historical approach cannot resolve the problem of validity (or that genealogical theories are also subject to criteria of validity). Psychology and history are no substitute for first philosophy and ethics. Only someone who does not distinguish between genesis and validity could claim that "with insight into this origin that belief falls away." Unfortunately Nietzsche did not know Vico, who deals with the evolution of morality in a strikingly similar way, but associates this approach with a universalist theory of natural law that is compatible with it. Kant and Schopenhauer wrongly ignored the historical development of our moral ideas, but it is a greater shortcoming to concentrate on the abundance of historically realized values while being unable to choose among them from the point of view of the theory of validity. And this shortcoming becomes intolerable when it claims to be superior to the effort to think in terms of the theory of validity, arguing that the latter's viewpoints developed historically, too—as if the same argument did not apply also to historicism, which also developed historically.

Nietzsche's attack on compassion goes well beyond the mere history of morality. Essentially, his claim is that the compassionate person enjoys his superiority and therefore is hardly capable of shared joy. But in his late works this observation, which in itself springs from a special kind of moral subtlety, turns into a rejection of sympathy with those who are suffering. Nietzsche's brutality is a compensation for his tenderness, but its admirable genesis does not make the end result any more palatable. And yet another ethical doctrine is proposed: that an unsatisfied hunger for vengeance produces a psychic poison that does not form if one immediately takes revenge. This is not false, but from it and from the critique of the modern penal system emerges a defense of duels, and later the glorification of the blond beast. Early on, there was already a tension in Nietzsche's writings on morals that arose from his deploring the disintegration of moral hierarchies while at the same time contributing to their disintegration, because they interpret greatness sarcastically: "One will seldom go wrong if one attributes extreme actions to vanity, mediocre actions to habit, and petty actions to fear." Even the difference between good and evil actions is no more than a matter of degree: "Good actions are sublimated evil ones." (Later, vices are interpreted as atavisms.) Nietzsche may have had a deep hatred for modern leveling down, but he is the writer who provided the resentment that cannot tolerate greatness with its most lethal weapon for taking a superior down a peg.

Nietzsche's critique of morality is further developed into a critique of religion, especially the Christian religion, which for him lacks the nobility of the Greek religion. It is in fact so irrational that one can hardly believe that it is still credited. Nietzsche recognizes, however, that Christianity is advantageous for certain persons and makes them more attractive (he had a weakness for aristocratic Catholic bishops), and like Feuerbach and Kierkegaard, he prefers the coherence of ascetic Christianity to the pitifulness of contemporary everyday Christians. Nor does he deny that some of the greatest works of art were made possible only by Christianity. However, if he complains that there is not enough love and kindness in the world to allow its being given away to imagined beings, one can easily reply that this delusion (if it is one) could definitely increase love; at least this is compatible with his theory of self-deception for the sake of life. More interesting is his explanation of asceticism on the basis of the will to power: someone who cannot tyrannize others satisfies his lust for domination on himself. As further weaknesses of Christianity he mentions the condemnation of the natural as bad, along with the emotional rollercoaster of arrogance and humility.

The fourth section of the first volume of *Human, All Too Human* is perhaps the most original, both because in it Nietzsche breaks with Romantic aestheticism on the ground of his disappointment with Wagner, and because his defense of the fragment and incompletion as a means of artistic expression is to be read self-referentially. For Nietzsche, art is not inspiration but hard work; at the same time, the artist's sense of truth, which is somewhat childish, is clouded and inferior to that of the scientist. He dismisses as absurd the metaphysical theory that art represents ideas. Instead, art is explained on the basis of individual needs. A further break with Schopenhauer is represented by the theory that the meaning of music depends upon its original unity with words in song. Absolute music is a late abstraction—and in this claim Wagner's theory of the *Gesamtkunstwerk* lives on. Most significantly, the concepts of greatness and genius are undermined. Not only does greatness cripple all imitators, but people seize upon the cult of the genius out of wounded vanity, because it relieves them of the necessity of competing with the genius. For the latter, however, that cult is extremely dangerous—"because he ceases to practise criticism of himself, at last one pinion after the other falls out of his plumage." It is an observation that applies to Nietzsche himself. Nietzsche's identification of what is individually and culturally questionable about genius is fascinating: on the one hand, it often arises out of an effort to compensate for weaknesses and out of the will to power; on the other, it presupposes the brutality of archaic discipline and necessarily atrophies in an ideal state.

After bidding farewell to metaphysics, religion, and morality, only one conception of value remains to Nietzsche, that of culture. He is concerned solely with demanding a higher culture; it does not occur to him that civil rights set a limit here. Like his favorite enemy, Rousseau, Nietzsche is absolutely certain that higher culture does not make people happier: he is a perfectionist, not a eudemonist. In the eighth section of "A Glance at the

State," Nietzsche gives expression to his scorn for modern representational democracies with their great "alfresco stupidities" and his longing for men of noble blood (in the end he invented a Polish aristocratic ancestry for himself). He mocks socialism's ideas of justice, which he thought would lead to terrorist despotism, declares admiration for the positive effects of even the most terrible wars (in which he also recognizes, however, negative effects), and, increasingly, he criticizes nationalism in the name of Europe, which for him should rule the world. His contempt for workers, whose sufferings are far less subtle than those of the idle free spirits, can also be explained by Nietzsche's own words: "Wherever there is a striving to exalt individual men into the suprahuman, there also appears the tendency to imagine whole classes of the people as being coarser and lower than they really are." An essential trait of nineteenth-century German culture is grasped when one notes that Marx overestimates the significance of the new social class of the proletariat from the standpoint of the philosophy of history, while Nietzsche scorns it. Charles Dickens's Christian answer to the social question has no real equivalent in the high literature and philosophy of Germany.

In the second and third volumes of *Human, All Too Human* these themes are developed further. For instance: "In the gilded sheath of pity there is sometimes stuck the dagger of envy." In addition, there is criticism of the mendacity of German education, which had begun to oblige people "to rejoice" in complex art works, criticism too of scholars whom he calls "skillful dwarves," as well as the praise of the Greeks as a foil to the present—"We employ our freedom to speak of them so as to be allowed to remain silent about others." And in counterpoint to attacks on socialism, there is polemic against plutocracy: "Only those who have intellect should have property." The demand for rule by those who have knowledge and not by political parties is Platonic, but the attack on reason in the world and a teleological interpretation of nature is anti-Platonic. This contrast could not go on indefinitely. The pathos of being close to the nearest and smallest things, instead of reveling in other-worldly spheres, grew stronger. At the same time, Nietzsche thinks he differs from earlier moralists because he dissects and does not preach.

In the preface to the second edition of *Dawn*, Nietzsche refers to the "thou ought," which also guides his subversion of morality—it takes place out of morality, out of honesty; and to that extent it is a self-cancellation of the moral. But an experienced logician would see in this rather a self-cancellation of immoralism, which presupposes what it challenges. On the other hand, no contradiction is involved when a theoretically valid position takes its own dim origins to heart. For Nietzsche, one of the origins of morals is respect for customs, whatever their content might be; they were challenged, for example, by the madness from which a moral evolution often began and which innovators have consequently yearned to have themselves. (We cannot escape the impression that Nietzsche also yearned for this.) What is new in this work is its program for a natural history of morality, which Darwin had already imagined in the 1830s and worked out on an incomparably more precise level. Darwin was not familiar with objective idealism's natural philosophy, which makes it possible to reinterpret a naturalization of the mind; but at least he did not confuse genesis and validity, and therefore the English nineteenth century did not experience the subversion of moral intuitions that Nietzsche set in motion. In this regard, he emphasizes the mind's inability to cause events; the mind appears only as an excess of vital performances. Later on, this view was expanded into an evolutionary theory of knowledge. Reasons are said to be rationalizations of aversions based on added lies. However, with time appearance is transformed into a believed habit. Nietzsche describes with relish the cruelty of archaic customs and warns against the view that the festering underground has now been conquered—for virtues are merely refined cruelties. And so the beauty and the happiness of evil people begins to fascinate him. He intensifies his attack on Christianity, whose founder he takes to be Paul. Toward Jesus Nietzsche throughout his life maintained a condescending but sympathetic attitude. The driving forces in Christianity are declared to be its hatred for Rome's greatness and its desire for revenge, the empty promise of chimeras in contrast to the Stoics' reconciliation with reality, subtle mental cruelty, hermeneutic sophistry (for instance in the typological interpretation of the Old Testament), antipathy toward the normal virtues in the name of conversion from sin, and self-immunization through the moral incrimination of doubts. But more important than this criticism is Nietzsche's sociological observation that he is standing at the deathbed of Christianity and the insight that modern philanthropy is a compensation for the twilight of Christian dogma.

La Rochefoucauld saw himself as a melancholic, but the German moralist did not want to have his joy in life spoiled, and so he published *The Gay Science*, in which, right at the beginning, he invites the reader to laugh at everything. At Nietzsche's inconsistencies as well? In the second aphorism, the demand for certainty is described as a mark of superior people; but how can anyone achieve certainty who denies truth and declares that consciousness is nothing but a late evolution of the organic, and thus not at the core of human being? To be sure, Nietzsche is right that there is unconscious thinking; but the problem of validity can be solved only by conscious thinking. The outline of a comparative science of social behavior "for the industrious" is fascinating—Max Weber, who read Nietzsche with great care, was to make it a reality and answered in the negative "the trickiest of questions," whether science itself can specify the goals of action. Since of course goals must come from somewhere, Nietzsche refers to a heroic experimentation "that could put all the great works and self-sacrifices of previous history in the shade"—it is tempting to interpret National Socialism as an attempt at heroism in evil, and to see Nietzsche as anticipating, even in content, some of its ideas. Thus he rejects the modern tendency to minimize pain, because it also depresses the capacity for joy, and he is prepared to endure any amount of pain as the price of an increase of delicious pleasures. To live means to "be cruel and merciless toward everything that becomes weak"; hence he suggests that handicapped children be killed. The theory of the feeling of power becomes central; it can sometimes be better satisfied by causing suffering than by doing good. The omnipresence of power is shown by the fact that even weaknesses are used as power factors, for example by women. Even love, and especially erotic love, is a form of greed, and selflessness is preached only by those who derive an advantage from it, because they themselves are weak. Morality is a herd instinct, and human dignity only a fiction. Nietzsche maintains that instead of teaching the categorical imperative, we should create ourselves. Without criteria, however, such a creation might well become a golem. Polytheism is considered superior to any monotheism because it is more individualistic. We no longer need *reasons* for rejecting Christianity—taste decides against it.

However, Nietzsche sensed that such a break would have enormous cultural consequences; his famous "madman" foreshadows the consequences of killing God: "Is the magnitude of this deed not too great for us?"

At the beginning of the last book of *The Gay Science*, which was added to the volume only in the second edition of 1887, we read that few people are aware of how much else must die along with the belief in God—"for example, our whole European morality." This shows that Nietzsche never understood that Kant's ethics was already independent of religious assumptions—to the contrary, the latter were supported by it. But Nietzsche was right: the loss of a religion does have far deeper effects than a change in hat fashions. His dramatizing of de-Christianization, which proceeded more swiftly and traumatically in Germany—partly thanks to Nietzsche—than in the rest of Europe, again won many religious people over to Nietzsche because he thereby attributed to Christianity a more essential importance than even lukewarm Christians usually do. For Nietzsche himself, the news that the old God was dead made him feel as if a new dawn had cast its rays on him. But its light was obscured by a cloud: how could Nietzsche recover his own claim to truth? Unlike his procedure in the earlier books and other works, Nietzsche now turned against not only morality, but also against science, which, as he rightly saw, has moral and metaphysical presuppositions; and this was accompanied by an upward revaluation of art. Science is viewed as a prejudice, and hence Nietzsche ridicules the intellectual mediocrity of savants such as the Darwinists who failed to see that the struggle was not for existence but for power, since the will to life is a will to power. Existing is essentially interpreting, and the world can contain an infinite number of interpretations. Nietzsche polemicizes with verve against universalist morality—a humanity in which egoism and altruism are reconciled deserves to be destroyed, and a kingdom of justice, as one of "the deepest mediocritization," is not to be desired; though it would certainly be worthwhile to reflect on new forms of slavery, without which Greece cannot be conceived. The National Socialist state seized upon this suggestion, too—though without managing a return to Hellenic greatness. Nietzsche declares himself free of misanthropy; he has decided to be from now on only a Yes-sayer because his contempt is too deep to remain compatible with hatred.

No one has heard as clearly as Nietzsche the magma of sub-dued malice and traumatic events from the past that seethes under the surface of modern culture. This is worthy of all our respect. But not satisfied with being a mere observer, he began, at the latest in *The Gay Science*, to spit fire himself, and thereby accelerated the doom that he sensed was approaching. At some point he must have become bored with merely describing human self-deceptions and the collapse of Christianity. He began to set up new tables of values. According to his own theory of knowl-edge, there could be no arguments for them; thus he had to write a literary work. *Also sprach Zarathustra* (*Thus Spake Zarathustra*, 1883–1885) presents the herald of a new ethics in its interac-tions with all possible human and nonhuman figures, a few of whom are allegories. This is Nietzsche's corniest book. It com-petes in language and structure with the Gospels, but the latter are—definitely better. There is nothing in the book that could be compared with the humanity of, say, Peter's denial of Jesus. Zarathustra's speeches are verbose and pretentious, and his char-acter is psychologically unsophisticated. This alleged genius, who is condemned to solitude and haughtily enjoys it, is inca-pable of true intersubjectivity. In terms of its content, the book contains mainly old ideas (the font of Nietzsche's originality was beginning to run dry) that are less enjoyable in sermon form than as aphorisms. What *is* new is the doctrine of the superman, which extended into the future Darwin's theory of the descent of man—a way of procuring legitimacy that reminds one of Marx-ism. Nietzsche also intensifies his theory of the will to power as the principle behind all positing of values and the injunction to remain true to the earth, that is, to reject transcendence for the sake of the world. Particularly novel is the theory of the Eternal Return, which had been merely hinted-at in *The Gay Science*. It probably goes back to ancient models and is turned against the Christian theology of history as well as against the optimistic philosophy of history that stresses progress. Nietzsche has no objective arguments for it, but it is the most extreme expression of his desperate desire to say yes to life—even the most terrible crimes in history will periodically recur, and it is good that this is so. In *Ecce Homo*, however, Nietzsche confessed that the stron-gest argument against the Eternal Return was not past mass mur-ders, but rather his mother and sister.

The psychology of everyday life had discovered, long before Nietzsche, that a person who is continually pointing out how healthy he is, is sick, and also somehow knows it. Nietzsche's stress on his physical health in his late works is thus an alarm signal, and the reference to his special status attests no less to deeper problems; indeed, his ever-shriller (and finally hoarse) voice is an unmistakable sign that this "dynamite" understood that with his denial of the capacity for truth he had left himself no leg to stand on. He was bleeding to death intellectually. By divulging the secret that he wore a mask, he indicated that his desire to mask himself did not go all that deep; presumably this pretension served to mislead the reader, who, when he encountered contradictions, was supposed to assume complex background ideas. Nietzsche himself was probably taken in by the deception. To that extent it may be, as he thought, that honesty was the last virtue remaining to him—but honesty without truth is not worth much. The late Nietzsche is still a first-rate source of inspiration for the psychopathology of the all-too-human—but now as an object of study, no longer as a teacher. In addition, he is still worth reading as a source of numerous cases of philosophical insipidness in the twentieth century; at least he is more original and more stylistically exciting than his epigones.

Jenseits von Gut und Böse. Vorspiel einer Philosophie der Zukunft (*Beyond Good and Evil: Prelude to a Philosophy of the Future,* 1886) is based, on the one hand, on a radical perspectivism that, unlike that of Leibniz, proposes no objective hierarchy of perspectives and therefore abandons the idea of truth. Behind logic lie "physiological demands for the maintenance of a certain kind of life"; falsehood is no objection, insofar as it promotes life (so why criticize religion, then?); there are only interpretations of reality, no genuine text. Instead of asking, with Kant, "How are synthetic *a priori* judgments possible?" the point is to answer the psychological question as to why a belief in such judgments is necessary. The mind is a multiplicity of drives, indeed, of subjects; to say "it thinks" would be more correct than "I think," a locution which in any case arises only from the peculiarities of our language and does not exist in other language families. On the other hand, Nietzsche hates the skepticism that springs from the weakness of will. Thus his perspectivism is integrated into an ontology according to which the whole of reality is a development of the will to power. This is a generalization of Schopenhauer's will with its focus on the sexual (which Nietzsche does not underestimate: "The degree and type of a person's sexuality reaches up into the furthermost peaks of their spirit.") To that extent, Heidegger was right when he classified Nietzsche as belonging to the metaphysical tradition. To be sure, theories are also power factors, as Michel Foucault has shown in detail, although it is not at all easy to quantify the concept of power, the social equivalent of the concept of force. But the dimension of validity cannot be made to disappear in this way, and Nietzsche's perspectivism undermines the status of his own metaphysics. He knows that, and his strategy is to relinquish a generally binding concept of truth and instead to blatantly underscore his own uniqueness, which consists precisely in his exceptional malice and dangerousness. Paradoxically, his blustering about new leaders whose hammer will shatter Christian and democratic Europe and introduce a revaluation of values is particularly attractive to the weak-willed, who with their admiration for Nietzsche dispel the fear that they might be the intellectual and moral dwarves whose rise Nietzsche foretells. Nietzsche was aware that the strategy of counting on such an audience was vulgar, and therefore he needed to end this work with a section entitled "What Is Noble?"—nobility being a quality that became all the more important for him as it became ever clearer that he had lost it forever. Nobility is not to be had without reliance on something larger than oneself; without that, the pathos of distance is nothing but pomposity. To single out the philosopher as distinguished from specialists in the particular sciences and to entrust him with the task of determining ultimate values makes sense when based on Platonic premises, but not when it is based on those of the late Nietzsche, who in the same book returns to the strongest concept of philosophy elaborated in the tradition in which he declares psychology to be the mistress of the sciences. No less erroneous is the historical explanation of noble values on the basis of the master morality that Nietzsche opposes to a democratic slave morality.

In *Zur Genealogie der Moral. Eine Streitschrift* (*On the Genealogy of Morality: A Polemic*, 1887), Nietzsche returns to the treatise form. It was not a good choice. Whenever Nietzsche foregoes ambiguity and even literary devices, still used in *Thus Spake Zarathustra*, he becomes banal. The original value-opposition is said to be that between "good" and "bad," that is, between "powerful" and "weak/cowardly." Only a slave rebellion of morality arising out of resentment replaced these concepts by "good" and "evil," the weak being described as good and their oppressors as evil. Analogously, "guilt" is said to have its origin in the law of obligations, in the revenge taken by the creditor on the debtor. For Nietzsche, the cruelty of archaic punishments served precisely to prevent the victim from having feelings of guilt. A bad conscience first emerged, he tells us, through an inward turn that took place when the will to freedom, repressed by blond beasts, could no longer be discharged toward the outside. The triumph of atheism, though, will restore a second innocence. Nietzsche explains ascetic ideals on the basis of the irreducibility of the will, which also underlies the phenomenon of active forgetting: people prefer wanting nothingness to not wanting at all. By depreciating asceticism Nietzsche burns the last bridge that linked him to Schopenhauer (the latter's theory of art is also rejected—people are interested in disinterested enjoyment only in order to escape the torture of the will). The ascetic ideal arises on the one hand from the instinct of self-protection in a degenerating life that seeks a meaning for its suffering, and on the other hand from the will to power of the priests who by assuming control of sufferers established the only empire they could. Although he concedes that the value of truth is ultimately cut from the same cloth as the ascetic ideal, Nietzsche wants to shake off the latter entirely, because it poisons psychological health.

In 1888 Nietzsche wrote his last works, two of which he was still able to publish: *Der Fall Wagner. Ein Musikanten-Problem* (*The Case of Wagner: A Musician's Problem*, 1888) and *Götzen-Dämmerung oder Wie man mit dem Hammer philosophiert* (*Twilight of the Idols, or How to Philosophize with a Hammer*, 1889). *Der Antichrist. Fluch auf das Christentum* (*The Antichrist: A Curse on Christianity*) appeared in 1895, *Ecce Homo* in 1908. Fragments written by Nietzsche for a planned but later abandoned work were published in 1901 under the title *Der Wille zur Macht* (*The Will to Power*). Nietzsche's sister claimed that this was his true magnum opus, but these fragments contain only a few ideas that are not found in the works he himself published. Nietzsche must have sensed that his time was running out; and simultaneously we note a wish to return to his beginnings, to Wagner and, in *Twilight of the Idols*, to the problem of Socrates and the untimely view of the present. In this work Nietzsche offered a potpourri of his favorite radicalized favorite themes that seemed marketable: Socrates's dialectic as plebeian revenge on the aristocracy; dualism as a flight from true reality, as in the wily Christian Kant; morality as a counter-nature hostile to life; religion, morality and free will as imaginary; selective breeding (as in the Indian caste system, with its rejection of the caste-less) instead of the Christian taming of the blond beast; the pedestrian character of the German tendency to merely accumulate facts; the sick as parasites on the successful who should not be allowed to survive "in a certain condition" (it does not get more specific); and Nietzsche as a disciple of Dionysus. *The Antichrist* mixes historical analyses of Christianity's genesis out of Judaism, the ways in which it differs from Buddhism, the fundamental break between national and universal religions, and the course of its later decay that led away from Jesus, with the promulgation of a new, anti-Christian morality: "The weak and the failures should perish; first principle of *our* love of humanity. And they should be helped to do this."

Enormous hermeneutic efforts are required—which are, in view of Nietzsche's willful and deliberately contradictory style of expression, admittedly not hopeless—to deny that there is any continuity between such statements and, for instance, the Nazis' *Aktion T 4*, the mass murder of the mentally ill. To be sure, there are differences from National Socialism; and the rejection of Wagner at the end was perhaps determined in part by an instinctive fear that a fusion of Nietzsche and Wagner might prove far more explosive than dynamite (even if one of his explicit reproaches is that in *Parsifal* Wagner returned to Christianity and its morality). A synthesis of Nietzsche's anti-Christian cult of power and the Wagnerian revival of old German mythologemes in the name of an aggressively anti-Semitic nationalism was in fact the collective experiment that the German people undertook under Adolf Hitler's directorship. This finding based on the history of ideas should not, however, keep us from tackling two philosophical questions that Nietzsche left behind. How can we account for the fact that so far as we know spirit evolved only late and in a few organisms with the notion that its claim to truth is irreducible? And how can the unconditional validity of a universalist ethics be reconciled with the not very appealing history and reality of our moral feelings?

The Exact Sciences as a Challenge and the Rise of Analytic Philosophy: Frege, the Viennese and Berlin Circles, Wittgenstein

In 1879, simultaneously with Nietzsche's first attempt to sound the depths of the human soul (an attempt that itself produced wholly new and unfathomable problems), Gottlob Frege (1848–1925) published his *Begriffsschrift, eine der arithmetischen nachgebildete Formelsprache des reinen Denkens* (*Concept Script: A Formal Language of Pure Thought Modelled on That of Arithmetic*). This work sprang from a desire, so unlike Nietzsche's, to achieve absolute clarity in forms of inference; the many formulas that adorn it are a counter-world to Nietzsche's expressive language of unmasking, which positively quivers with excitement. Since Frege's book, logic has been not only a deductive science (it was already that in Aristotle) but also a formalized discipline: earlier efforts at formalization were insufficient, whereas not much separates the procedure of the *Begriffsschrift* from that of today. Frege had a doctorate and was qualified as a lecturer of mathematics, but, like Windelband, he had studied with the philosopher Hermann Lotze (1817–1881); and since Husserl was also influenced by Lotze, we see in the latter the ancestor of the philosophers in this chapter and the next (which proceed according to schools, and therefore discuss the older Husserl after Wittgenstein, who continued the tradition founded by Frege and is far more critical of metaphysics than is Husserl). Although today hardly anyone reads him, Lotze was one of the most influential German philosophers of the nineteenth century. Perhaps still more important than his attacks on Hegel's and Schelling's natural philosophy in the name of modern scientific physiology (which however did not make Lotze a materialist; on the contrary, his metaphysics shaped cultural Protestantism), or even his introduction into philosophical discussion of the concepts of validity and value, was Lotze's radical change in style: instead of the genius-like thinkers of German idealism whose characteristic style was continued by Schopenhauer, Marx, and Nietzsche, there now appeared the university professor who no longer addressed a wide audience but wrote only for colleagues, and often in professional journals. The 1920s were to revolt against these academic philosophers, but without even coming close to achieving once again the intellectual richness and moral differentiation that marked the heroic age of German philosophy.

Frege's concept script was a precision instrument, designed primarily to clarify the question whether it was possible to ground arithmetic in logic. For that purpose, "the completeness of the chain of inference" had to be verified, and that could only be achieved by separating oneself from everyday language and grammar. "If one of philosophy's tasks is to break the dominion of the word over the human mind . . . then my concept script . . . will be able to become a useable tool for philosophers." Through the logical language of the concept script a logical calculus became possible, which Frege laid out both for propositional and for first- and higher-order predicate logic, and in fact including relational logic, whose development was at that time only beginning. The truth value of compound propositions is a function of the truth value of elementary propositions. Frege proved that his calculus is consistent, but not that it is complete; moreover, his axioms are not all independent of each other. His two-dimensional notation is more complicated than the later unidimensional notation, which in addition foregoes the judgment stroke and the content stroke (*Urteilsstrich* and *Inhaltsstrich*). *Die Grundlagen der Arithmetik* (*The Foundations of Arithmetic*, 1884) seeks to show that the laws of numbers, including the principle of mathematical induction (later in Peano the fifth axiom), are *a priori* as well as (contra Kant) analytic; that is, that they can be reduced to logic. With regard to geometry, Frege follows Kant's theory of pure intuition and is hostile to non-Euclidean geometries and the use of implicit definitions in David Hilbert's (1862–1943) *Grundlagen der Geometrie* (*Foundations of Geometry*), one of the greatest advances in the axiomatization of the exact sciences, which reached its apex in this period. But arithmetic is more general than geometry, since everything that can be thought can be counted. Whereas the two volumes of the *Grundgesetze der Arithmetik* (*Basic Laws of Arithmetic*, 1893 and 1903) are "derived using concept script" and are therefore difficult to read, *The Foundations of Arithmetic* develops its arguments in ordinary language, and because of its defense of a Platonic philosophy of mathematics and the concrete explication of the concept of number, it is probably Frege's most important work. Frege strongly opposes a psychological rather than logical foundation of arithmetic, maintains that the meaning of words is to be found solely in the context of the sentence, and insists on the distinction between concept and object. For Frege, as for Plato, concepts are timeless entities without which "the world would cease to be intelligible." According to him, there can be no genuine history of concepts—it is only "a history either of our knowledge of concepts or of the meaning of words." Frege does not think that we could form the concept of number without sense experience or time. But the fact that one must have had experiences in order to *become aware of* the content of a proposition does not in any way mean that it could not be *a priori*. For him, it is clear that numbers cannot be subjective in nature, even if they are not independent of reason—they are given to reason directly. The mathematician creates nothing—"he can only discover what is there." Consistency is not sufficient for mathematical existence; indeed, even consistency does not result from merely not finding any contradiction. Numbers are obviously not to be confused with symbols for numbers; neither are they properties of single things or of agglomerations of them, as can be immediately seen from 0 (zero), which is not different in kind from other numbers. In the expression "four noble steeds," "noble" is a conceptual characteristic; whereas the number "four" expresses a property of the concept "noble steed," namely, that four objects fall under it.

However, the concrete execution of Frege's logicistic program collapsed when in 1902 Bertrand Russell wrote him about the antinomy named after him, which can be constructed in classical set theory. Frege was unable to provide any lasting solution to this problem, and therefore later turned away from logicism, perhaps too quickly. But both his reflections on the philosophy of language—especially his distinction between sense and reference (*intension and extension*) in names and sentences—and his *theory of concepts* (laid out in essays written between 1891 and 1892) rank as classics. According to Frege, "the morning star" and "the evening star" refer to the same object, and thus have the same reference, but they do not have the same sense. Frege also compares concepts with functions, because both of them are "unsaturated," that is, they both include a gap and yield a complete sense only when the gap is filled in with a proper noun. In the case of concepts, not only numbers but also objects are allowed as arguments. If one takes "Germany" as the argument of the function expressed by "the capital city of x," then the function value is "Berlin." One result of Frege's rigorous distinction between concept and object is that "the concept 'horse'," for example, is not a concept, but rather an object, because the corresponding proper noun may not be used predicatively. In his three late studies "Der Gedanke: Eine logische Untersuchung" ("The Thought: A Logical Inquiry"), "Die Verneinung" ("Negation"), and "Gedankengefüge" ("Compound Thought"), which appeared posthumously under the title *Logische Untersuchungen* ("Logical Investigations"), Frege grounded his break with traditional logic and presented his own philosophy of logic, which assumes the exclusive validity of classical logic. Impressive in these works are distinctions such as that between thinking, judging, and asserting, descriptions such as the one that presents the sentence as the sensible garb of the insensible thought, and the defense of the peculiar mode of being of thoughts (e.g., the Pythagorean theorem). These are neither things nor subjective ideas, Frege insists, because otherwise the intersubjective validity of science would be endangered. "A third domain must be recognized." The task of logic is "to investigate the spirit, . . . not spirits." Thoughts are timeless and can operate in the world of experience only because they are "conceived."

The elaboration of artificial languages, whose limits Kurt Gödel (1906–1978) made clear, has undoubtedly made it easier to test philosophical arguments. However, learning these languages is very time-consuming, and as a result philosophers influenced by Frege are often ignorant of other areas of knowledge that up to Frege's time were considered essential for a philosopher. One may have doubts as to whether this exchange has been useful to philosophy. Despite his admiration for mathematics, Frege did not sufficiently know or value even the great advances made in the mathematics of his time. And outside logic, mathematics, and philosophy of language, he achieved nothing; indeed, his political diary of 1924, first published in 1994, is a disturbing document of the German radical right, with calls for a war of revenge against France, violent tirades against universal suffrage and social democracy, and anti-Semitic slogans that demand, among other things, that the Jews be driven out of Germany. It may seem unfair to introduce private notes into a brief history of philosophy, but they shed light on the philosophy of the twentieth century, showing that acuity in the creation of a concept script is compatible with ethical and political blindness.

Frege's logical revolution produced a philosophical school that is now dominant in the Anglo-American world, so-called "analytical philosophy." In its origin, it is at least as German-Austrian as it is British, and thus should not be opposed to "continental" philosophy, even though it is true that most of its representatives emigrated to Anglo-American countries after 1933 (and their later works are therefore not dealt with in this book). The first form taken by analytic philosophy, now long since abandoned, was logical positivism or logical empiricism (the former sympathized with phenomenalism, the latter was more realistically oriented). The enthusiasm for the overwhelming advances that were achieved in the natural sciences during the nineteenth century— advances whose technological application altered people's lifeworlds more drastically than any other event since the invention of agriculture—was in a certain sense only increased when evolutionary biology began to throw light on human behavior and when, in the early twentieth century with the special and general theories of relativity and quantum theory, centuries-old assumptions about space, time, matter, and causality were questioned or even refuted. Philosophical reflections on fundamental principles played an important role in this process, whether regarding the nature of geometry (especially after the development of consistent alternatives to Euclidean geometry, in which the Germans Carl Friedrich Gauß and Bernhard Riemann were significantly involved), the nature of measurement procedures, or the general principle of relativity of movement. Albert Einstein's (1879–1955) special theory of relativity began with the problem of the measurement of simultaneous events spatially distant from each other, that is, with a transcendental reflection on the conditions of the possibility of physics; his ideas were influenced, among others, by the philosophizing physicists Hermann von Helmholtz (1821–1894) and Ernst Mach (1838–1916), as well as by the French mathematician and philosopher of science Henri Poincaré. Einstein's book, *Über die spezielle und die allgemeine Relativitätstheorie* (*Relativity: The Special and* the *General Theory*, 1916) remains a masterpiece of popularization that made difficult theories accessible to the general public. The scientifically exciting atmosphere of this time is part of the crisis of classical modernity, which at the beginning of the twentieth century also produced an art, music, and literature whose originality is comparable only to that of the *Sturm und Drang* movement, as well a new art form, film, whose aesthetic analysis soon followed, for instance in the works of Béla Balázs (1884–1949) and Rudolf Arnheim (1904–2007). The dissolution of clear wholes into unfamiliar elements is common to cubism and quantum theory. It is striking, for instance, that logical empiricism, in calling for rigor and turning away from the ballast of tradition, coincided with modernist architecture, from Adolf Loos (1870–1933), the author of *Ornament und Verbrechen* (*Ornament and Crime*, 1913) to the Bauhaus. At the same time, the fascination with science and technology meant a reduction of the classical concept of reason. However, since the concept of reason was monopolized by the triumph of science and technology, criticism of the high price of modernization—a price felt more deeply in Germany than in countries like Great Britain, where industrialization had begun much earlier, or Italy, where it proceeded at a more leisurely pace—could only present itself as irrationalist, as, for example, a protest in the name of life.

The possibility immediately suggested itself of using Frege's new logic, on the one hand to provide a foundation for the new science, and on the other to assimilate one's own philosophical convictions to the methods and results of natural science. For natural science was now the gold standard of knowledge. The feeling of being a witness to both the most important scientific revolution since the seventeenth century and to a wide-ranging collapse of traditional aesthetic, religious, and political values and hierarchies (which became unmistakable in 1918 with the breaking apart of four empires) escalated to become the hope that it might be possible to effect a correspondingly radical change in worldview. For instance, the realization that Kant had wrongly passed off as *a priori* valid some convictions of his own period that had now been falsified led to a fundamental rejection of the possibility of synthetic *a priori* judgments, which would threaten the progress of physics. Though, in truth, the assumption that the world is governed by natural laws is just such a judgment. Only judgments based on experience and the tautologies of logic were thought to be legitimate. This empiricism was called "logical" because like Frege and in contrast to, say, John Stuart Mill, it argued that logic was irreducible to experience.

The centers of logical positivism were Berlin and, especially, Vienna. At least since the work of the mathematician, philosopher, and Catholic priest Bernhard Bolzano (1781–1848), who was harassed by both the state and the Church and to whom we owe a more rigorous grounding of logic and of the infinitesimal calculus, as well as an initial approach to the problem of infinite sets that was solved by Georg Cantor (1845–1918), there has been an independent philosophy in Austria. (In contrast, German-speaking Switzerland has up to now hardly produced an important philosopher, presumably because its success in isolating itself from the rest of Europe favored peace and prosperity, but not intellectual adventure.) We owe to logical empiricism first-rate works on the philosophy of mathematics and physics, but in the end it extended its claims far beyond this area to questions it was not competent to address, and in the process underestimated earlier philosophy in disturbing ways, even if it imagined that it had forever replaced "speculative" philosophy with a "scientific" discipline. However, it is to be noted that the movement was more heterogeneous than it appears at first glance; it included not only positions that sought to reduce everything to elementary sense data, but also the insight that this program was doomed to fail. For example, in 1924, long before Willard V. O. Quine's holistic criticism of the dogmas of empiricism, Hans Reichenbach (1891–1953) wrote with reference to the use of measuring instruments: "Any assertion regarding facts, even the simplest . . . is already an interpretation . . . and therefore itself already theory." His book *Philosophie der Raum-Zeit-Lehre (The Philosophy of Space and Time*, 1928) remains a classic of the philosophy of physics. Unlike Frege, Reichenbach emphatically defended the legitimacy of non-Euclidean geometries by endorsing a formalist philosophy of mathematics—according to which if-then relationships, which are the only ones with which mathematics is concerned, are analytic, and therefore different theorems are valid given different axioms. Synthetic *a priori* judgments are not necessary in geometry. The question regarding the truth of axioms is not a mathematical problem; the basic concepts of mathematics are implicitly defined by the totality of the axioms. Against Kant, Reichenbach points to the fundamental difference between mathematical and physical geometry. In order to describe physical space-time adequately, coordinating definitions are needed that describe the procedures by which the corresponding values are measured. Reichenbach acknowledges that a certain metric can always be assigned to physical space if one is prepared to change the coordinating definitions accordingly. But against a radical conventionalism he insists that this freedom ceases when one settles on a definition and decides, for example, on measurement by rigid bodies. Definitions are said to be neither true nor false, but the combination of coordinating definitions and measurements produces testable results. In doing so, universal forces, unlike differential ones, are to be disregarded, because their presence could in principle not be noticed—because they would also alter the standards. Reichenbach's proof that non-Euclidean geometries (though not four-dimensional geometries, whether Euclidean or non-Euclidean) could be visualized is particularly fruitful. Visualization is based on a normative force that has its origin in logic and is therefore capable of realigning a particular visualization. So-called pure intuition does not prescribe anything to nature; instead, it is the result of an adaptation to real, existing space. In discussing spaces with non-Euclidean topology, Reichenbach examines causal anomalies that are encountered if one continues to interpret these spaces in Euclidean terms, which is in itself always possible. For him, this amounts to a refutation of Kant's system of *a prioris*, because in this case the principle of causality and Euclidean metric contradict one another. But from this we can infer only that these two principles cannot both be valid in a specific case. In reality, Reichenbach's readiness to sacrifice Euclidean topology in such a case points to the fact that synthetic *a priori* principles guide him as well. His own reflections on the connection between causality (which is an invariant) and temporal orientation are not so far removed from Kant. A hierarchization of the criteria that make possible a choice from among the various interpretations compatible with the empirical data is lacking, because according to Reichenbach descriptive simplicity has nothing to do with truth. His attempt to distinguish between definitions and empirical statements and the philosophical and physical components, respectively, of the special and general theories of relativity is impressive. The superiority of Einstein's theory to that of Hendrik Lorentz consists precisely in the fact that Einstein foregoes an explanation of the constancy of the speed of light. In the general theory of relativity, however, the metric of physical geometry is explained by gravitational fields. It is noteworthy that a broad consensus regarding the correct interpretation of the two theories of relativity was achieved early on, whereas in the case of quantum mechanics, despite the work of important philosophers and physicists such as Carl Friedrich von Weizsäcker (1912–2007), there is up to now no such consensus; indeed, its formalism has favored the most arbitrary ontological assumptions.

Alongside its constructive work in the field of theory of science, logical positivism has a critical aspect that found expression, for example, in *Wissenschaftliche Weltauffassung. Der Wiener Kreis* (*The Scientific Conception of the World: The Vienna Circle*, 1929), a manifesto dedicated by its coauthors Hans Hahn (1879–1934), Otto Neurath (1882–1945) and Rudolf Carnap (1891–1970) to their mentor, Moritz Schlick (1882–1936), and in Carnap's famous essay "Überwindung der Metaphysik durch logische Analyse der Sprache" ("The Elimination of Metaphysics through Logical Analysis of Language," 1931) in the journal edited by him and by Reichenbach, *Erkenntnis*. In terms of the history of consciousness, this aspect was far more influential than the first one, simply because it was accessible to a much broader audience than the inevitably more esoteric debate with modern mathematics and physics. That is too bad, because it is by far the poorer of the two. Ultimately it is based on a radicalization of the criterion of significance in Kant's first *Critique*—but it omits the synthetic *a priori* judgments in theoretical and practical reason and thus any attempt, no matter how modest, at pursuing the problems raised in the third *Critique*. Personally, the logical positivists were mostly respectable people, and politically they often supported social reform programs. But the majority of them insisted that moral statements were not judgments that could have truth value, but only expressions of subjective preferences. In this they were following a late nineteenth-century tendency attributable to the increasing historical knowledge about alternative systems of value and to the crisis in the theory of natural law, which issued in the jurisprudence of legal positivism.

Logical positivism's goal is a unified science modeled on physics. The intended system of constitution seeks to move from one's own mental qualities to physical objects, from these to the mental qualities of others, and finally to the objects of the social sciences. With regard to the mental qualities of others, behaviorism, which reduces the mental to externally observable behavior, is considered a scientific conception of the world. The true enemy of this new conception is metaphysics. Its statements are not false, but rather meaningless. They are pseudo-statements, in which words without meaning are used or constructed contrary to the rules of syntax. In order for a word to have meaning, we have to know how to verify a sentence that contains it; ultimately, such sentences have to be reducible to protocol sentences. Since the metaphysical conception of God cannot be empirically verified, the word "God" is meaningless. Carnap's logical analysis of why Martin Heidegger's hypostatization of "nothing" (*nichts*) into "Nothingness" (*das Nichts*) is based on a misunderstanding of the nature of negative existential statements is impressive. But he moves up from such individual analyses to the generic claim that all metaphysics is meaningless, because its judgments are neither analytic nor empirical. Like music and lyric poetry, metaphysics is the expression of a feeling of life—metaphysicians are "musicians without musical ability."

It is not hard to see that here Carnap is himself guilty of a broad generalization of the kind that characterizes a few metaphysicians in the tradition, but only the worst of them. He is concerned at the beginning to prove concretely that some metaphysicians' individual arguments are logically invalid. Such a proof is always meritorious, but two things must be kept in mind. First, there are now many logics, and they partly exclude one another (the choice among them has to be made by philosophical arguments that in a certain sense precede logic itself), and partly have different areas of validity. It is certainly not logic as such that speaks against the use of normative or intensional terms; on the contrary, the obvious indispensability of such terms has led to the elaboration of new systems of logic. Second, an interpreter should make an honest attempt to find meaning in what is to be interpreted—for example one can understand the phenomenon of the fear of "nothingness" as fear of one's own death or fear of the loss of meaning in one's own culture. But what Carnap says in the course of his article makes his analyses of arguments completely superfluous: according to him, all metaphysical statements are meaningless insofar as they are verifiable neither analytically nor empirically.

Why was this thesis abandoned by analytic philosophy, which now recognizes a broad field of analytic metaphysics? On the one hand, positivism did not succeed in demarcating science and metaphysics in the way that its program required. In view of the difficulties of the problem of induction, what the verification of scientific theories means cannot be made clear. Even Karl Popper's (1902–1994) critical-rational falsificationism in his *Logik der Forschung* (*Logic of Scientific Discovery*, 1935), according to which scientific theories can only be refuted, never proven, did not solve the problem of induction; for how do we know that a successful falsification will also be valid for the future? On the other hand, however, this question arises: What is the status of the judgment that only statements that are either analytic or can be validated by experience are meaningful? It is ridiculous to claim that it is the result of logical analysis. Logical analysis can only allow us to distinguish between different kinds of statements. The statement that only the previously mentioned kinds of statements are acceptable is certainly not an analytic statement, because its negation is not a contradiction, and neither can it be grounded in experience, because it is normative in nature. Herein lies a fundamental self-contradiction in the theory that points to its ultimate irrationality. In logical positivism, insight into the logical structure of modern scientific theories was not accompanied by the sense for self-grounding that characterized classical metaphysics, and since this insight was mostly a compensation for not being able to make a creative contribution to the further development of physics, we can return Carnap's compliment by saying that he was a physicist without ability in physics. Although philosophy's study of modern science is non-negotiable, it was naïve to think that scientific theories would resolve old philosophical controversies such as that between realism and idealism, precisely because these theories could be differently interpreted philosophically; and it was no less a mistake to reduce epistemology to the theory of science. Science is only *one* form of knowledge, alongside which there is also ethical and philosophical knowledge; and in fact the epistemological weaknesses of the theory of science were revealed in the 1970s, when the historical turn with its concept of differing paradigms led to a rapid loss of significance for this discipline, whose influence on productive scientists had in any case not been great.

However, logical positivism produced one philosophical genius, and that was Ludwig Wittgenstein (1889–1951). His work is slender—his two main books are the *Tractatus Logico-Philosophicus* (1921) and the posthumous *Philosophische Untersuchungen* (*Philosophical Investigations*, 1953); of many notebooks published only after his death the last, *Über Gewißheit* (*On Certainty*, 1970), is the most fascinating philosophically, because it seeks to limit the language game of doubt by drawing attention to the fact that doubt can begin in the first place only in relation to background knowledge; a transcendental justification of this knowledge is not, however, considered. Though Wittgenstein did not understand some crucial philosophical questions and certainly is not in the same league as Kant or Hegel, his appeal was considerable, and it can be explained as follows: first, Wittgenstein's ascetic life, which for a period caused him to completely abandon academic activities because he thought that in his *Tractatus* he had solved all philosophical problems, manifested an existential conclusiveness that is found in no other twentieth-century philosopher, least of all in any existentialist. Second, although this engineer who had stumbled into philosophy had only a modest familiarity with the philosophical tradition—he was mainly influenced by Frege and Bertrand Russell—this proved to be a blessing, for it enabled him to make a new beginning. Third, Wittgenstein outlined the program of logical positivism earlier, more clearly, and more comprehensively than the other members of the Vienna Circle, and at the same time he immediately recognized its internal self-contradiction, which most of the positivists had long hidden from themselves. That the "scientific conception of the world" left unsolved the true questions with which a human life is concerned, Wittgenstein felt with an intensity that completely escaped the logical positivists, and therefore, fourth, in his second phase he propounded a philosophy which, compared with his early work, represents a break of a radicalness that only a few thinkers have ever endured. (Continuity being important to every person, and probably to philosophers even more than to others.) Finally, the literary form of Wittgenstein's two main works is highly innovative: the chilly abstraction of his metaphysics of logic goes hand in hand with the most apt metaphors and images; and Wittgenstein expresses himself regarding the great worldview problems of the time precisely by saying nothing about them—in an age characterized by a form of mass-media discourse entirely new in world history, he adopted a countercultural form of communication that is able to fascinate us more than the presentation of long treatises. It suited the linguistic skepticism of the period around 1900: think of Hugo von Hofmannsthal's "Letter of Lord Chandos."

The central point of departure of the *Tractatus* is the idea that the world consists not of things but of facts. Facts are existing states of affairs, and states of affairs are possible facts; Wittgenstein is working on a semantics of possible worlds that deviates from later ones. He defends a form of atomism—so-called atomic facts are independent of all others, and with their establishment the world is determined. For Wittgenstein the central question in epistemology and the philosophy of language is: how can we form a picture of the world, for example, a proposition? By "picture" Wittgenstein does not mean something that outwardly resembles the world; instead, what is crucial is that there be an isomorphic relation between picture and fact, i.e., there must be a biunique correlation between the individuals and attributes that constitute the fact and the elements of which the picture consists. (Think of the projections of geometry or musical notations.) "These correlations are, as it were, the feelers of the picture's elements, with which the picture touches reality." Such a correlation is possible only thanks to the logical form that is common to the world and the picture; this is the sole regularity of the world. We can recognize something objective-idealist in this idea; and that explains why Wittgenstein has been interpreted as both a metaphysical realist and as a transcendental philosopher—as a transcendental philosopher of language, however, because he would like to eliminate all psychological categories such as self-evidence. "*The limits of my language* mean the limits of my world."

The transcendental content is minimal in comparison with Kant, because Wittgenstein recognizes no synthetic *a priori* judgments and interprets causality, for instance, as Hume did. The sense of a picture lies in what it represents; whether it is true can be determined only by comparing it with reality. But a proposition can be understood without knowing whether it is true. Whereas elementary propositions are logically independent of one another, and the statement of all true elementary propositions provides a complete description of the world, other propositions are truth functions of elementary propositions. An artificial language is best suited to the representation of such relationships, for its use avoids the logical confusions that characterize traditional philosophy, in which ordinary language reflects thoughts in a distorted way. Most propositions that were written about philosophical questions are nonsensical (*unsinnig*), because they run counter to the logic of language. In contrast, tautologies— that is, the propositions of logic—and contradictions are called "senseless" (*sinnlos*). The ban on reflexivity is crucial for Wittgenstein's theory of propositions—no proposition can refer to itself. Philosophy clarifies only thoughts; it "is not a body of doctrine but an activity." Only questions that can be answered can be legitimately asked. The entirety of true propositions is the entirety of the natural sciences (including psychology); there can be no ethical propositions. But what, then, is the status of the propositions in the *Tractatus* itself? Wittgenstein acknowledges their nonsensical nature: in order to see the world correctly, one should throw them away like a ladder after one has climbed it. And yet Wittgenstein seems not to demand simply the value-free observation of a reality that is structured by formal logic, but in which not even Kant's analogies of experience can still be presupposed. In his view, even if God no longer reveals himself in the world, something mystical is yet manifested in the simple fact of its existence. But it is pointless to theorize about it: "What we cannot talk about we must pass over in silence." Wittgenstein's religiousness is diametrically opposed to Hegel's panentheism. Residues of a negative theology are opposed to a cool observation of a world emptied of meaning and held together solely by logic and mathematics. If Goethe's worldview largely corresponded to Hegel's, then the writer who most powerfully expressed the new dualism is probably Franz Kafka.

"The tacit conventions on which the understanding of everyday language depends are enormously complicated." This sentence from the *Tractatus* seems to anticipate the program of the *Philosophical Investigations*, which seeks to trace ordinary language's subtle ability to adapt itself, rather than attempting to judge how far it deviates from an ideal logical language. However, it remains striking how little Wittgenstein knows about the linguistics of his time; in knowledge about linguistic phenomena he certainly cannot compete with Humboldt, or with the splendid *Sprachtheorie* (*The Theory of Language*, 1934) of the philosophizing psychologist Karl Bühler (1879–1963), whose "Organon model" distinguishes between the expressive, representative, and appellative functions of language. Even after Wittgenstein finally moved to Cambridge in 1929, he remained, unlike most of the emigrants, true to German, but his view of language and the world changed, and once again he set a trend that thousands of epigones still emulate. The philosophy of the ideal language was followed by "ordinary language philosophy," which had, however, been practiced before his change of direction by authors like John L. Austin and Gilbert Ryle at Oxford. In terms of the history of consciousness this change of direction must be regarded with ambivalence. On the one hand, enthusiasm for the new axiomatic logic and the ideal language modeled on it was the last normative linchpin still recognized by these highly intelligent intellectuals who had lost their belief in God and in the advance of history, or in some cases had even grown up without it; and the fizzling out of this enthusiasm set the stage for the postmodern indifference that paralyzes philosophy today, especially since the fundamental contradiction in the *Tractatus* is in no way transcended in the later work, and the possibility of a binding ethics still remains unclarified. Philosophy is supposed to be able only to describe the factual use of language: "It leaves everything as it is." Therefore one maxim is: "Don't think, but look!" On the other hand, the humbleness of recognizing that, despite all its violations of logic, there are more reasonable achievements in ordinary language than in the Esperanto of artificial languages, commands respect. "For the crystalline purity of logic was, of course, *not a result of investigation*: it was a requirement." The change in content corresponds to a change in form: the carefully numbered and hierarchically ordered propositions of the *Tractatus* are now succeeded by a loose series of aphorisms in which the author sometimes wearily argues with an imaginary interlocutor, perhaps his own earlier self.

The concept of the language-game is crucial; it represents a break with the Platonic and Cartesian theories of meaning (including that of the *Tractatus*). Language is essentially a social process, part of a form of life; instead of an autonomous relationship to elementary objects, a process of "training" or "conditioning" takes place. From the outset, the acquisition of language is interwoven with certain activities, and every historically developed language contains levels of differing abstractness: "Our language can be seen as an ancient city: a maze of little streets and squares, of old and new houses, and of houses with additions from various periods; and this surrounded by a multitude of new boroughs with straight regular streets and uniform houses." Even if the diverse language-games, such as commanding, questioning, and chatting, change through history, they have a basis in human "natural history." What is decisive for Wittgenstein is the rejection of the idea that the acquisition of language is preceded by a mental mastering of intellectual relations, an act of "meaning," that is then expressed in language: "Thinking is not an incorporeal process which lends life and sense to speaking, and which it would be possible to detach from speaking." Here Wittgenstein underestimates small children's cognitive achievements, which on transcendental grounds have to precede the acquisition of language, and without which the identification of things could never even begin. For Wittgenstein, the understanding of a meaning is shown only in the concrete use of language; there is no inner image that guides its use. His reflections on rule-following are particularly famous, and have been interpreted by Saul Kripke, probably correctly, in the following sense: according to Wittgenstein, there are infinitely many legitimate ways of continuing the previous application of a rule, and therefore only what is socially established can be seen as the right continuation. For that reason Wittgenstein rejects the possibility of a private language, for example a private language for one's own feelings, and he tends to reduce pain to pain behavior. The rediscovery of the mind-body problem in the analytic philosophy of recent decades was therefore a revolt against Wittgenstein. A recurring theme is his polemic against essentialism; instead of seeking a common essence, for example of language-games, Wittgenstein refers to family resemblances, which through continuous intermediate forms also bind together very different objects. The relativistic consequences of his concept of language-games were soon drawn in many disciplines, from the social sciences to the history of science. But Wittgenstein's most radical suggestion is his new concept of philosophy itself. For him, the results of philosophy are "bumps that the understanding has got by running its head against the limits of language," and his goal is "to shew the fly the way out of the fly-bottle." As in the *Tractatus*, the point is still ultimately to free oneself from the torment of reflection. Anyone who is unhappy in philosophy will obviously prefer Wittgenstein to Hegel. But someone who is attached to autonomy and takes into account the possibility that the individual might be right to oppose the social world's conditioning would be well-advised either to go back to the classics or to adopt Husserl's theory of meaning rather than Wittgenstein's.

❧ 12 ❦

The Search for a Foundation of the Human Sciences and the Social Sciences in Neo-Kantianism and Dilthey, and Husserl's Exploration of Consciousness

---

Before taking up the other major movement of the first half of the twentieth century, Neo-Kantianism must be mentioned, even if it does not display the same originality as positivism and phenomenology. After the end of German idealism and the rise of a materialist worldview—e.g., in the work of Ludwig Büchner (1824–1899), the brother of the great poet Georg Büchner—an obvious middle way presented itself in the form of a return to Kant that carried transcendental thought further and thereby raised, for instance, the history of philosophy and of science to a new level. The founder of the Marburg School was Hermann Cohen (1848–1918), and he was followed by a large number of other German-Jewish thinkers. On the one hand, this is the expression of the outwardly successful recognition of Judaism by the German middle class that had occurred in the meantime. On the other hand, the large number points to a special sensitivity with regard to the dangers of modernity that Judaism, like Catholicism, sensed earlier than did Protestantism. The hegemony of the latter over the German spirit decreased noticeably in the early twentieth century, even though it was precisely in this period that its central contribution to modernity was clearly articulated by Weber and Troeltsch. Whereas Edmund Husserl converted from Judaism to Lutheranism, and Max Scheler and Edith Stein (1891–1942) converted to Catholicism, Cohen is perhaps the best example of someone who brought the Jewish spirit into the German university, while at the same time remaining true to his own tradition. After emeritus status was conferred on him in Marburg, Cohen taught at the Berlin "Lehranstalt für die Wissenschaft des Judentums"; in a brochure published in 1915, he defended the essential affinity of the German and Jewish spirits. According to him, ethical universalism demands a democratic socialism and a league of states, each of which could include different ethnic groups. In the Prussia of the Second Empire, Cohen was active in support of universal suffrage and workers' rights; his student Paul Natorp (1854–1924) cofounded social education. Cohen's last and probably most original work, *Die Religion der Vernunft aus den Quellen des Judentums* (*The Religion of Reason Out of the Sources of Judaism*, 1919), ends with a stirring invective against "the specter of hatred among peoples," that angel of death "who strides through the world with his scythe." Whereas a large number of European intellectuals not only welcomed the First World War when it broke out but also stumbled, filled by hatred, into the Second World War after the First was over, Cohen, like Pope Benedict XV, saw this war as the moral catastrophe that it was. Both of them were inspired by the high regard for human life that both Judaism and Christianity taught, and both are, paradoxically, better representatives of reason than the radical modernists who swept away all normative claims in the name of life or history.

Cohen's last book is an interpretation of his own religion using Kantian concepts, repeatedly strengthened by intelligent critiques of pantheism as well as of Christian dogma and ethics, for example, of the doctrine of substitutionary atonement. Out of zeal both a religious Jew and a Kantian, Cohen argued against the absorption of Judaism into the general culture, thereby reminding us of the simultaneous revolt of dialectical theology against cultural Protestantism. However, unlike the latter, Cohen is rationalistic, like the greatest Jewish philosophers of religion in the Middle Ages. Various monotheistic religions might be interpreted as religions of reason, but according to Cohen Judaism is distinguished by its originality. But why is religion necessary at all, if ethics is to be grounded autonomously?

Cohen sees ethics as characterized by its universality, while law and the state mediate between the I and humanity. But in addition there is the concrete relation between I and Thou, who is not reducible to a "He," and here religion intervenes with sympathy for the suffering of the Thou and the perception of one's own guilt (whereas in Judaism merit is attributed not to oneself, but to the patriarchs). In addition, only God guarantees the unity of theoretical and practical reason. Cohen interprets Jewish monotheism, the Law (which he understands symbolically), and the Old Testament prophets, as expressions of a universalist ethics, even if isolation from the rest of humanity was in the beginning unavoidable. The Messianic time is understood immanently, as the epoch, occurring within history, of the realization of social justice. For Cohen, eternal punishment in Hell is incompatible with God's love, and even rewards in the beyond ought not to play any role, since doing one's duty is its own reward—a saying from the Mishnah that Spinoza had adopted and which indicates the affinity between Judaism and Kant's anti-eudemonism. Cohen's knowledge of the Old Testament and Jewish tradition is most thorough; but his work suffers from the fact that the systematic development of the attributes of God or of human virtues is so interwoven with the interpretations of texts that neither the philosopher of religion nor the historian of religion gets his money's worth. Cohen repeatedly underestimates the extent of development over time within Judaism (even if he brilliantly works out the distinction between social prophecy and the emergence of the I in Ezekiel). Thus it is unfortunate that he did not live long enough to read Rudolf Otto's (1869–1937) *The Idea of the Holy* (1917), which unsurpassably describes the slow moralization of the numinous, which was originally not a moral category. Cohen strongly emphasizes Judaism's social justice and the place of non-Jews in the Torah—the concept of the Noahide is the predecessor of natural law, and the rights of resident aliens are very wide-ranging. Cohen's rejection of Zionism is bound up with this view: it would "contradict the Messianic task of Judaism to isolate it in a special state." The rise of a genocidal anti-Semitism in Germany, without which the Zionist ideal would hardly have been realized, was clearly unimaginable for this Maimonides of the twentieth century, no matter how much he saw Jews as the people of suffering.

Wilhelm Windelband (1848–1915) and Heinrich Rickert (1863–1936), the most important representatives of the second branch of neo-Kantianism, the Baden School, were concerned with a subject that Kant had not taken up—the philosophical grounding of the human sciences and the social sciences as distinct from the natural sciences. This desideratum was particularly urgent in view of the enormous progress made by these disciplines, and especially by the theoretical sociology practiced by philosophical minds such as Ferdinand Tönnies (1855–1936), Georg Simmel (1858–1918), and Max Weber (1864–1920). In *Gemeinschaft und Gesellschaft* (*Community and Society*, 1887), Tönnies worked out, using polar oppositions in a way reminiscent of Hegel, basic structures of the social, and ranked the community, which experiences the social bond as an end in itself, over the atomistic society, thereby involuntarily preparing the way for the opposition, hyped in the "ideas of 1914," between Anglo-American individualism and the German ethnic community. To this opposition Thomas Mann (1875–1955) added, in his *Betrachtungen eines Unpolitischen* (*Reflections of a Nonpolitical Man*, 1918), the opposition between civilization and culture. Simmel was closely associated with *Lebensphilosophie*; his main work is probably his *Philosophie des Geldes* (*Philosophy of Money*, 1900), which brilliantly analyzes the consequences for the social value system of the triumph of the money economy. Max Weber presented—especially in the first part of his masterwork later titled *Wirtschaft und Gesellschaft* (*Economy and Society*, 1921–22), what is still the most comprehensive theory of sociological categories, with an abundance of enduring definitions of social phenomena. Although he was himself religiously tone-deaf, he thoroughly investigated the contribution made by religions to the development of the economy and the state (for instance, in *Die Protestantische Ethik und der 'Geist' des Kapitalismus* [*The Protestant Ethic and the Spirit of Capitalism*, 1904–05]). At the same time, he articulated the modern demand for value freedom in the classical essays "Die 'Objektivität' sozialwissenschaftlicher und sozialpolitischer Erkenntnis" ("Objectivity in Social Science and Social Policy," 1904), "Der Sinn der 'Wertfreiheit' der soziologischen und ökonomischen Wissenschaften" ("The Meaning of 'Ethical Neutrality' in Sociology and Economics," 1917) and "Wissenschaft als Beruf" ("Science as a Vocation," 1917). All this did not prevent him from demanding from politicians (in his lecture "Politik als Beruf" ["The Profession and Vocation of Politics," 1919]) an ethics of responsibility instead of an ethics of conviction that preserves the purity of one's own inwardness. In general he describes as an "iron cage" the loss of meaning and freedom that was setting in with the modern processes of rationalization and bureaucratization, and, paradoxically, designates as the end result of this "disenchantment" a polytheism of abstract values that can no longer be hierarchically ordered. His melancholic analysis of the costs connected with the inescapable process of modernization is reminiscent of Wilhelm Raabe, who may have been the subtlest of the German writers of the late nineteenth century. Precision in concept construction, mastery of countless sources from the most varied cultures, and an existential suffering at the hands of modernity make Weber the greatest social scientist of the twentieth century.

In addition to the problem of the role of values in the social sciences, the pair of concepts "nomothetic" and "idiographic" played an important role in the Baden School after Windelband's address as rector of the University of Strasbourg entitled "Geschichte und Naturwissenschaft" ("History and Natural Science," 1894); for him, the natural sciences were concerned with general laws, while the human sciences described individuals. But it was soon objected that in natural history there was certainly a description of individual natural objects and that economics, for example, sought to establish general laws. In the methodological controversy over Karl Lamprecht's (1856–1915) *Deutsche Geschichte* (*German History*, 1891–) the question was to what extent even historical science was required to seek to establish laws; but Lamprecht was unable to overcome the notion, which was predominantly idiographic and influenced by Leopold von Ranke (1795–1886). The last great neo-Kantian was Ernst Cassirer (1874–1945), one of the last thinkers who was familiar with both the natural and the human sciences of his time. Against Schlick, he defended an interpretation of the theory of relativity that was Kantian in the broad sense of the term, and in which thought experiments were central (Kant's forms of intuition were formalized and opened to historical concretization). In his *Philosophie der symbolischen Formen* (*Philosophy of Symbolic Forms,*1923–) he presented an integrative philosophy of language, myth, and knowledge. By referring to a plurality of approaches to reality he left the narrow-mindedness of positivism behind him, but the inevitable question arises as to why there are precisely these specific approaches, whether they are equally justified, and how they are to be ranked in the event that they conflict.

Before neo-Kantianism, Wilhelm Dilthey (1833–1911) had already undertaken a "Critique of Historical Reason," that is, an attempt to ground the human sciences in an "understanding psychology" (*verstehende Psychologie*) (as opposed to an "explaining" psychology) that was not based on laboratory work but guided by a philosophy focused on the meaning of life (*Lebensphilosophie*). His first major work on this subject, *Einleitung in die Geisteswissenschaften* (*Introduction to the Human Sciences*, 1883), seeks to distinguish the human sciences (*Geisteswissenschaften*), which for him include the social sciences, from the natural sciences (*Naturwissenschaften*) on the one hand, and from metaphysics on the other. Hence Dilthey waged a two-front war against German idealism and positivistic naturalism, and in the process contributed to the formation of the specifically human-sciences consciousness that now graces not only universities but also publishing houses and the feature pages in newspapers. It is comprised of enormous historical erudition with, however, an aversion to rigorous philosophical arguments, incompetence in mathematics, and a limited understanding of the exact natural sciences. Dilthey's "introduction" remained, like many another in post-classical philosophy, unfinished, presumably because it lacked a generating architectonic principle. The first book offers an abundance of important insights: human nature includes not only thinking, but also willing, feeling, and imagining; the human sciences are concerned with facts, theorems, and also value judgments, which must be clearly distinguished from statements about reality; society cannot be explained solely on the basis of the individual; studies of cultural systems (for instance, art) are opposed to studies of external organization (for instance, the state) with law connecting the two of them. Sociology and philosophy of history are criticized for their abstractions; instead, Dilthey argues for "historical research which is based on a mastery of the individual human sciences that is as comprehensive as possible" and which culminates in a universal history. Dilthey claims that there is more certainty in the human sciences so understood than in the natural sciences.

In the second book, there is a destruction of the history of metaphysics that anticipates Heidegger and is more dilettantish than
that of Logical Positivism, because there is hardly any analysis of
arguments. What is more, Dilthey does not understand that he
himself harbors metaphysical assumptions, for example in his
critique of Comte's naturalism: the assertion that mind is irreducible to nature is itself a statement about Being. *Der Aufbau
der geistigen Welt in den Geisteswissenschaften* (*The Formation of
the Historical World in the Human Sciences*, 1910) clearly goes
beyond the first work, among other reasons because Dilthey is
working on a hermeneutics that seeks to do justice to the understanding of the expression of what is experienced, in both its life-
world form and its scientific form.

The human sciences deal with objectivizations of the mind;
characteristic of them is the movement back and forth between
the whole and its parts, between universal history and individual sciences such as linguistics or legal studies. Through an abundance of studies on the history of philosophy and the history of
literature, Dilthey inspired concrete research in intellectual history more than almost anyone else; his works on Schleiermacher
as well as on the young Hegel are still trailblazing. However, what
is untenable in his approach is that in his essays on the theory
of worldviews (*Weltanschauungen*) he observes philosophy from
the outside: metaphysical systems are classified as works of art
and deprived of their own claim to truth. Dilthey's objectively
fruitful typology of philosophical systems that divides them
into naturalism, the idealism of freedom, and objective idealism
and that was sketched by his teacher, the important Hegel critic
Friedrich Adolf Trendelenburg (1802–1872), takes no interest in the question as to which of the systems stands out from
the point of view of its theoretical grounding; and Dilthey also
fails to explain which type of system his own typology belongs
to. Metaphilosophy becomes a kind of hovering over philosophy
instead of its crowning achievement. The end result of Dilthey's
approach was a historical relativism that is aware of everything
that has ever existed in the intellectual world without being
able, or even wishing, to decide what is true in these intellectual
structures. The modern scholar in the human sciences deals in
ideas, and thus overcomes the parochial prejudices of the naïve
religious consciousness, which holds that its own tradition has

access to the word of God. But not only does he lack the vitality and the ethical seriousness of the naïve religious consciousness; his approach guarantees that, inevitably, his own activity must appear to be only one way of proceeding among many. Certainly Dilthey suffered from this result, and sought to overcome relativism; the human sciences are supposed to lead back to life. But as Gehlen correctly writes, the imitation and vicarious living of another person's mental energy is not the emergence of the same energy in oneself, since "there is no more radical chasm than that between the imagined will and the real will." This relativistic consideration of worldviews continued to be influential on an intellectually much lower level in Oswald Spengler's (1880–1936) *Der Untergang des Abendlandes. Umrisse einer Morphologie der Weltgeschichte* (*The Decline of the West: Outlines of a Morphology of World History*, 1918–), and was later accompanied by the noisy demand that a decision finally be made. How the increasingly more extensive historical research on one's own tradition and on other cultures could be reconciled with the religious and ethical claim to absolute truth that characterizes Christianity, became a painful question for Protestant theology, which, especially in the work of Adolf von Harnack (1851–1930), had in the meantime raised historical theology to the level of the other human sciences. Ernst Troeltsch (1865–1923) was the writer who discussed this question most intensively, without, however, being able to provide a satisfying answer, because the cultural Protestantism of his time no longer had any available philosophical foundation. In *Das Wesen des Christentums* (*The Essence of Christianity*, 1900), Harnack presented one of the most honest appraisals of Christianity, and as a cofounder of the Kaiser-Wilhelm-Gesellschaft, which in 1948 became the Max-Planck-Gesellschaft, for a time he made German science preeminent worldwide.

Edmund Husserl (1859–1938), the most important critic and stimulator of Dilthey in his last decade, was probably the twentieth-century thinker who remained most loyal to the traditional concept of reason. Like Frege, Husserl had a doctorate in mathematics and thus fascinates analytic and continental philosophers alike. The pertinence and clarity of his works, his distinctions, which are always essential (hardly any philosopher's corrections to his work in later editions are so worth careful study), his sounding of the inner life of the mind with mathematical precision, the pathos of his belief in philosophy, the originality of his combination of a form of Platonism with a neo-Cartesian theory of subjectivity as the ultimate founding authority, as well as his personal integrity, make him the most relevant thinker of the twentieth century. However, two important reservations are to be made. First, Husserl is thematically much narrower than the great philosophers of the classical age. Though first-rate in theoretical philosophy, he wrote nothing on ethics, aesthetics, or philosophy of religion; his knowledge of the history of philosophy was very selective, and his understanding of the political changes of his time was minimal. The quality of his enormously extensive private notes, which were published posthumously in *Husserliana*, is uneven. Second, Husserl's students undertook, even during his lifetime, a radical deviation from his own understanding of phenomenology. This was not, of course, Husserl's fault, but it does show that his broad ignorance of the empirical sciences of his time, for instance of Freud's analysis of the unconscious foundations of our consciousness, remains unsatisfactory despite his obvious superiority on the level of theoretical validity.

Husserl was the student of Franz Brentano (1838–1917), the nephew of the poet Clemens Brentano and his sister, Bettina von Arnim, and thus a scion of what is probably the most famous German-Italian family. A priest, Brentano resigned after the announcement of the dogma of papal infallibility in 1870. His most important achievement consisted, first, in a reappropriation of Aristotle, who was used, as in Trendelenburg's work, against German idealism (in this connection Brentano developed a fascinating theory according to which the history of philosophy passes through four phases that repeat themselves), and second, in a refoundation of philosophy thanks to an analysis of human consciousness. Though Brentano welcomed the development of experimental psychology, which took place in the late nineteenth century with the active collaboration of philosophers like Wilhelm Wundt (1832–1920) and Carl Stumpf (1848–1936), he himself did not work experimentally and insisted on the intrinsic legitimacy of a first-person psychology (along with an approach in the third person). His discovery that acts of consciousness are intentional, that is, are related to something, is crucial. (He wrongly thought that everything psychic was intentional.)

However, what the precise status of this something is, whether it is immanent in consciousness or transcends it, is not easy to determine. In the first case, it would seem impossible that different subjects could establish relations to the same object, while in the second it remains unclear how a relation to a fictive structure is possible. In *Vom Ursprung sittlicher Erkenntnis* (*The Origin of our Knowledge of Right and Wrong*, 1889) Brentano defends, against subjectivism, a moral realism in ethics that is based on elementary self-evidence. Love and hate are seen as basic moral acts, and Brentano develops a few fundamental axiological principles for identifying objectively right love and preferences. Despite his critique of Kant's formalism, Brentano shares his conviction that threats of punishment, even if made by God, cannot be a legitimate sanction of morality. Knowing and loving, for instance, are valuable on intrinsic grounds.

Husserl owed his philosophical awakening in part to Frege's critical review of his book *Philosophie der Arithmetik* (*Philosophy of Arithmetic*, 1891), which reproached him for his mixture of logical and psychological observations. In his *Logische Untersuchungen* (*Logical Investigations*, 1900–1901), he himself became the severest critic of psychologism, which was then the most widespread theory of logic. No other work of the twentieth century is as good an introduction to philosophy as its "Prolegomena," because no other work argues its case so successfully on the subject of one of the fundamental problems of philosophy. Whereas psychologism claims that logic, even if perhaps embedded in a normative dimension, is reducible to psychology, which investigates the ways people judge and draw conclusions, Husserl shows with ever new arguments that although logic as the theory of the art of knowing is partly based on the psychology of the human mind, it is absurd to base *a priori* logic on empirical facts or to try to derive the latter from the former. On the contrary, logic is the science of the ideal conditions of the possibility of science itself, and as such it is the foundation of psychology, as of the other sciences. Building not on Fichte but rather on Bolzano, Husserl develops a theory of science that seeks to determine the fundamental form specific to all the sciences. He argues partly that the prejudices of psychologism (such as confusing laws that serve as the basis of normativization with those that contain this normativization itself as content) are false, and partly that as a skeptical relativism, psychologism leads to self-contradictory consequences. Anyone who confuses logical truths with real laws has to assume that the laws of truth regulate their own coming and going. Even species relativism—which claims that logic holds only for human beings—is untenable, because it confuses the act of judgment with the content of the judgment. Husserl understands logic on the analogy of mathematics and insists on a radical distinction between ideal assessment and causal explanation. Psychology has to explain all acts of judgment, even false ones, which it, *qua* psychology, cannot distinguish from correct ones. Evolutionary explanations of human cognitive behavior definitely have a legitimate place, but the problem of validity cannot thereby be resolved. Husserl conceives logic much more broadly than Frege, or even Frege's epigones, who see it as a theory of inferences; much later, he was to write a book attacking the replacement of transcendental logic by formal logic. Unlike mathematics, pure logic raises the question of the essence of the thing, the event, space, time, etc., and why this essence can be conceived. It is thus both an ontology and a transcendental theory of science, not very different from what we find in Hegel, but without theological ambitions. For Husserl does not want a worldview philosophy, but a "scientific" philosophy. However, his misgivings regarding Hegel's theological roots led him to overlook the fact that, from the point of view of the theory of foundation, Hegel's triadic system of objective idealism has advantages over the dualism of ideal and real science.

Unlike Hegel, Husserl had no architectonic talent, and never sought to systematically exhaust what belongs to logic in this broad sense; indeed, even the nature of inferential relationships is not made the subject of any of his investigations, because Husserl considers mediate knowledge as secondary with respect to self-evident knowledge. (In actuality, a logic that no longer addresses the problem of clarifying the premises of philosophy suffers from the unfortunate consequence that every argument by contrapositon can be transformed into a *reductio ad absurdum*.) His six studies seek to prepare pure logic only in terms of critical epistemology and also discuss in that connection subjects in the philosophy of language. In order to proceed scientifically and without presuppositions, philosophy has to analyze the phenomena of consciousness that are going on in the course of knowing something. Husserl begins with the relationship between expression and meaning. He distinguishes meaningful expressions from indicative signs, and within the former their physical side from the psychic experiences attached to them. In the case of monologic discourse, words would certainly not function as indicators for the existence of psychic acts. Instead, the physical phenomenon, which is often no longer perceived at all, is accompanied by acts that give it meaning and intuitive fullness, that is, meaning-bestowing and meaning-fulfilling acts, respectively. The individual act of judgment should not be confused with what it says; its meaning, which it, as a single act, can share with many other acts, is an ideal unit. Husserl compellingly rejects the notion that meaning is identical with the illustrative mental images produced by the imagination. Long before speech act theory, Husserl recognized the existence of expressions that simultaneously intimate what they name (for example, wishes as contrasted with declarative statements), as well as the peculiarity of essentially occasional expressions such as "I" and "now," whose meaning is achieved through two factors, the word and the situation. The so-called fluctuation of meanings is always a fluctuation of the acts of meaning, because ideal units are immutable. Concepts, judgments, and inferences are such ideal units, which are never made, but only discovered; many of them remain unknown and unnamed. Meaning is the logical content and not, for instance, a real part of the corresponding psychic process. In the second investigation, this leads to the problem of the unity of the species. Even if he rejects the metaphysical hypostatization of the universal, Husserl insists on the incontrovertibility of the discourse on universal objects: the ideal cannot be interpreted away psychologistically, as it is in British empiricism, whose confusions he subjects to a brilliant critique. The existence of a content in a psychic context is not already its being meant; sensations are not the object of the perception.

The third investigation, on the theory of the whole and the parts, connects up with the discussion of the concept of abstraction, but it also has a general ontological meaning. What is central is the difference between independent and non-independent contents, or between pieces and moments respectively. In addition to analyses of the relationship of foundation, the investigation contains a defense of synthetic *a priori* necessities. Natural laws, however, are mere factual truths: to that extent Husserl occupies a middle position between the *apriorism* of German idealism and Logical Positivism. In the fourth investigation the distinction between independent and non-independent contents is applied to language, in which there are also simple and complex meanings, indeed a few expressions, such as "and," that are syncategorematic, that is, have meaning only together with other words. Like Wittgenstein in the *Tractatus*, Husserl seeks laws in the compounding of meanings; what contradicts them is senseless (*sinnlos*) or nonsensical (*unsinnig*). He calls contradictions (but not tautologies) "absurd" (*widersinnig*). In addition to empirical linguistics, Husserl calls for an *a priori* linguistics, knowing well that the sense for such disciplines "is almost threatening to wither away in our age, even though all fundamental insights go back to them."

The fifth and probably most important investigation concerns intentional experiences and their contents. In opposition to Brentano, Husserl draws clear distinctions between three conceptions of consciousness; first, consciousness as the whole inventory of the empirical I; second, as the inner perception of one's own experiences; and third, as the quintessence of intentional experiences. The moments that constitute an act are not its intentional content; we do not see our sensations of colors, but rather colored things, and therefore the long-standing image theory of cognition is wrong. The analysis of complex acts—e.g., the pleasure taken in a state of affairs or the understanding of an expression—is impressive. The quality and matter of acts are considered as dimensions of them—we can relate to the same state of affairs in different ways, for example in a wish or a question. The representing content through which we relate to the matter is added later. As objectifying acts, nominal and propositional acts play a special role.

In the sixth investigation Husserl outlines his theory of knowledge. Knowledge is present when the meaning-intention is fulfilled through adequate intuition—the former exists independently of the latter, of course, since we can understand something before we consider it to be true. What is crucial here is that there is not solely a sensuous but also a categorial intuition, for instance the general intuition of universal kinds. Whereas Husserl argues, with Kant and against Hegel, that everything categorial is based on sensory intuition, he rejects, with Hegel and against Kant, the theory that categories falsify objects. No appeal to a noncategorial act is possible; and there is nothing that in principle could not be perceived. What distinguishes Husserl from both Kant and Hegel is that any attempt to derive the categories is alien to him: the categories have their origin in an intuition. That is unsatisfactory, as is the appeal to self-evidence as the ultimate criterion of validity. To be sure, the theory of knowledge may not be able to dispense with intuitions, but it is hard to understand how a fruitful conversation could take place between two persons who appeal to contradictory self-evidences, as quite often happens in the case of categorial intuition as well as in that of value intuitions. The phenomenon of errors of evidence is also a greater problem than that of a mistake made in a proof, because there is no procedure for clearly distinguishing errors of evidence from real evidences.

Husserl's second masterpiece is his (never completed) *Ideen zu einer reinen Phänomenologie und phänomenologischen Philosophie* (*Ideas Pertaining to a Pure Phenomenology and to a Phenomenological Philosophy*, 1913). This new science, which is conceived as a first philosophy without presuppositions that also takes itself as its object, is distinguished from psychology by two characteristics: it is a science of essences, not of facts; and its phenomena are seen, in contrast to the earlier work, as unreal. Husserl speaks of eidetic and of transcendental reduction, which together make up phenomenological reduction. The first reduction continues Plato, but with the modern concentration on consciousness, which is considered the ultimate foundation. The real existence of its contents is not a matter of interest; it is "bracketed" in the so-called *epoché*, but the contents of consciousness are undoubtedly given as such, independent of the question as to whether they relate to something physical or psychic. Husserl's Achilles' heel is his method of determining the essence of a thing, of for example an act of consciousness, by fictively "varying" the object until one reaches a point where it no longer has the same essence. This procedure seems undeniably circular; that is, it seems to depend on a preconception of the essence. But holding fast to the knowledge of essences, against empiricism and skepticism, is crucial for his project. According to Husserl, regional essences ground regional ontologies and their own categories; in addition, there is a formal ontology that thematizes the forms of all possible ontologies. The regional axioms are said to be synthetic *a priori* cognitions. The bracketing of the world (later compared to a religious conversion) is neither a denial nor a doubt regarding its existence; it consists solely in putting the natural attitude out of action, as it were. By analyzing the stream of consciousness with its peculiar temporality, its retaining of the past, and its anticipation of the future (retention and protention, respectively), Husserl points to the halo of unactual experiences that surrounds the actual one; he shows how the perception of spatial objects takes place in off-shadings, even if they relate to the same object; he distinguishes between acts that are directed to something immanent (to one's own acts) and those directed to something transcendent (to essences, things, acts of other I's); and he argues in a very Cartesian way that the positing of the world is accidental, while that of the pure I is necessary. Even the annihilation of the world of things would only modify the I's stream of experience, not suspend it. For Being is in itself secondary with regard to the I. Even God cannot be assumed to be transcendent in the same sense as the world, though Husserl is open to an original source of transcendental subjectivity. A causal explanation of the transcendental I is excluded, since causality occurs only within the intentional world. Certainly, in the psychological attitude that exists parallel to the phenomenological one, consciousness is an occurrence within the world, but this relationship ultimately makes sense only in relation to the transcendental I. Husserl's transcendental idealism is an important advance over earlier forms, especially those of Berkeley and Hume, because it is not based on confusing the act of thinking and the object of thinking, which in *Ideas* are distinguished in an exemplary way as *noesis* and *noema* correlated with one another. Intentionality separates consciousness, the "source of all reason and unreason, all right and wrong, all reality and fiction," from mere bundles of sensations.

Husserl's differentiations between *noeseis* and *noemata* are masterful and are modeled on the things themselves. He is right that in philosophy arguments lead to interesting results only if there is a method for coming to agreement on the premises; being masterful in argumentation without access to the phenomena is insufficient for philosophy; in fact, it produces freewheeling. But there is no seeing without categories, and so the absence of a method of concept formation remains a disturbing lack in phenomenology. In particular, it seems impossible to circumvent logic, although Husserl would like to "bracket" it also. One has to insist on transcendental arguments, especially where consciousness is not simply being described but the legitimacy of its claims to validity is presupposed.

Any first-person philosophy is threatened by the danger of solipsism, and it speaks in Husserl's favor that he himself acknowledged this problem. The five *Cartesianische Meditationen* (Cartesian Meditations) given as lectures in 1929 in Paris (published in French in 1931 and in German only in 1950) are a splendid introduction to phenomenology. They emphasize, among other things, Husserl's innovations with regard to Descartes, who gambled away his discovery by reifying the ego into a thinking substance that interacted with others causally. The decisive last meditation seeks to replace transcendental solipsism with a monadological intersubjectivity. By constituting a sphere of ownness that separates my I from other contents within the contents of consciousness, I become aware of the peculiar status of my body, which is related back to itself insofar as, for example, one hand feels the other. But I experience entities with a body similar to my own as experiencing the same world as I do; indeed, as experiencing me, among other things. Within the world I also find objects such as tools, which in origin and meaning point to other subjects. On the one hand, according to Husserl it is central that other I's can appear to me only through the mediation of the body—"if what belongs to the other's own essence were directly accessible, it would be merely a moment of my own essence." On the other hand, only the monadological community, the recognition of other I's, leads to the constitution of the objective world. The higher levels of the community have to do with the common relationship of the monads, not to the objective world, but rather to one another. The study of the I-Thou-acts and the various types of social communities is considered an important task. By using the term "monadology" Husserl deliberately harks back to Leibniz. Even if he does not share the latter's philosophical theology, he emphasizes that the different monads do not each have their own worlds; it could happen only accidentally that the horizons of individual monads would not be mutually accessible, for example because they operated in different cultural environments or "life-worlds."

The concept of the life-world becomes a "universal philosophical problem" in Husserl's last work, *Die Krisis der europäischen Wissenschaften und die transzendentale Phänomenologie* (*The Crisis of European Sciences and Transcendental Phenomenology*, 1938). Its first part describes brilliantly the breakdown of belief in reason in an age of unbridled irrationalism, and traces it back in part to a truncated concept of "objective" science, as it was manifested, for example, in the value-free human sciences: "merely fact-minded sciences make merely fact-minded people." According to Husserl, this is only a residual concept of a comprehensive philosophy, which was beheaded by Positivism, even if in truth the sciences are its branches. The technical aspect of the sciences is not affected by this process, but its sense of truth is shaken. With moving emotion the aged Husserl, "who has lived in all its seriousness the fate of a philosophical existence," invokes philosophers as humanity's officials; only if they restore the comprehensive concept of reason is the Europeanization of humanity more than a historical folly. In this work Husserl, who had earlier already taken an interest in a philosophical history of philosophy, offers an outstanding analysis, based on the history of philosophy and science, of the changes that took place in the early modern period and that produced, from Galileo on, the new natural science. Through momentous abstractions it distanced itself from its life-world basis, for example by mathematicizing qualities and by arithmetizing geometry, and thus made it possible to dominate nature. Husserl sees Galileo as both a discovering and a concealing genius, and Descartes's saving insight as being first correctly worked out in phenomenology. What is striking in this interpretation is the connection between deconstruction and a teleological orientation toward phenomenology. Husserl strongly insists that all the sciences, including logic, must be based on the life-world. Genetically, he is surely right, but one wonders how science can criticize the life-world if science cannot emancipate itself in terms of theoretical validity at least a little from the life-world. Whether the nonintuitive theoretical concepts of science or the qualities of the life-world have priority is not easy to decide, even if physics is dependent on the perception of marks on measuring sticks. Contrary to what Husserl maintains, in the case of geometry there seems to be no such dependency. Finally, there is the question of whether the program of a philosophical foundation in the life-world does not itself transcend the life-world, and thus contradict itself performatively. Seeking a theoretical foundation for the sciences in factual opinions seems paradoxical, though here Husserl links up with Heidegger and anticipates the later Wittgenstein—but it is more plausible that these two also abandon the classical conception of reason. Husserl continues to struggle with the relationship between subjectivity and intersubjectivity: the point of departure is supposed to be the transcendental *epoché*, without whose loneliness he does not consider radical philosophy possible, even if in an inner-worldly perspective, individual subjectivity is part of an intersubjectively shared life-world. The transcendental I is precisely something other than the inner-worldly I, for which only a Thou and a We exist. But at the same time the transcendental I is already supposed to constitute in itself a transcendental intersubjectivity.

A master is not helped by students who are epigones; and when original minds break with the master's teaching, he is seldom happy about it. Presumably the best possible student is one who applies the teacher's principles in new domains. That may be difficult in the case of encyclopedic philosophers, but Husserl's ideas could be extended to aesthetics and practical philosophy by analyzing the corresponding acts. The Polish thinker Roman Ingarden (1893–1970), who often wrote in German, rejected the late Husserl's transcendental idealism and can be seen as the most important realist phenomenologist, but his most original book is probably *Das literarische Kunstwerk. Eine Untersuchung aus dem Grenzgebiet der Ontologie, Logik und Literaturwissenschaft* (*The Literary Work of Art: An Investigation of the Borderlines of Ontology, Logic, and Theory of Literature*, 1931). *Untersuchungen zur Ontologie der Kunst* (*The Ontology of the Work of Art*), which deals with the visual arts, music, and film, appeared in 1962. Adolf Reinach (1883–1917) wrote on the philosophy of law, Alfred Schütz (1899–1959) on sociology, and Oskar Becker (1880–1964) on mathematics. But the most brilliant among the phenomenologists who remained loyal to Husserl's theory of validity is undoubtedly Max Scheler (1874–1928).

Originally a student of Rudolf Eucken (1846–1926), whose "activism" satisfied a worldview-related need and who in 1908 was rewarded for this when he became the only German philosopher to be awarded the Nobel Prize for literature, Scheler became a convinced phenomenologist after studying Husserl's *Logical Investigations*: his existential need for spirituality was now combined with greater precision. Late in his life he became an influential public intellectual (unfortunately, during the First World War he was, like many another German intellectuals, a propagandist for German violence; but after the war he became a proponent of a Christian socialism). Today, Scheler is definitely underestimated. His eccentric character and his way of writing are both to blame for this; he often argued carelessly, and he never made stylistic revisions to his quickly written works. But the abundance of ideas he offers is overwhelming, and his view of phenomena is penetratingly original, almost like that of the Greek philosophers. His greatest achievement consists in his synthetic power, especially in combining a Platonism of values with a competent analysis of the social development of value-attitudes: Scheler was also an excellent sociologist and was, among other things, the founder of the sociology of knowledge. What makes him so exciting intellectually is that he was one of the first to accept Nietzsche's and Freud's challenges and managed to combine their enduring psychological insights into a moral realism. *Das Ressentiment im Aufbau der Moralen* (*Ressentiment*, 1912) acknowledges the importance of ressentiment in the formation of moral judgments. Thus for Scheler the establishment of the modern welfare state is a substitute for the personal love relationship between one person and another; indeed, philanthropy in general is an expression of a counterimpulse against God and against superior people. Those who demand that we be humane often have only the animal side of human beings in mind. Subjective theories of value are an expression of ressentiment; their only remaining criterion of morality refers to what people generally do. "So the herds filled with ressentiment flock more and more together and consider their herd consciousness a substitute for the initially denied 'objectively good.'" Against Nietzsche, however, Scheler emphasizes that the revolution in the Christian conception of God does not arise from ressentiment—God is no longer the idea of the good to be loved, but rather himself a loving person. However, this "reversal in the movement of love" can be instrumentalized by ressentiment if the orientation toward the weaker does not arise from the fact that their inherent worth is recognized, but rather has its ultimate ground in a repugnancy for anything greater. Certainly one thing that is problematic about the theory is that Scheler cannot, and does not want to, ground ultimate decisions regarding values—for instance of the superiority of vital values over values of utility, which he sees as being undermined by modern capitalism—but wants instead to present them as self-evident.

Zur Phänomenologie und Theorie der Sympathie und von Liebe und Haß (On the phenomenology and theory of sympathy and of love and hate) followed in 1913 (since 1923 it has borne the title *Wesen und Formen der Sympathie* [The essence and forms of sympathy]), and up to that point, indeed even today, it is the most comprehensive and most subtle analysis of these phenomena. Scheler's distinction between vicarious feeling (*Nachfühlen*) and empathy (*Mitfühlen*) is classic: in the former we grasp another person's feeling without an analogous feeling being produced in us; thus the cruel person subsists on vicariously feeling with others but does not empathize with them. Whereas feeling with one another (*Miteinanderfühlen*) relates to the same fact— for instance, the death of a person similarly loved—in fellow feeling (*Mitgefühl*) the other's pain becomes the explicit object of the intention. On the other hand, emotional contagion (*Gefühlsansteckung*) is a causal process that operates unconsciously, in which there is no intention directed to the states of consciousness of other people. Finally, its limit case is identification (*Einsfühlung*), in which, as in hypnosis, another subject absorbs the I, or the I takes control of another subject. Love is essentially distinguished from fellow feeling; it is based on the perception of values (in oneself, for example, so that self-love, unlike fellow feeling with oneself, is possible). This thesis leads to the rejection of naturalistic theories of love. The search for a higher value of the beloved object sometimes encounters pre-existing structures and is sometimes creative, that is, it produces the higher value precisely through its expectation: "*Love is the movement in which every concrete individual object that carries values attains the highest possible values it can have in accord with its ideal vocation.*" Here Scheler distinguishes between vital, psychic, and spiritual love. Finally, a theory of the perception of others is laid out, according to which the mental states of others are not first made known solely through outward behavior; instead, certain experiences are given without yet being separated into our own and those of others. This is phenomenologically correct, but the presence of unconscious inferences is compatible with this finding.

Scheler's magnum opus, *Der Formalismus in der Ethik und die materiale Wertethik* (*Formalism in Ethics and Non-Formal Ethics of Values*)—which rightly can be considered the twentieth century's richest axiology, at least in German—was published between 1913 and 1916. The goal of this work is to overcome Kant's formalism without, however, abandoning his apriorism: this is supposed to be made possible by a material *a priori* that is grasped in acts of feeling. It may be doubted whether feelings are a better foundation for ethics than reason and will. But in recognizing that our emotional life is morally relevant, Scheler noted an important truth and brilliantly categorized an important field. Shortly before him, G. E. Moore worked out in England an intuitionist value ethics, but his universe of values is narrower than Scheler's; in addition, historical processes play no role in Moore. Scheler distinguishes sensory, vital, cultural, and religious values. Good and evil are said to consist in the right and wrong ranking of these values. Values are related to goods as colors are related to colored objects. In rejecting an ethics of goods like that of Nicolai Hartmann (1882–1950), Scheler remains a post-Kantian ethicist and is thus clearly superior to all neo-Aristotelians whose critique of Kant usually denies the intrinsic rights of an autonomous normative sphere. In particular, happiness is not the goal of virtue—but it is its source. The criticism bears not only on Kant's normative formalism, but also on his descriptive theory that the lower faculty of desire is driven by inclinations indifferent to value. In truth, the conations are always directed at values; what matters is the order of preference. Scheler's argument that values precede imperatives is important. For him, imperatives are appropriate only when there is a tendency to act in violation of them; but that is an empirical precondition that is not always fulfilled. On the basis of this distinction Scheler also has room for a relativism not of values, but of imperatives, which can turn out differently under different conditions. The work ends with a complex theory of the person, which is distinguished from the I, character, etc. It is the person who executes intentional acts and cannot be psychologically objectivized; one can only co-execute or re-execute his or her acts. In the absolute value he attributes to the person, Scheler remains true to Kant, with however the difference that according to him acts of feeling, and not only those of thinking and willing, are a central part of the person. Neither does he want to exile the realm of ends to the noumenal world. His theory of social units, which differentiates between mass, life-community, society, and solidaric love community (which preserves the spiritual individual person), goes even farther than Tönnies. For Scheler, the love community is realized in the Catholic Church, which fascinated many phenomenologists; but toward the end of his life Scheler broke with the Church because he felt that it was too repressive with regard to the individual. Scheler's personalist phenomenology nonetheless gave Catholicism an opportunity for a more timely self-interpretation: one has only to think of Karol Wojtyła (later Pope John Paul II).

In 1928, Scheler's *Die Stellung des Menschen im Kosmos* (*The Human Place in the Cosmos*) appeared simultaneously with *Die Stufen des Organischen und der Mensch* (The levels of the organic and man) by Helmuth Plessner (1892–1985), who had studied with Driesch, Windelband, Weber, and Husserl, and as a critic of totalitarian thinking about community shaped German sociology. These are two classics of philosophical anthropology, a discipline that has never gained a foothold in the Anglo-American world because it seeks a balance between the German tradition of natural philosophy and the orientation of transcendental philosophy toward the subject. Its goal is to discern the essential characteristics of human beings that distinguish them from other organisms. It emerged, after central preparations in the work of Herder, in a period when, thanks to Darwin's theory of the descent of man and, for example, Wolfgang Köhler's famous experiments with chimpanzees (published in 1917), the demarcation between animals and humans had ceased to be self-evident. Whereas Plessner, in the framework of an *a priori* but not vitalist philosophy of biology, discussed in detail the distinguishing characteristics of plants and animals, Scheler's short treatise is at the same time a metaphysics, because the special status of the human being sheds light on the whole of the cosmos. Only a feeling-impulse without sensations or representations is attributed to plants, which lack the feedback of organic conditions to a center; the more individualized animal has instincts, drives, and sensations; indeed, the higher animals have intelligence and are capable of making choices. So what is new in humans cannot lie in that area. Instead, it consists in a principle antithetical to life, the spirit. The spirit is more than drive-motivated intelligence; it is the "the capacity to be determined by the way things themselves are." For that reason human beings have a world, and not only an environment. In fact, humans can even objectify their own bodies and their own souls thanks to their self-consciousness. The empty forms of space and time and the category of substance emerged from this objectivity. The ability to rise above oneself leads to humor and irony; indeed, the human being is "the eternal Protestant against all mere reality," a being who can sublimate his drives. In connection with his distinction between essence and reality, Scheler emphasizes that the spirit has its own laws, but no energy of its own. For that it needs the drives, which it directs toward its goals. In itself, the spirit is impotent; only through the process of sublimation can it gain power. The dependency of the upper sphere on the lower is a general law of nature. Spirit and life-urge are even said to be the two attributes of the ground of the world, and the spiritualization of drives and the bringing to life of the spirit are the goal of everything that happens—not the beginning, as claimed by theism, from which the late Scheler distances himself. Only through the act of commitment, not through objectivization, can a human participate in the ground of the world. Against Descartes, Scheler defends the identity of the physical and the psychic sides of the life process, which are different only phenomenally. But he offers instead another dualism, which seems to mediate Hegel and Schopenhauer. Of special interest is Scheler's debate with Ludwig Klages (1872–1956), whose main work, *Der Geist als Widersacher der Seele* (The Spirit as adversary of the soul) appeared a year later. Scheler understood that the *Lebensphilosophie* of the 1920s, despite its not unjustified revolt against an excessive rationalization of society, was a romanticizing flight toward youth and a primitive past that was arbitrarily constructed in order to compensate for suffering caused by one's own over-intellectualization. Unlike the neo-Kantian critics of *Lebensphilosophie*, however, Scheler recognized the power of the life-urge and tried to make it subservient to the spirit.

A strong interest in reflection on validity may lead to a loss in the perception of reality; and just after the irruption of the most brutal corporality into reflection, as occurred in the horror of the trenches in the First World War, a revolt against

Husserl's neo-Cartesianism seemed natural: his belief in reason was no longer in tune with the new age of crisis. This revolt
found its most powerful expression in his best-known student,
who will be discussed in the following chapter. But we must note
that the problem of intersubjectivity, with which the late Husserl and Max Scheler struggled, led in the 1920s to a trend that
declared, against any transcendental idealism, that the I-Thou
relationship was the center of reality, and was for the most part
religiously inspired. Martin Buber's (1878–1965) *Ich und Du* (*I
and Thou*, 1923) is the best-known book of this "dialogic philosophy," whose weaknesses it shares: phenomenological power
and poetic language influenced by expressionism at the expense
of conceptual and argumentative clarity. It draws its life from the
opposition between the It-world and the Thou-world; in the It-
world everything is objectified, whereas the fundamental word
"I-Thou" establishes "the world of relation." The fellow human
being is the most important but not the only Thou—both nature
and intellectual structures, such as characters in literature, can
become Thous; and God is pure Thou. Buber realizes that the
Thou-relationship's symmetry cannot last long: "Without It man
cannot live. But he who lives with It alone is not a man." Relation is more than feelings, which are in reality well adapted to the
soulless bureaucracy of modernity: "If, like the modern man, you
have learned to concern yourself wholly with your own feelings,
despair at their unreality will not easily instruct you in a better
way—for despair is also a feeling and thus something interesting."
In 1938, Buber was still able to emigrate to Palestine. Among
Zionist intellectuals he had a special status because of his tireless
activity, from Brit Shalom's founding in 1925 until his death, on
behalf of a bi-national state that would include Arabs and Jews
on equal terms. *Die Schrift* (*The Scripture*), his translation of the
Old Testament written together with Franz Rosenzweig (1886–
1929), is intended as a German-Jewish alternative to Luther's
Bible.

৵ 13 ৼ

Is Philosophy Partly to Blame
for the German Catastrophe?
Heidegger between Fundamental
Ontology and History of Being

No one concerned with German intellectual history can avoid confronting the question as to why precisely this culture is responsible for what are probably the most atrocious crimes of the modern age. How could this people of poets and thinkers so quickly come to be seen by its neighbors as a people of mass murderers and accomplices? It is absurd to maintain that the study of Germany has to concentrate on the period between 1933 and 1945. To the contrary, the Nazi terror is so enigmatic because it was supported by a culture that had made great and unique intellectual achievements, also and precisely during the Weimar Republic. The abundance of first-rate German scientists, artists, and philosophers during the first three decades of the twentieth century is astonishing, as the last two chapters have demonstrated. And it is above all for that reason that we find ourselves facing the question as to whether the "German spirit" contributed to the resistible rise of National Socialism. It is hard to answer this question in a systematic way, because the manifold factors that play a role here can hardly be weighed against one another; indeed, it is even a matter of debate whether ideas exercise a causal effect at all. But anyone who maintains that they do can hardly avoid looking around for the ideas that promoted the advance of National

Socialism or at least hindered the opposition to it—even while keeping always in mind that other factors were far more important: the military defeat of 1918, which the country had still not gotten over; the lack of acceptance of the republican form of government amid widespread crises in long-standing views of political legitimacy and in the Weimar institutions themselves; the internal and international tensions that arose partly from the emergence of the Soviet Union, and the economic depression that began in 1929. But even if fascism was not confined to Germany, National Socialism was so different from fascism's other forms that it is natural to seek in it a connection with specific German traits, among which, along with thoroughness even in evil, are also philosophical ones.

Anyone who wants to answer the question as to why so many Germans followed Hitler would do well to distinguish three levels of followers. First, there was a relatively small minority that supported the National Socialist policy of annihilation out of deep conviction. Second, there was a large group that did not approve of mass murder as a political means, but in 1933 was willing to bring to power a government from which every kind of brutality could be expected, so long as it could be hoped that it would make Germany strong again, ward off the communist threat, avenge the country's defeat at the hands of France, and destroy the British hegemony that Germany had observed with increasing envy ever since its unification in 1871. Third, there was a large number of people who did not vote for Hitler, but nonetheless obeyed him, not only because they did not want to take any risks, but also because they were convinced that they owed obedience to the legal government.

The last group followed an old German tradition in which Luther and Kant are the central figures. A plausible theory of resistance was hardly offered by German philosophy, and the disappearance of the doctrine of natural law did not make it easier to reformulate such a theory. The second group had lost the belief in the intrinsic worth of the rule of law, as well as in the moral command to avoid war as much as possible; it was, like Spengler or Carl Schmitt, for example, fascinated by power politics and thus as far distant from Kant as could be imagined. The decline of Enlightenment ideals was connected with the limit-experience of attrition warfare of the First World War, which mocked the early modern state's promise to keep violence within bounds. This was in no way limited to Germany. In Germany, however, nationalism could pride itself on an exceptional culture that had to be protected against being infested by Western European values. "The Destruction of Reason" (to borrow the title of György Lukács's [1885–1971] well-known book of 1954, *Die Zerstörung der Vernunft*) took place in the 1920s on various levels. Universalist ideals had been undermined by Nietzsche and the anti-democratic right, but Logical Positivism (which was situated on the political left) also argued that ethical propositions were only subjective, and thus made its contribution to weakening, within the history of German consciousness, the conviction that people are bound to an ethical order that transcends their self-interest. The Marxist alternative was no more attractive; and Lukács's book suffers from the fact that he sees continuities from Schelling to Hitler, because for him anything that is not Marxist is irrational; indeed, for him, even intuitionism is suspect. Lukács was an important aesthetician (his 1916 *Die Theorie des Romans* [*The Theory of the Novel*] is still a classic), but as an epistemologist he is irrelevant, and his polemic against unreason contradicts both of reason's first commands, namely to listen and to criticize immanently. A conversation was thus no longer possible—and in fact one of the reasons for the fall of the Weimar Republic was its inability to converse. So far as the first group is concerned, Nietzsche had justified the killing of people "unworthy of living"; he was followed by the Darwinian biologist Ernst Haeckel (1834–1919), whose monism was, however, rejected by the Nazis. Finally, in the 1920s there was fateful debate among penologists and psychiatrists regarding this subject. This does not mean that any philosopher deserving to be taken seriously urged or condoned the murder of the Jews and Gypsies (though the German tradition of anti-Judaism is certainly ancient, and the successful emancipation of the Jews at the end of the nineteenth century had set in motion a verbally eliminationist anti-Semitism). But Nietzsche contributed like no one else to the moral cynicism without which this enormous rupture in civilization would hardly have occurred, because he made it intellectually and stylistically acceptable. Moreover, he accelerated de-Christianization, which had gained far more ground in Germany, even before him, than it had in Great Britain, for instance. Without this de-Christianization, it would have been nearly impossible to establish a totalitarian state that was based on power and that promised to fill the void of meaning in which people cannot live for long. Not only did the genocide of the Jews involve breaking a taboo, but this taboo was broken through actions against the religion that had prohibited killing more strongly than had the pagan cults.

It goes without saying that the Nazis' "philosophy," in so far as it can be determined from the writings of Adolf Hitler and Alfred Rosenberg, is beneath the intellectual and moral level of this writer. But it would be false to exclude for that reason all philosophers who were not, like the majority of German university professors, simply fellow travelers, but for a time lent National Socialism enthusiastic support. Moral cowardice, malice, and even partial intellectual blindness are compatible with great intellectual achievements. We cannot deny the value of Konrad Lorenz's (1903–1989) biological discoveries, even if there are obvious links between his biologism and his commitment to National Socialism (and in general the biologistic form of naturalism is more dangerous than the physicalistic one, because physicists, thanks to their mathematical training, prize logical clarity, whereas the biologist may be fascinated by the brutality of the struggle to survive). Lorenz has to be mentioned because in 1941, when he was a professor of psychology in Königsberg, he reinterpreted Kant's transcendental epistemology in a biologistic way and conceived the *a priori* as innate structures that can be traced back to phylogenetic experiences. This does not allow the solution of the problem of validity, but his book *Die Rückseite des Spiegels—Versuch einer Naturgeschichte menschlichen Erkennens* (*Behind the Mirror, a Search for a Natural History of Human Knowledge*, 1973) remains one of the best introductions to the evolutionary theory of knowledge, whose basic ideas go back to Darwin himself.

Thus we cannot dismiss Husserl's most famous student by pointing to the speech he gave as a National Socialist university rector in 1933. Anyone who compares Martin Heidegger (1889–1976) with Karl Jaspers (1883–1969) will immediately see that of the two philosophers of existence Jaspers was an outstanding philosopher of psychiatry, a diagnostician of his time (*Die geistige Situation der Zeit* [*Man in the Modern Age*, 1931] remains diagnostically relevant, precisely because Jaspers did not foresee

National Socialism), a cultural philosopher with a sense for the dawning global dimension of philosophy, and a public intellectual in the young Federal Republic who was aware of his responsibilities, and who had behaved impeccably during the Third Reich. Heidegger, on the other hand, who had already become a Nazi sympathizer shortly before Hitler took power, pathetically failed to lead the Leader as he had intended, and became entangled in the guilt of the National Socialist state. And yet it is—unfortunately—Heidegger, and not Jaspers, who deserves to be called a "philosophical genius." Anyone who maintains that he is a moral and intellectual disaster has a duty nonetheless to understand his central importance in the history of twentieth-century philosophy. The decoupling of phenomenology from rigorous reflection on validity, such as also occurred in France, was begun by Heidegger. And as a teacher in Marburg and Freiburg he soon showed himself capable of attracting, through the originality of his questioning and his magnetic personality, outstanding students, four of whom were liberal or left-wing Jews: Karl Löwith (1897–1973), Herbert Marcuse (1898–1979), Hans Jonas (1903–1993), and Hannah Arendt (1906–1975).

Creative achievements seldom consist in discovering entirely new elements, but rather, for the most part, in bringing together different currents—with a resulting synthesis that is something absolutely new. *Sein und Zeit* (*Being and Time*, 1927), although it was never completed, is just such a path-breaking book. It integrates into a single, unified conception five tendencies that at first glance seem very different from one another. As the title indicates, Heidegger seeks first of all to ask anew the question as to the meaning of Being; with his commitment to ontology he turns against Husserl's transcendental idealism. Second, an approach to Being is supposed to become possible through an analytics of human existence. This is essentially temporal—and thus Husserl's legacy continues. But third, Heidegger uses the theory of the temporality of existence to present one of the most intensive analyses of mortality since the ancients, for which there was no place in Husserl's theory, since the interruption of the stream of consciousness can hardly be explained idealistically. Furthermore, he sets out to base the German discipline of hermeneutics on the life-world. It is not only Schleiermacher's subtle interpretations of Plato that are hermeneutic achievements, but existence itself is, as such, a form of understanding. Finally, Heidegger built the bridge between temporality and historicity that had been a very important German theme since the eighteenth century, although it was only seldom connected with the temporality of our consciousness. However, since Nietzsche's and Dilthey's historicism represented the position opposed to Husserl, this synthesis arouses the suspicion of some inconsistency.

Nonetheless, it is not only this connection of lines of thought that made *Being and Time* explode like a bomb; the mood of the book was right. The First World War had made death very present to people's minds, but unlike literature (especially Tolstoy, to whom Heidegger owes more than he acknowledges), philosophy had largely ignored it. The association of temporality and historicity suited the period's sense that it was witnessing a major break in world history; and the book's unique language, full of German chauvinist neologisms, as well as its revolt against the anonymous "they" (*das Man*) in the name of resoluteness had resonance for the generation that fought in the trenches. The search for a life-world foundation for the sciences, which for the most part confused genesis and validity, mirrored the petty bourgeois anxiety aroused by a science and technology that were understood by fewer and fewer people, especially since this archaism, like that of the Nazis, was accompanied by a highly modern trait, which was however easily overlooked because it consisted in an absence: the book has no concrete ethical content to offer. Now, in itself that is not a reproach. A philosopher is not required to express himself on every subject. But the insidious thing about this work is that it undermines, through its redefinition of terms such as "conscience" and "guilt," the traditional moral sense and very clearly suggests that resoluteness, no matter what for, is the only thing that matters. One might, like Scheler, accuse Kant of formalism, but the *Metaphysics of Morals* is certainly not as formalist as Heidegger's anti-ethics. Even if the book intends only a destruction of the history of ontology, it offers no less a destruction of ethics. However, since Heidegger's language is much less clear than Nietzsche's exemplary prose, which was honed on the French moralists, and because he throws around watchwords of the tradition, such as "Being" (*Sein*), and makes no bones about his antipathy to modernity, he is much more dangerous than Nietzsche. Generations of Christian theologians of all confessions have absorbed him with a good conscience. The end result is a postmodern theology that no longer sees the rational clarification of the concept of God as its task, congratulates itself on the confusion of hermeneutic standards because that is a way to put Bible criticism in its place, looks down on the natural sciences because they all emerged historically, and rejects any normative ethics as no longer in tune with the times. It is appropriate to doubt whether this remedy benefits the intellectual status of theology or is in keeping with the theological tradition of the Enlightenment or even the Middle Ages.

Heidegger's rapidly acquired and pervasive influence on the theology of the twentieth century was made possible only by the fact that he himself was reacting to Søren Kierkegaard's theological and philosophical revolution, which led, immediately after the First World War, to the so-called "dialectical theology." The name is peculiar when we consider that the central idea of the movement is the opposition—and precisely not the mediation, as in Hegel—between the finite and the infinite. I have already mentioned that Hegel's rationalism undermines traditional Christological orthodoxy. In contrast, Kierkegaard wants to maintain the latter at any cost, and since he clearly recognizes that Jesus's unique status, and his radical difference from Socrates, cannot be rationally grounded, he rejects any attempt at a rational justification of theology. We can grant him that the moral appropriation of the Christian message transcends speculative understanding, and we can certainly grant that progressive Hegelian theologians' feeling of superiority over earlier, existentially deeper appropriations of the Christian message was unjustified. But if Christianity can be grasped only through a leap of faith, if it is not only paradoxical in the original sense of the Greek word—that is, because it collides with common opinion—but is in fact absurd and prides itself on its absurdity, then we must ask a simple question: how is a reasonable person supposed to accept it? On the one hand, traditional Catholic theology had sought a rational justification of the belief in God, and on the other had offered historical arguments for the validity of what was accepted as revealed truth. Kierkegaard rejects both paths (the latter, because he had studied Lessing in depth); indeed, he does not even have a fully elaborated intuitionist epistemology. Therefore he can ultimately appeal only to a subjective decision. While we can certainly find

Biblical passages, for instance in Paul, that refer to the irrationality of belief, there is, already in the Old Testament, a whole tradition that identifies God with wisdom, and Kierkegaard broke
with it long before Heidegger and his epigones. But in this connection he analyzes subjective mental states with enormous precision and a—dialectical—sense for how they can flip over into
opposed psychic conditions. But this is a tack that turns theology
into the psychology of the religious, and one that can be grounded
on atheistic foundations as well.

Heidegger's fundamental ontology is based on an existential
analytics of existence. In his work, "existence" (*Dasein*) does not
refer simply to the human mode of being, for the analytics of existence is irreducible to anthropology and psychology. Moreover,
it stands in opposition to the philosophical definitions of the
human being in the Greek and Christian tradition as a rational
being or an image of God. It is true that of all entities that we
know *Dasein* is realized only in human beings, who not only have
a special ontic status, but are also ontologically oriented—*Dasein*
comports itself toward *Sein* (Being). But Heidegger subsumed
under the concept of *Dasein* a plenitude of traits that could in
principle also be found in unknown species, whereas at the same
time he left out essential characteristics of human beings, ranging from sexuality to religiousness. Against Husserl's eidetic orientation, Heidegger emphasizes that the essence of *Dasein* lies
in its existence, which is precisely not characterized by specific
properties, but is instead in each case mine (*jemeinig*): *Dasein* is
concerned with its own Being. Thus *Dasein* is not part of what
is present-at-hand (*vorhanden*); it is to be grasped through so-
called existentialia, not through categories. Heidegger's fundamental existentiale is Being-in-the-world—a determination that
turns Husserl's transcendental reduction on its head, so to speak.
In knowing, for example, *Dasein* does not reach out from its inner
sphere; instead, it is always already "outside"—and with that the
epistemological problem is supposed to be solved.

In sharp distinction to Descartes, but drawing on a suggestion made by Husserl, Heidegger works out worldhood, which
according to him is originally characterized by readiness-to-
hand (*Zuhandenheit*), the mode of being of equipment such
as pencils and desktops, hammers and nails, each of which
forms a context of assignments or references. This sounds like

pragmatism—knowledge is first formed on the basis of our dealings with things. Heidegger rejects the notion "as if an initially objectively present world-stuff were 'subjectively colored.'" Instead, presentness-at-hand is a deworlding [*Entweltlichung*] of an original readiness-to-hand. Later in the book he tries to show that modern natural science could be successful only in the light of a mathematical projection of nature: the science of facts became possible only because researchers understood that there were no mere facts. In the original Being-in-the-world, space is not an abstract three-dimensional framework, but rather place is the "there" of an item of equipment's belonging-there. "From already being in a 'familiar' world" *Dasein* orients itself through circumspect de-distancing (*Ent-fernen*). The world is neither in space, nor is the latter in the subject—rather, space is in the world, since only Being-in-the-world discloses space. In a similar way *Dasein* encounters others, for instance those who provide equipment. Others are precisely not what is opposed to me, but rather those among whom I also am. Their Being is *Dasein*-with (*Mitdasein*), while Being-in is Being-with-others. These others cannot be taken care of (*besorgen*) like equipment, but instead are objects of concern (*Fürsorge*) that can paternalistically leap in or leap ahead of the Other, in order to return to him care (*Sorge*) as such. Analogously, the circumspection (*Umsicht*) with regard to equipment corresponds to considerateness (*Rücksicht*) and tolerance (*Nachsicht*) with regard to others. The existentiale of the *they* (*Man*) is central; *Dasein* is subject to it. This is certainly also an unburdening—we will encounter this determination again in Gehlen—but being authentically oneself consists in a modification of the *they*. *Dasein* experiences itself as "thrown" (*geworfen*)—it is subject to attunements and moods, such as fear, for instance; equiprimordially it is understanding. This does not refer to an intellectual operation that is opposed to explaining; rather, it refers to a basic mode of *Dasein*, namely the disclosing of world. The ready-to-hand is explicitly understood and explained as something; and once again mere staring is a no-longer-understanding, that is, a privation of understanding, and in no way more primordial. Only *Dasein* can be meaningful or meaningless, depending on whether it understands its own Being and the disclosed world or not. There is a circle in understanding, but it is a question of getting into it "in the right way."

Heidegger then tries to interpret the elementary logical concept of the statement as a derivative mode of interpretation. In his analysis of language we must emphasize especially his judgment that language is not a means of conveying experiences (passing on information, for instance, presupposes Being-with), and also his interpretation of keeping silent as an essential possibility of speech. Returning once again to the *they*, Heidegger introduces idle talk, curiosity, and ambiguity as forms of the falling prey of *Dasein*; there had been no equally sharp critique of existential superficiality since Pascal. In his profound observations on *Angst*—which unlike fear is anxious not about something within the world, but rather about Being-in the-world as such, and thus reveals partly the freedom of choosing oneself, and partly falls into the mode of not-being-at-home—the influence of Kierkegaard is obvious, but it is deprived of its theological and moral substance. As often happens in Heidegger, theologoumena are so skillfully secularized that they do not lose their electrifying effect. Finally, the structural whole of *Dasein* is conceived as being-ahead-of-oneself-already-in (the world) as being-together-with (innerworldly beings encountered). But that is the essence of care, in which the possibility of project (*Entwurf*) is grounded. The idealism-realism problem can be solved only by recourse to the care-structure of *Dasein*; and it is not a scandal in philosophy, as Kant thought, that no proof of the reality of the external world has yet been achieved; the scandal is that such proofs have been repeatedly attempted. We should not take any more seriously the "formal-dialectical efforts" to catch skepticism unawares: according to Heidegger, all truth is relative to the Being of *Dasein*, and therefore the claim to eternal truths is only a not-yet-eliminated residue of Christian theology (which is seldom a good argument, and is positively tasteless in a work that is so parasitical on the Christian fund of ideas). The propositional concept of truth is said to be derivative with respect to an ontological concept of truth as discoveredness.

The temporality of *Dasein* is central in the second section of the work. Heidegger begins with existential-ontological reflections on death, which can be experienced only in regard to the other, whose corpse is an object to be taken care of. However, no one can relieve the other of his dying, at most one can die for him; one has to relate to death as the ownmost, nonrelational possibility

that cannot be bypassed. The *they* sees to it that there is an eva-
sion of death that covers it over, it does not allow the courage of
developing *Angst* in face of death to arise. But authentic Being-
toward-death (*Sein zum Tode*) consists in an anticipation of this
possibility (*Vorlaufen*; literally "running ahead toward"), and in
this freedom toward death a detachment from the illusions of the
they is achieved. Once again we see the marketable secularization
of theologumena by the Catholic sacristan's son who no longer
believes in eternal truths. (Rainer Maria Rilke proceeds with similar skill, but in a lyric poet such a procedure is unassailable.) The
memento mori is a central Christian practice, and the expectation
of Divine Judgment certainly has a purifying effect. But since in
Heidegger there is no longer any talk about the immortality of
the soul, one wonders what this running ahead toward death,
which once took place in every *Ave Maria*, might now be. The
serenity of the Epicureans seems wiser: If I am, then death is not,
and if death is, then I am not. It cannot be understood what this
anticipation is supposed to produce other than a cheap thrill that
gives one the feeling of being more authentic than others, because
one embarks heroically on nothingness.

With the concept of resoluteness (*Entschlossenheit*), Heidegger develops the ethical heart of his work. First of all, it is striking how he completely formalizes and subjectivizes the concept
of conscience, which is to be understood neither theologically
nor biologically. It calls, but it says nothing (Heidegger acknowledges no ideal truths); instead, it speaks in the mode of silence.
If we interpret conscience as an objective power, we only subject
ourselves to the *they*, whereas the call asks us to choose ourselves.
Still more irritating is the reinterpretation of the concept of guilt,
which consists in the fact that as "thrown," one is not one's own
ground, and in the existential project we inevitably forego some
possibilities. This ontological interpretation of conscience and
guilt is distinguished from the "vulgar," that is, ethical, which
moves under the spell of an ontology of the present-at-hand.
But we are well advised when we, despite the predicate "vulgar,"
defend the stubborn feeling that someone who foregoes the possibility of a career as the commander of a concentration camp
is less guilty than someone who plans such a career for himself.
However, Heidegger's resoluteness, like that of Jean-Paul Sartre's
existentialism, which is so different in kind politically, is empty.

"Resoluteness is certain of itself only in a resolution." Granted, this does not necessarily lead to National Socialism, but it also has to be granted that it does nothing to block the road that leads in that direction—and in general it encourages a radicalization of irrational convictions.

The anticipation of resoluteness heralds the theme of temporality, which lends unity to the structure of care: the being-ahead-of oneself [*Sich-vorweg*] is grounded in the future, while the already-being-in (*Schon-sein-in*) manifests having-been (*Gewesenheit*, Heidegger's equivalent for *Vergangenheit*, i.e., past), and being-together-with is made possible by making present. What is crucial here is the priority of the future. All existentialia are now revisited and deepened with regard to temporality; in fact, even the spatiality characteristic of *Dasein* is supposed to arise from temporality. Out of the temporality of *Dasein* its historicity finally arises. Here Heidegger is writing in the wake of Dilthey's historicism, which is, however, valorized in terms of existential philosophy. The movement away from the individualism of authenticity to concepts such as destiny, community, and people is striking. The resoluteness of a whole nation is not discussed, but one senses its possibility. Heidegger's concept of world history has nothing to do with Kant's or Hegel's constructions in the philosophy of history; there is no talk of either progress in history or the formation of a world-historical consciousness. Heidegger's observations on history reject efforts at "objectivity"—he is concerned with the potentialities of existence, of *Dasein* that has-been-there, and in no science is universal validity less at home than in history. The historian's choice of materials arises from the existential choice of *Dasein*'s historicity. We will see that Gadamer's founding of hermeneutics is based on a similar idea, which however rejects, through the extension of reception history, the provinciality of Heidegger's suggestion, to which any chauvinistic cobbled-together historical construction can gratefully appeal. The work concludes with reflections on the constitution of public time through time measurements and on the genesis of the vulgar—that is, the scientific—conception of time. Time is said to be more objective than any possible object, because it is found in the psychic as well as in the physical; and it is more subjective than any possible subject, because it makes the latter possible in the first place. Given the broad identification of time and being, one wonders what kind of ontic status timeless entities like mathematical structures or values have; in the latter, Plato—and metaphysics after him—saw the paradigmatic existent; and we are painfully touched to find the natural sciences and ethics, to whose grounding Kant devoted his magnificent work, now both considered, in the twilight of the state based on the rule of law, as "vulgar." Shouldn't we rather describe as vulgar the phasing out of the best heritage of the West?

Like Wittgenstein, Heidegger reconceived his philosophy in a radically new way. In the 1930s there occurred what he called a *Kehre*, or "turn," which took shape, for example, in his *Beiträge zur Philosophie. (Vom Ereignis) (Contributions to Philosophy [Of the Event]*), first published in 1989. But unlike Wittgenstein, Heidegger was no longer able to work up his new conception into a classic text; instead, he published a large number of articles and essays, all of which revolve around a few interconnected themes, but whose level differs greatly. Anyone who reads the collection entitled *Holzwege (Off the Beaten Track*, 1950) is disturbed to find a text like "Der Spruch des Anaximander" ("Anaximander's Saying"), which mocks all hermeneutic standards, placed next to two undeniably brilliant articles—"Der Ursprung des Kunstwerks" ("The Origin of the Work of Art," 1935–36) and "Die Zeit des Weltbildes" ("The Age of the World Picture," 1938). It is unlikely that there has ever been an important thinker who was less capable of self-criticism than Heidegger—he produced important and confused works alongside one another and was himself not able to distinguish between the two. The crucial basic insight of the *Kehre* consists in a retreat from the residual transcendentalism of *Being and Time*: not *Dasein*, but *Sein* (Being) is now the decisive fundamental notion—the human being is the "shepherd of Being" (note the plagiarism of the Bible). But this is not for all that a return to the metaphysical tradition, first because, like Spinoza, Heidegger conceives Being in a fully amoral way, and second because he only elevates metaphysically Dilthey's historicism: Being manifests itself in different periods in entirely different forms, and between these no continuous, that is argumentative, transitions are possible. The history of Being, which is supposed to be essentially a history of the various conceptions of Being, is thereby understood as a history of decline and withdrawal, because Being increasingly conceals itself; and with his

turn away from metaphysics to the philosophy of history of metaphysics, Heidegger seeks to contribute to the "transformational
recovering" (*Verwindung*) of this misleading metaphysical tradition that is characterized by its oblivion of Being. However, given
Heidegger's own oblivion of the *logos*, there can be no method
of recovering his own claim to validity, because Being is opposed
to all conceptual structures, as it is not in the tradition from
Plato to Hegel. How, after two and half millennia of decline,
Heidegger's sudden insight is supposed to have become possible, is not conceivable—and it ought not to be. Against Hegel's
progress-schema, Heidegger sees an ever-increasing estrangement
from the original unconcealment that is supposed to have been
approached most closely by the pre-Socratics—the philosophical
interest in the latter had begun with Nietzsche, whereas classical
German philosophy had given priority to Plato. Thus, with the
passing of time, we reach further and further back. Plato already
put Being under the yoke of the Idea, and the Middle Ages paved
the way for modern rationalism. "The Age of the World Picture"
is a crudely simplifying, but nonetheless splendid analysis of the
transformation of the world by the concept of the picture, as it
underlies modern metaphysics. Modern science, which culminates in machine technology, the aestheticization of the work of
art, the interpretation of human activity as culture, and finally the
loss of the divine, are all offshoots of this will of modern metaphysics to make the world available; and indeed objectivism and
subjectivism are only two sides of the same epochal upheaval that
culminates in the gigantic. "Die Frage nach der Technik" ("The
Question Concerning Technology"), a lecture first delivered in
1949, deepens this stance and offers one of the most brilliant
analyses of modern technology. Thus Heidegger rightly rejects
the thesis that technology is something neutral; it is not a mere
means; instead it makes manifest a way of relating to the world.
Whereas the wooden bridge is built in the Rhine river, the river
is dammed up into the modern hydroelectric plant, and the
Rhine itself is "an object on call for inspection by a tour group
ordered there by the vacation industry." Heidegger calls modern technology "enframing" (*Ge-stell*), for which everything is
standing-reserve (*Bestand*), and thus usable; this is already inherent in modern natural science as its secret *telos*. And the danger of this technology—which one could at most encounter by

bringing its essence into view—in no case consists only in the "potentially lethal machines and apparatus of technology," but rather in the change in the human essence. In the context of his philosophy of history, which sees history as a decline, Heidegger also made room for the National Socialist will to power—already in the 1930s, because he soon distanced himself inwardly from the NSDAP (though he remained a member to the end). That was an achievement considerably diminished by the fact that he considered the Nazis' techniques of mass murder to be in essence the same as motorized agriculture—neither before nor after the *Kehre* did Heidegger have categories that would have allowed him to move beyond "ontological statements about essences" so as to note the morally relevant differences.

Heidegger's rejection of subjectivist aesthetics enabled him to make the ontology of the work of art central once again. The work of art is not about beauty or even eliciting experiences, but rather about the setting-into-work of truth [*Ins-Werk-Setzen der Wahrheit*]. Unlike equipment, the work of art sets up a world. Here, truth is not understood as mimesis, and that is why Heidegger analyzes a Greek temple as one of his examples, in addition to Vincent Van Gogh's "Still life, a Pair of Shoes." The essence of truth includes concealment; and yet the work of art founds community. It should surprise no one that Heidegger's late philosophy often consists in interpretations of poetry, most of which slap the methodology of literary studies in the face, even if he rightly saw in Hölderlin a predecessor, in tune with his critique of modernity. An idiosyncratic form of polytheistic pseudo-religiousness, a philosophy of language that subordinates the autonomous will of the individual to the happening of language, and finally a quietist ethics of "releasement with regard to things" (*Gelassenheit zu den Dingen*) as a "simultaneous yea and nay to the technological world" characterize the late work. To be sure, it remains Heidegger's world-historical achievement to have been one of the first to conceptualize the increasing discomfort with modern subjectivity and with unbridled technology, even if he lacked any ethics such as might have allowed him to propose a therapy once he had diagnosed the disease.

❧ 14 ❧

National Socialist Anthropology and Political Philosophy: Arnold Gehlen and Carl Schmitt

Probably the most important philosophical book published under the Third Reich is Arnold Gehlen's (1904–1976) *Der Mensch. Seine Natur und seine Stellung in der Welt* ("Man, His Nature and Place in the World," 1940), which went through several expanded editions (I take the last as my basis here). Like *Being and Time*, Gehlen's book concentrates on the peculiar mode of being of a finite, rational being that knows it is finite: an obvious subject when belief in God has ceased while at the same time a thirst for reality prevails that is not satisfied by the subtle foundational ideas of Frege and Husserl. Gehlen and Heidegger are, moreover, connected by their pragmatism, which associates knowledge with action (but only Gehlen refers to its American predecessors). In 1933 Gehlen wanted to write a "philosophy of National Socialism," but Heidegger's linguistic German chauvinism was alien to him, and he was also free of anti-Semitism. It is not only in his style, which rivals that of the great European prose writers, that Gehlen is superior to Heidegger, whom he does not cite even once in his main work. Characteristically, Gehlen takes into account a broad range of results from the various sciences: he was the student of the biologist and vitalist philosopher Hans Driesch (1867–1941), and from 1938 to 1940, he was Konrad Lorenz's predecessor in Königsberg. Although the epistemological status of his "empirical philosophy" is unclear, after abandoning transcendental reflection, a reliance on experience is more honest than Heidegger's indulgence in unverifiable statements about essences. Gehlen seems to have seen his task as making the abundant results of the various sciences intelligible on the basis of one *single* principle.

As someone who after an existentialist phase was for a time strongly influenced by Fichte, Gehlen foregrounds the concept of action; on its basis the system of human characteristics is supposed to be grasped. What distinguishes human beings from other animals is that human beings have to act, because their instincts are greatly reduced and, in fact, they are already deficient beings (*Mängelwesen*) in their physique, retarded development, and secondary altriciality. Action is understood here as something that goes beyond the mind-body opposition: Gehlen has no hope of solving that problem, and instead looks for psychophysically "neutral" categories. In opposition to any metaphysical dualism, he points out that human beings' special status does not consist solely in "spiritual" qualities which, as in Scheler, are superimposed on animal qualities; rather, the specifically human also permeates the physical, the "reason of the body," and expresses itself in, for instance, the enormously adaptable movements that have to be learned in coping with objects. (One consequence of this way of seeing things is paradoxically that Gehlen distinguishes humans from animals more radically than Scheler, Lorenz, and contemporary ethology do). The decoupling from instinctive impulses, and thus from the situation, represents an unburdening, or relief (*Entlastung*; that is the new key concept); but the sensory overload that goes hand in hand with disclosing the world, in contrast to the animal's dependence on its milieu, along with the excessive nature of impulses as the flipside of the inhibition of impulses, constitute a burden that also has to be managed. Culture is the quintessence of "nature reworked in the service of life," and humans are by nature cultural beings. Thus even acts that appear in animals as end phases, such as eating or sexual intercourse, can in humans be carried out as means and receive a symbolic meaning. Through their ability to rest, human beings can objectivize the world, associating data from the various senses with each other; and through this process they arrive at a concept of things. However, it is crucial that the thing be the object of a possible action—as something that can be changed, for example, repaired. Gehlen's analyses of the development of language are particularly convincing; for him, it runs parallel to that of perception and action. He distinguishes five different roots of language. First, there is a life of self-produced sounds, to which motor and sensory functions equally contribute. Second, the expression of sounds after visual impressions is the result of unburdened movement. Third, the satisfaction of needs that follows a child's cry soon leads to the expectation that his next cry will produce the same result. Fourth, the sound gesture is the sound-motor musical accompaniment to a mainly playful movement. Only in fifth place comes the recognizing sound described by Herder, which also includes distant stimuli in the self-enjoyment of active participation. Gehlen's theory of meaning, directed against Husserl, is considerably weaker; it identifies the timelessness of the *noema* with the iterability of the *noesis*. So far as pragmatism is concerned, Gehlen is certainly right genetically in saying that conscious thought is a late product of evolution, and in terms of the theory of validity we can grant him that thoughts are actions and that the consequences of a thought are part of its meaning. But in this sense Hegel's philosophy is also a form of pragmatism. In addition, the explanation of inner life, of silent thinking, representation, and imagination suffers from the old problem that a biological function of consciousness is possible only if epiphenomenalism is false; but that presupposes a complex alternative: the mind-body problem cannot be simply evaded or cybernetically short-circuited. Gehlen borrows from George Herbert Mead the significance of role-playing in the constitution of self-consciousness, which presupposes a social dimension; he also sees imagination as an elementary social organ (consider Charles Taylor). Most likely to intersect with fascism's self-image are Gehlen's reflections on the irrational certainties of experience without which action, and especially group action, would not be possible at all. "There is an experimental way of thinking in which, reversing Goethe's saying, the observer and not the actor becomes unconscionable." This can be prevented only by discipline and habits that shape character. So far he is absolutely right, but Gehlen fails to see the distinction between discipline in an ancient school of philosophy and discipline within the SS. For him ultimate certainties "reflect the vicissitudes of the instinct," and when certainties conflict, only history can decide where the truth lies. Also, historical significance is more a matter of dynamic effectiveness than of the originally intended meaning—Gadamer was to weave his hermeneutics out of this idea.

Urmensch und Spätkultur (Primordial man and late culture, 1956) completes Gehlen's philosophical anthropology by adding the social dimension, and offers a theory of institutions that alone could contribute to an inner stabilization of the endangered human being: by the automatization of social behavior, thus making it predictable, by the background satisfaction of the need to preserve a situation that ensures that future needs will be met (when I see a full grain storehouse the future hunger that characterizes human beings no longer pains me) and by channeling the feeling of indeterminate obligation that ultimately leads to morality. Tensions arising from ambivalent feelings can also be stabilized in this way: funerals are an institutional response to the mixture of attachment to the dead and fear of the corpse. Gehlen's attempt to reconstruct the social evolution of primordial man is especially fascinating—since Vico, there had been no philosopher who dealt so penetratingly with this subject. One of Gehlen's important insights is that by no means all institutions owe their existence to goal-directed action, even if reciprocity is a crucial principle—sometimes they result from quite different goals. The transition to agriculture and livestock-breeding, for instance, was a secondary result of the practice of keeping animals for religious purposes, which had is origin in totemism; not immediately eating the caught animal, but rather feeding it, presupposes the recognition of its intrinsic value and a control over drives that only a religion could have exerted. Analogously, the artificial (i.e., one-sided) attribution of kinship relations is supposed to have sprung from imitative animal rituals; only the repetition of concrete acts could provide institutions with continuity. "The group encounters itself, a group experience can be set apart in its purity, precisely because it is not a matter of practical cooperation to achieve goals." Naturally, Gehlen's interest in primordial man was prompted by his increasing disgust at the subjectivism of the late culture of his time.

Like the pagan-immanentist counter-Enlightenment that has come into being since Nietzsche, Gehlen complains about the destruction of the archaic "metaphysics of agreeing and quarreling powers of life," first by monotheism, then by scientific-technological mechanism: "God and the machine have survived the archaic world and now encounter each other alone." A nature deprived of its divine essence corresponds to late-period subjectivity's inner world of mental facts, which is decoupled from actions, and lives on second-hand experiences (for instance, those provided by the mass media). "Now the subjectivization and softening of art, of law, and also of religion necessarily begins. Everywhere 'ideas' shoot up with which we can do nothing but discuss them." Philosophy itself has dissolved into ideas, "ever since Dilthey studied every conceivable standpoint and imagined how it would be if one had one of them and then additionally understood the others." With this compensatory attitude, all institutions are noiselessly eroded from within, and even if Gehlen quite sincerely hopes it will be possible to overcome the scourge of war, he has nothing but scorn for a consumerism organized by a welfare state that has abandoned the goal of self-improvement. True philosophy can survive only if it exercises inner asceticism with regard to discussion, film-incited emotion, and busyness. What he is asking for is "the renunciation of the advantages of public opinion, the constructions of consent, and the facilities of low-voltage substitutes for life." In 1957, *Die Seele im technischen Zeitalter* (*Man in the Age of Technology*) appeared in the series called *Rowohlts deutsche Enzyklopädie*, one of the best book series in the young Federal Republic, to which today there is no equivalent for there is no longer a comparable number of important intellectuals. Perhaps still more important than its social-psychological analyses are its reflections on the anthropology of technology as organ substitution, organ strengthening, and organ relief, as well as the characterization of the modern age by the superstructure of science, technology, and capitalism. Through the use of fossil energies modernity has detached itself from the organic basis of nature—what grows back every year.

In *Zeit-Bilder. Zur Soziologie und Ästhetik der modernen Malerei* (Time-pictures: on the sociology and aesthetics of modern painting, 1960) and *Moral und Hypermoral* (Morality and hypermorality, 1969), Gehlen further articulated his dislike of the present age, and though in his last book he did throw light on the social causes of the phenomenon of irresponsible moralizing since Antisthenes, it does not amount to an ethics of ethics, precisely because for that purpose an ethics is needed. But this cannot be acquired on an anthropological basis alone. Gehlen, furthermore, seems never to have understood that there is a moral duty to question unjust institutions, no matter how right it is that humans need institutions if they do not want to wither away in their respective mindscapes. But to develop a normative theory of institutions, such as was proposed by Hegel, for instance, this philosophical cavalier—who saw the dignity of human beings as consisting in letting themselves be consumed by an institution and who, at the end of his life, sympathized with the Soviet Union—would have needed metaphysical assumptions, which he utterly lacked. Nonetheless, many of his prognoses have been confirmed; the Internet, for instance, has globalized life at second hand, and its usefulness ought not to make us forget that we have to pay a high cultural price for it. The problem with every criticism of the modern culture industry is that to get a hearing it has to depend on the latter and, paradoxically, suffers a defeat if it gains the attention of a culture industry that has grown bored with its own banality. Then comes the time of authors like Gehlen or Gottfried Benn—but it is a short time.

Sometimes one is inclined to lament that Dante did not live in the twentieth century, because the addition of numerous figures from that period to the moral fauna of the *Inferno* would have made it even more abysmal. In particular, one wonders where Carl Schmitt (1888–1985) would have been lodged, since of the three National Socialist thinkers in these two chapters, he was doubtless the most morally repulsive. In making this judgment I am referring not only to his justification of the murders in connection with the so-called Röhm Putsch in 1934, which he offered in the scandalous article "Der Führer schützt das Recht" ("The Führer Protects the Law") published in the *Deutsche Juristen-Zeitung*, which he edited from 1934 to 1936, when he himself was overthrown. His inability to feel remorse after the war, his mawkish self-pity regarding his own fate (he was a potential defendant in the Nuremberg trials until Robert Kempner decided against arraigning him), his complete lack of sympathy for the victims of the Holocaust, and indeed the ostentatious display of his Catholicism, with whose ethical core his original political ideas were in the most blatant contradiction, are enraging. And yet we cannot avoid acknowledging that this jurist was one of the most important political thinkers of the past century,

and in fact the political judgment to be passed on him is so difficult because during the Weimar Republic he was on the right, to
be sure, but did not belong to the NSDAP, which he, like Gehlen
and Heidegger, did not join until early May 1933. In 1932 he was
still arguing, in *Legalität und Legitimität* (*Legality and Legitimacy*), against the prevailing opinion of the constitutionalists
of his time that a legal abolition of the Weimar constitution
in accord with article 76, which both the communists and the
national socialists sought, could not be permissible: the "eternity
clause" in article 79 III of the Basic Law for the Federal Republic of Germany makes this essential insight explicit. Schmitt was
the most brilliant of a group of jurists and philosophers of law
in the Weimar period, many of whom were influenced by Neo-
Kantianism. For instance, Gustav Radbruch (1878–1949), who
became, as a Social Democrat, minister of justice in 1922 and
1923, published a *Rechtsphilosophie* (Philosophy of law, 1932), in
which, making a sharp distinction between "is" and "ought," he
ranked justice, expediency, and legal certainty beneath the idea
of law, as its components. Even if he showed how individualistic,
collectivistic, and transpersonalistic conceptions are reflected in
the very different forms that the various legal institutions such
as property and marriage receive, this relativism did not prevent
him from expressing himself clearly on particular questions—his
arguments against capital punishment, for example, are classic;
for him, it is not based on the right of self-defense. His famous
article "Gesetzliches Unrecht und übergesetzliches Recht" (Stat-
utory injustice and suprastatutory law, 1946) breaks with legal
positivism, which "weakened any ability to defend oneself against
the misuse of National Socialist legislation." According to him,
there are unjust statutes: "Where equality, which constitutes the
heart of justice, is deliberately denied in the passing of positive
statutes," the statute lacks even the character of law. However, in
the case of judges who knew only legal positivism it was hard to
prove intentional perversion of the course of justice, and without that they could not be punished. On the other hand, the
Neo-Kantian Hans Kelsen (1881–1973) remained a pure legal
positivist (even if he introduced an ideal basic norm in order
to ensure the validity of any given legal system). Schmitt's most
important legal opponent, especially in the legal controversy over
the dismissal of the Prussian state government by Papen's federal

government in 1932, was Hermann Heller (1891–1933). In his synthetic *Staatslehre* (Theory of the state, 1934), Heller developed constitutional law into political science and integrated into a descriptive political theory strongly inspired by Hegel the insights into the ontology of law and the state that had been achieved in the meanwhile.

No work of Schmitt's approaches Heller's in categorial abundance; his *Verfassungslehre* (Constitutional theory, 1928) considers only the constitutional law approach to the state and leaves out political sociology. But the combination of doctrinal acuity with a truly comprehensive knowledge of the history of European law makes the book still one of the best introductions to the structural principles of modern constitutions. In particular, the clear distinction between the rule of law and the political components of a constitution is successful; one of the political components, for instance, is the commitment to democracy, which is logically independent of the principle of liberalism, but is naturally compatible with it. What made Schmitt most famous, however, were two brilliantly written essays that showed a competence in intellectual history very unusual in a jurist: "Politische Theologie" ("Political Theology," 1922) and "Der Begriff des Politischen" ("The Concept of the Political," 1927). These were further developed in *Theorie des Partisanen. Zwischenbemerkung zum Begriff des Politischen* (Theory of the partisan: intermediate commentary on the concept of the political, 1963) and *Politische Theologie* II (*Political Theology* II, 1972). *Political Theology* defends the plausible thesis in legal history that central legal concepts are transformations of theological concepts: the metaphysical world-picture of a period is also reflected in its political ideas of legitimacy. Among these legal concepts, Schmitt is particularly fascinated by that of sovereignty. The sovereign is the person who makes the decision whether to declare a state of emergency. This is connected with an interest in political institutions in emergency situations (in 1921 he published his study *Die Diktatur* [Dictatorship]) and in a theory of decision-making. The final ground of law is neither an abstract normative principle, as in Kelsen, nor a complex social process, as in Heller, but rather an ungrounded and ungroundable decision to which an almost theological dignity is ascribed. This seems clearly to resemble Heidegger's "resoluteness"; in the work of Ernst Jünger and in the dialectical theology of these same years we find something similar. Nothing of the Catholic natural law tradition remains in this conception, which presupposes not a Thomistic, but rather a voluntarist conception of God. The 1927 article, expanded into a book in 1932 after a debate with Leo Strauss (1899–1973) and others, sees the specific difference of the political in the distinction between friend and foe. The merely descriptive reference to the persistence of enmities is intellectually honest; no theory of the struggle for power can avoid the category of the enemy. But the problem with Schmitt's essay is that he provides the declaration of enmity with a special moral consecration: it alone leads the way out of the flattening liberal age of neutralizations. In particular, it is intolerable to define the political not, as did the tradition, through the common good, but through demarcation lines drawn both inside and outside, for such a definition naturally renders the idea of a universal state self-contradictory. Schmitt legitimates politicians for whom struggles for power are not a means of solving an objective problem, but rather an end in themselves. We find nothing in him that resembles the desperation in Matthias Claudius's poem "Kriegslied" ("War Song") or in Kant's response to the horror of wars. It would be legitimate to argue, following Schmitt's late writings, that open and clear declarations of enmity can be better than moralistic demonizations of the opponent: international law of war, which in the early modern period imposed restrictions on war, was a progress that was undermined by the figure of the partisan. "Only the repudiation of real enmity opens the way to an absolute enmity's work of annihilation." But Schmitt never laid out a theory of just war, because he limited his concern to *ius in bello*, without facing the issue of *ius ad bellum*; and his fascination with the absolute sovereignty of states, with the state of emergency, with dictatorship, and with war did more than quicken Germany's tumble into totalitarianism and a second world war. His ideas had an "inspiring" effect after 9/11/2001 even in the homeland of classical liberalism.

﷼ 15 ﷼

The Federal Republic's Adaptation
to Western European Normality:
Gadamer, the Two Frankfurt
Schools, and Hans Jonas

The victims of mass murder and the Second World War were the two most appalling consequence of National Socialism. However, in the framework of this history, we must also emphasize that the National Socialists destroyed, along with many other things, the special status of German culture. And they did so on at least three levels. By driving out and murdering its Jewish and critical intelligentsia, Germany inflicted upon itself an intellectual bloodletting from which it has not yet recovered—in part because this group took refuge in Anglo-American countries, and especially the United States, enormously benefiting those countries' scientific development, helping to make their universities the best in the world, and enabling them to continue to attract the best thinkers from Germany. Second, the German policy of occupation had the result that Scandinavia, central Eastern Europe, and the Benelux countries, where German had often been a scientific lingua franca, turned resolutely toward English. Third, however, even after the restoration of constitutional government based on the rule of law in the Federal Republic—an astonishingly rapid and successful process given the enormity of the events—further travel along specifically German philosophical paths was no longer possible. The transition from the first to the second Frankfurt School corresponds philosophically quite exactly to the integration with the West that Germany undertook under Adenauer, finally and, presumably, irrevocably. But even if the philosophy of the Federal Republic never again reached the level that German philosophy had enjoyed since Kant, it nonetheless attracted selective international attention—in contrast to the philosophy of the German Democratic Republic, about which it suffices to say that its *Marxistisch-leninistisches Wörterbuch der Philosophie* (Marxist-Leninist Dictionary of Philosophy) does not include an entry for the word "*Geist.*" And it was not only the word that was lacking in the book. In what follows I can name only those thinkers who won wide international recognition. A few comparatively little-known philosophers of the Federal Republic were objectively no less important, but their achievement cannot be discussed in this introduction.

The 1950s were strongly influenced by Heidegger and his epigones; oohing and aahing about the history of Being conveniently diverted attention from a search for more complex political causes of, or even individual guilt for, National Socialism. It is probably correct that without the integration of former Nazis the reconstruction of the Federal Republic would not have succeeded, but that does not mean that it was a credit to Germans that most of the murderers escaped punishment—Kant would have seen blood guilt coming over the country. Purely philosophically, one of the subsequent costs of Heideggerianism was that the core disciplines of philosophy, epistemology and ethics, lay fallow; only in the 1970s did a rehabilitation of practical philosophy take place. Neo-Kantianism and the Husserlian tradition in phenomenology were largely wiped out, for even the most talented of Heidegger's students had emigrated, and logical positivism continued to develop abroad. Anyone who wants to know why German philosophy still has not recovered, need only look over the list of emigrant philosophers and philosophically-inspired scientists who are mentioned elsewhere in this book, most of whom did not return to Germany: Theodor Adorno, Günther Anders, Hannah Arendt, Rudolf Arnheim, Walter Benjamin, Ernst Bloch, Martin Buber, Karl Bühler, Rudolf Carnap, Ernst Cassirer, Sigmund Freud, Hermann Heller, Max Horkheimer, Hans Jonas, Hans Kelsen, Karl Löwith, Herbert Marcuse, Helmuth Plessner, Karl Popper, Hans Reichenbach, Eugen Rosenstock-Huessy, Edith Stein, and Leo Strauss.

A strong focus of the young Federal Republic was on the historiography of philosophy, to which thinkers attached their own, usually modest systematic ambitions—as in the case of Joachim Ritter (1903–1974), whose liberal-conservative group of students in Münster was influential, especially in jurisprudence. Typically, it was in the old German disciplines of hermeneutics and aesthetics that a new philosophical breakthrough was made. And its maker was, in fact, a student of Heidegger who, partly as a result of his comprehensive studies on Plato and upper-class urbanity, had early developed inner reservations about Heidegger's most disastrous aspects, and who behaved, not heroically, but still decently during the National Socialist period. With *Wahrheit und Methode. Grundzüge einer philosophischen Hermeneutik* (*Truth and Method: Outline of a Philosophical Hermeneutics*, 1960), Hans-Georg Gadamer (1900–2002) published one of the most influential books of the postwar period: the subtlety of his analyses of the ontology of the artwork and his comprehensive reconstruction of the history of the human sciences guaranteed this work the status of a classic. And yet it must be conceded that the book did not do justice to the task, set since Dilthey, of producing a critique of historical reason. Instead, it significantly increased confusion in the human sciences, because it definitively abandoned the question as to how one can distinguish true understanding from false—even though the scientific character of the human sciences depends on a plausible answer to this question. Gadamer inherited from Heidegger his aversion to transcendental reflection on validity, and with Heidegger he sought the final answers in history. All the same, his concept of effective history (*Wirkungsgeschichte*) is more accessible to empirical control than that of the history of Being (it has inspired, among other things, literary studies on reception history). But about the idea of *Wirkungsgeschichte* one must also say that the fact that an interpretation is widely accepted does not suffice to prove its validity.

Gadamer's decision to begin the first part of his hermeneutics with an "excavation of the question of truth in the experience of art" led on the one hand to the book's containing first-rate aesthetic analyses that campaign, against Kantian subjectivization, for an aesthetics of the artwork: in particular, his ontology of play and image is magnificent. On the other hand, the danger of beginning with the artwork lies in the fact that the latter invites the most complex form of understanding, because, among other reasons, it has a very special intrinsic right with regard to the author's intention and thrives on ambivalence. That does not hold for all forms of understanding, and it is a wise maxim that one had better begin with the simpler cases. Instead, in the central second part of his book, Gadamer extends what he has already developed to the human sciences. His true concern is to break out of the aporias of historicism in which hermeneutics had become completely entangled since Dilthey. By carefully tracing the historical genesis of historicism, Gadamer tries to relativize the latter itself; but genesis and validity must always be kept separate, even in the case of a movement that constantly confuses the two. However, Gadamer's enduring achievement is to have challenged the historicist perspective that would like to learn only *about* the *interpretandum*, by arguing that understanding is possible only when we learn *from* the *interpretandum*, when we assume that, in principle, truth is to be found in it, and ask questions about the subject matter itself to which it may be able to provide answers. "It is undoubtedly true that, compared with the genuine hermeneutical experience that understands the meaning of the text, reconstructing what the author really had in mind is a limited undertaking. Historicism tempts us to regard such reduction as a scientific virtue."

One of the positive consequences of this change in perspective was that after Gadamer historians of philosophy read the classics again with the desire to learn from their arguments rather than simply to report on them. The little book you are now reading would not be conceivable without Gadamer. No less fruitful are his reflections on what distinguishes a true conversation from deficient forms, such as pedagogical and therapeutic conversations. And yet we must lament the fact that Gadamer at the same time gave up the intentionalist standards of historical understanding that since the nineteenth century had won worldwide recognition for the German human sciences. It is completely legitimate, and often philosophically fruitful, to sound out the unintended consequences of an idea, but one must be aware of the point at which one transcends the *mens auctoris*, the authorial intention. To do that, one needs method; but the "and" in Gadamer's title means "instead of": truth is supposed to occur without method. In this, Gadamer follows Heidegger, whom he wrongly believes to have phenomenologically overcome historicism; indeed, the whole deconstructivist undermining of the human sciences in recent decades is ultimately inspired by Gadamer, according to whom "one understands *differently, if one understands at all.*" The protest made by the important Italian private law scholar and historian of law Emilio Betti (1890–1968) in his book *Die Hermeneutik als allgemeine Methodik der Geisteswissenschaften* (*Hermeneutics as a General Methodology of the Human Sciences*, 1962) was absolutely legitimate—the approach of the historian of law is distinct from that of the dogmatic jurist, even if Gadamer assimilates the two because for him any understanding is an "application" of what is understood. Nonetheless, we can compare Gadamer's famous concept of the "anticipation of completeness" (*Vorgriff der Vollkommenheit*) with Donald Davidson's "principle of charity," the principle of sympathetic interpretation that on transcendental grounds attributes to the *interpretandum* as much truth and consistency as it can. In addition, Gadamer's defense of prejudices as conditions of understanding is not erroneous—every act of understanding also assumes principles that are not themselves subjected to criticism; and, similarly, his rehabilitation of authority and tradition is in itself not hostile to reason because he considers tradition to be "not the defense of the conventional and time-honored, but rather the ongoing shaping of ethical-social life."

The third and last part of the work offers—apparently in the wake of the late Heidegger, against whom, however, the grandeur of ancient *theoria* is defended—a philosophy of language that is supposed to prove the universality of hermeneutics, because "*Being that can be understood is language.*" This thesis cannot be correct as it stands. First of all, nonlinguistic things, such as a sculpture, can be understood (in the narrower sense of the word); and second, everything may be capable of being articulated in language, but it does not thereby *become* language: physicists use language, but unlike linguists they do not deal with it. Nevertheless, this part of the book remains readable not only because of its numerous insights into linguistic anthropology, its defense of the irreducibility of language (which is never identified with a specific language), and its analysis of the concept-construction that takes place in it. Beyond those achievements, Gadamer seeks to construct an equivalent of first philosophy, a logic in Hegel's or Husserl's sense, and in fact echoes of the Christian theology of the *logos* play a role in his long investigations of the history of concepts. As he gropes his way into the metaphysical tradition, Gadamer leaves his teacher far behind him, even if his polemic against Hegel's philosophy of reflection deprives him of all argumentative means for constructing a plausible new first philosophy.

It is hardly surprising that the horror of two world wars and of totalitarianism inspired four German Jews to make a radical break with the progress-oriented philosophy of history that emerged in the eighteenth century. The theses put forward by Walter Benjamin (1892–1940) in his essay "Über den Begriff der Geschichte " ("On the Concept of History"), written shortly before he committed suicide as he was fleeing France, combine messianic hopes with a rejection of the Marxist belief in the inexorability of progress (on the grounds that this belief forgot about the victims of history). "The current amazement that the things we are experiencing are 'still' possible in the twentieth century is *not* philosophical. This amazement is not the beginning of knowledge—unless it is the knowledge that the view of history which gives rise to it is untenable." Compared with this linguistically prodigious and existentially shattering text, Karl Löwith's *Meaning in History* (1949) seems professorial, but it is in fact similar in character because it offers a disillusioned history of the philosophy of history that, with a brilliant accordance of form and content, moves chronologically backwards, from Jacob Burckhardt's (1818–1897) skeptical *Weltgeschichtliche Betrachtungen* (*Reflections on History*, 1905) to the theology of history of the Bible, in whose transfer to immanent temporal schemas Löwith saw the origin of the belief in progress. (Löwith returned to Germany in 1952—Gadamer brought him to Heidelberg—so that his work, although written in English during his exile in the United States, belongs to German philosophy.)

The most important work by this group is certainly Max Horkheimer (1895–1973) and Theodor Adorno's (1903–1969) *Dialektik der Aufklärung* (*Dialectic of Enlightenment*, 1947). Since 1931 Horkheimer had led the Institute for Social Research, founded in 1923 at the University of Frankfurt. During the National Socialist period it moved first to Geneva, then to New York, and finally returned to Frankfurt in 1951. In his inaugural lecture, " Die gegenwärtige Lage der Sozialphilosophie und die Aufgaben eines Instituts für Sozialforschung" (*The Present Situation of Social Philosophy and the Tasks of an Institute for Social Research*), Horkheimer still demanded a social philosophy inspired by Marxism, that instead of reconciling itself to the injustice of history, as Hegel had done, was to devote itself to eliminating concrete suffering through interdisciplinary cooperation with the empirical sciences. The central work of the first Frankfurt School, however, written "amid the present collapse of bourgeois civilization," is a profoundly pessimistic work. Like Horkheimer's *The Eclipse of Reason*, which appeared at the same time and contrasted melancholically the irretrievably lost belief in an objective reason from Plato to Hegel, the *Dialectic of Enlightenment* describes the triumph of an abbreviated concept of reason, according to which it essentially serves self-preservation, but in the process of conquering external nature also mutilates inner nature. Thus crucial aspects of the present are adequately grasped, but the diagnosis suffers from three defects. First, Horkheimer and Adorno use an ingenious interpretation of Homer's *Odyssey* to shift the fall into sin—even more radically than did Heidegger, who saw the process of decline as beginning with Plato—to the beginning of Western culture; in fact, myth is supposed to be already a product of the Enlightenment, which made its conversion into myth easier: "Enlightenment is mythic fear turned radical." This does not account for the specifics of the industrial age, and the fact that the latter appears as the logical endpoint of a development that began very early does not make the criticism any more promising. Second, we can say analogously that the brilliant analysis of the culture industry as mass deception, which is based on an aristocratic conception of art, is disturbing in the context of the book, because the culture industry's banality is of an entirely different order than the Nazis' radical evil. Both authors display a striking antipathy toward the United States, which was the only place where they could survive. Their inability to relate their work to empirically oriented American sociology or economics convinced them of their rootedness in the German cultural milieu and explains their rapid return to Germany after the war. Third, their criticism lacks any clear normative foundation, because they reject Kantian ethics, which they see as a form of human self-repression and compare somehow to de Sade's ideas. In fact, even self-contradiction is accepted because it corresponds to the objective contradiction of the society. Finally, their negative philosophy of history destroys the futuristic form of justification peculiar to Marxism. This mixture of undeniable moral sensitivity with a total absence of ethical-logical foundation underlies the expressive revolution that in 1968 gripped Germany more powerfully than it did other Western states, because Germany had to confront its atrocious past—in the fifth such revolution, after the Reformation, *Sturm und Drang*, Romanticism, and the crisis of classical modernity, though it was far less productive culturally than these predecessors. Perhaps one of the reasons for that was the thoroughgoing loss of reality exuded by, for example, *Eros and Civilization* (1955), a work by another Critical Theorist, Herbert Marcuse. In opposition to Freud, it sets its hopes on a broad satisfaction of needs, including sexual needs, while refusing to pay the necessary price in individual and social control.

As an aesthetician, Adorno still remains outstanding, especially since as a composer himself, he was able to penetrate deeply into the essence of modern music—it was not for nothing that he was Thomas Mann's advisor when the latter was writing *Doctor Faustus*. But his one-sided preference for Schoenberg over Stravinsky in his *Philosophie der neuen Musik* (*The Philosophy of New Music*, 1947) is elitist, and in fact elitist in a sense in which the great artists of the past were not, for they knew that they could not do without a general audience. With twelve-tone music the question arises, is it not, despite the brilliance of its creators, a dead-end? It led to an irreparable estrangement of serious music from a broad audience, and that had as its inevitable consequence an increasing trivialization of popular music. The posthumous and unfinished *Ästhetische Theorie* (*Aesthetic Theory*, 1970) is Adorno's best book, because it instantiates, in its mannered but highly impressive prose, precisely the concept of art that it defends—namely, that great art expresses dissonance and not harmony. "Disintegration is the truth of integral art." Here Adorno radically contradicts Hegel, who nonetheless remains a model insofar as Adorno clings to the priority of the artwork over production and reception. Adorno maintains that the work of art has a twofold nature—on the one hand it is autonomous, on the other it is part of the social world. Unlike Hegel, Adorno does not propose a systematization of the arts or any philosophy of history of the development of art; he remains focused on modernity. But he conceptualizes the latter, while at the same time adapting himself to it mimetically. Unlike Benjamin, who in "Das Kunstwerk im Zeitalter seiner technischen Reproduzierbarkeit" ("The Work of Art in the Age of Mechanical Reproduction," 1936) set high hopes on the new mass media such as film and photography, and sought to answer the aestheticization of politics in fascism with a politicization of aesthetics, Adorno is skeptical with regard to the new developments and rejects a political instrumentalization of art. His *Negative Dialektik* (*Negative Dialectics*, 1966), conceived as his theoretical magnum opus, does not in the least do justice to the questions it broaches, because it denies, by introducing in direct opposition to Hegel the slogan of the nonidentical, any possibility of a conceptual categorization of reality and *a fortiori* any reconciliation with it, which Adorno grotesquely compares to the music the SS used to drown out the cries of their victims. The reference to the universal context of delusion (apparently a functional equivalent of Heidegger's oblivion of Being) helps one live with one's own contradictions; for Adorno himself inevitably uses concepts. Even if it solves none of the world's problems, and in fact looks with contempt on those who try to alleviate them, Adorno's suffering from the atrocities of the twentieth century is genuine. This makes his book valuable and at the same time more dangerous: anyone who at the beginning of his career as a thinker falls under the spell of this philosophical expressionist dance will find it hard ever to learn to analyze a problem clearly (for example, the problem of freedom, around which Adorno aporetically circles).

The first Critical Theory had run out of steam because it had no normative foundation; providing one became the main concern of Jürgen Habermas (born 1929). The collaboration of his Frankfurt colleague Karl-Otto Apel (born 1922), who worked out discourse ethics with Habermas, was essential—and thus the second Frankfurt School also came to be represented by a pair of thinkers. Apel wrote only a few philosophical monographs (one of which was on the distinction between the explanatory natural sciences and the understanding human sciences); instead he wrote, like most of the analytic philosophers, many articles, including a few that became classics (the first and most important collection of these is *Transformation der Philosophie* [*Towards a*

Transformation of Philosophy, 1973]). Still more impressive than his constructive ideas is his performance as a critic of contemporary philosophy, which rests on his exceptional sense for performative inconsistencies, that is, for contradictions between what one says and what one thereby presupposes, contradictions such as those that characterize both Heidegger's and Wittgenstein's philosophies alike. In the masterly article "Das Apriori der Kommunikationsgemeinschaft und die Grundlagen der Ethik" (The *a priori* of the communication community and the foundations of ethics), Apel made the crucial point that the two diametrically opposed mainstreams in contemporary philosophy, scientistic Logical Positivism and Existentialism, were in fact complementary, because both limited the concept of reason to technological-scientific reason and attribute merely a subjective status to values (in contrast to the Eastern European Marxists' untenable system of integration). Ethics could now be understood again as rational if one grounded it transcendentally, that is, showed that it is a presupposition of logic and argumentation. But in his view, this is an ultimate grounding that, unlike a grounding that is dependent on arbitrary premises, cannot be further questioned. According to Apel, the fundamental ethical norm results when one conceives argumentation as an intersubjective process taking place in speech acts: argumentation thus considered presupposes both a real and an ideal communication community, and that produces both the basic duties to ensure the survival of the human species and to produce the ideal communication community within it. The relationship of tension between the two communities constitutes human history, in which Apel sees, in later works, the realization of a phylogenesis of moral consciousness that is analogous to the ontogenetic logic of development discovered by Jean Piaget. Apel's claim to have found an ultimate ground triggered a great deal of irritation (even Habermas rejected this claim), but Apel's methodologically most important article, "Das Problem der philosophischen Letztbegründung im Lichte einer transzendentalen Sprachpragmatik" ("The Problem of Philosophical Foundations in Light of a Transcendental Pragmatics of Language," 1976), remains one of the clearest texts on this fateful philosophical question, which requires a positive answer if there is to be any chance of an alternative to relativism (at least so long as one is not willing to be content with unmediated institutions).

Apel acknowledges that ultimately grounded propositions cannot be proven without being already presupposed; but this must be distinguished from a vicious circle because the negation of these propositions also presupposes them. Anyone who denies truth inevitably makes a truth claim, but someone who contests Euclid's parallel postulate does not presuppose it.

However, Apel's program of transforming Kant's transcendental philosophy on the basis of a theory of intersubjectivity influenced by the American pragmatism of Charles Sanders Peirce is laid out only in more and more facets; a systematic elaboration is lacking. This has to do with the fact that discourse ethics is reduced to the command to seek a consensus; it does not want to anticipate the concrete results of the discourse. On the one hand, it is certainly right to leave neighborhood or marriage conflicts to those concerned. On the other, it is illusory to think that moral conflicts can be resolved simply by having the parties talk to one another: it is impossible to see how a consensus could ever be achieved, for example in questions regarding the distribution of resources, without substantive principles such as promoting the greatest happiness of the greatest number or the performance principle. Discourse ethicists are not wrong in saying that such principles must also prove their worth in dialogue—and this holds no less for scientific ideas. But just as someone who only organizes conferences for mathematicians does not make any mathematical achievement, so even with the discourse principle no concrete ethical insight is gained (other than the correct but not original insight that consensus is usually better than violence). Discourse ethics likes to appeal to Kant's universalist formalism, but it is wrong to do so. Kant's formalism is not proceduralist, and developed (even if perhaps with subreptions) the categorical imperative into a system of natural law and virtues. There is nothing approaching an equivalent of this in discourse ethics, and therefore it encourages, against its own intentions, the kind of person who justifies his moral decisions not on objective criteria, but on his assumptions as to what the majority would probably decide, and no longer sees this as opportunism precisely because consensus is the ultimate criterion of truth. One can reasonably doubt whether a democracy dominated by such people will be able to cope with the enormous objective challenges of the coming decades. Within the history of consciousness, discourse ethics is best suited to an age that sees the idea of an objective order of values as an affront to its own emotional commitment to freedom and at the same time, after the experience of National Socialism, fears ethical nihilism. People want to believe in the possibility of a rational ethics, so that it is possible to keep talking, but such an ethics must not come with strict obligations. It is improbable that an ethics without connection to the unconditional could ever mobilize the kind of moral resources that were liberated by Kant's ethics of autonomy or, earlier, by religions.

The reference to the "real communication community" leads to a legitimation of democracy, which postwar Germany desperately needed. Therein lies an important advance beyond Kant: the politically just is supposed to be communicated in public discourses. With its connection to democratic consensus-building, the new conception of legitimacy also moves a step beyond legal positivism. But the help against the abuse of majority decisions that is supposed to lie in the appeal to the ideal communication community is empty so long as the criteria according to which the latter makes decisions remain unknown. But if they are presented, then the individual can also decide on his own responsibility what is right, after he has ascertained the legitimate needs of others. The communicability of one's own ideas is a necessary, not a sufficient condition of morality; in addition, it is always the individual who must determine whether a consensus was truly achieved and whether this consensus could stand its ground before the ideal community. In fact, the philosophy-of-history thesis according to which a paradigm of intersubjectivity has now superceded the paradigm of objectivity of Antiquity and the Middle Ages, as well as the post-Descartes paradigm of subjectivity is both illuminating and misleading. The increasing significance of the philosophy of language and social philosophy in the twentieth century is unmistakable, and it is associated with a development of democracy, the welfare state, and international integration that must be positively valued. But intersubjectivity is more than subjectivity only when it preserves the latter within itself. Thus for example a speech act theory without an intentionalist theory of meaning is devious, because sound waves become speech only when interpreted by speakers and listeners. It counts in John Searle's favor that after having done important work on speech acts, he worked out a theory of intentionality that is strikingly similar to Husserl's, whereas discourse ethics does not come up to the level of Husserl's outstanding work of distinction-making, because the three-paradigms doctrine allegedly allows it to treat shabbily the philosophy of mind (including the mind-body problem) and ontology. A consciousness of having made progress becomes counterproductive if it invites us to underestimate the achievements of the past.

If we compare Apel with Habermas, the first thing we notice is that Habermas published many more books. Hardly any other intellectual in the Federal Republic has published so much. In fact, in the history of German culture there are few public intellectuals who have shaped social debate for as many decades, and throughout the world, as has the Kyoto Prize winner Habermas. He is also a master of journalistic expression, as witnessed by his pointed summary of conclusions drawn by others, their rapid application to current problems, compromises between widespread but also inherently incompatible positions in public opinion, and at the same time a sharp distinction between allies and opponents. On the one hand, Habermas has lent eloquent expression to the feeling of the time, and on the other he has both studied (since *Strukturwandel der Öffentlichkeit* [The Structural Transformation of the Public Sphere, 1962]) and forcefully promoted the democratization of the German spirit. His sense of mission in this regard is explained in part by the year of his birth, 1929; that cohort was particularly important for the intellectuals of the Federal Republic because of the group that still had very consciously experienced National Socialism, it was the first that was no longer drafted: it spent no time fighting on the front lines nor did it have experience of the prisoner of war camps that often followed on combat, and thus it had little reason to critically examine or repress its own role. On the other hand, Habermas stood for the integration of leftists into German scholarly institutions, where they remained marginalized before 1968—an injustice that had to be fought, but which led to a politicization of the universities that was not good for their scientific quality. Early on, Habermas rejected the irrational aspect of the student revolution of 1968, which he at the same time inspired, and his political involvements, most recently on behalf of the process of unifying Europe, are almost always intelligent and responsible. However, in the so-called "historians' quarrel" of 1986–87 he failed, out of the respectable motive of maintaining the uniqueness of the German crimes, to differentiate sufficiently between the very different positions of his opponents. What distinguishes Habermas from Apel is his enormous capacity for work, which he retained even into old age and his immense knowledge of the various social sciences, from psychology to political science (not including economics, however). He offered a new normative foundation for these sciences, which since Émile Durkheim, Max Weber, and Vilfredo Pareto had set out on the path toward becoming value-free. This explains the worldwide success of his work—in the sociologists' positivism dispute of 1961 between Adorno and Popper, Habermas supported Adorno.

And yet, despite our admiration for Habermas, the limits of his achievement cannot be overlooked. In the central philosophical disciplines of epistemology and ethics, Apel is much more precise technically than Habermas, for the clarity of the latter's arguments is more often obscured than increased by the abundance of his sociological knowledge. Even if we compare Habermas with the first Frankfurt School, despite all the undeniable progress made, we can also draw up a list of losses. Adorno's aesthetic sensitivity is absent in Habermas; despite his battle against it, Adorno grudgingly acknowledged the complexity of the theoretical foundations of the great systems of objective idealism, whereas Habermas considers them refuted by a simple reference to the views that social scientists now hold; and, finally, the slender normative basis of discourse ethics no longer allows any criticism of the vulgar aspects of late modernity that Horkheimer and Adorno unsparingly analyzed—relying not so much on the conceptual tools of Critical Theory as on the upper bourgeois education that both of them had still enjoyed. If we compare Habermas with the great German philosophers of the past, we see that the individual sciences with which he is familiar include neither mathematics, which Frege and Husserl possessed, nor the natural sciences of physics and biology that informed Logical Positivism and Hans Jonas, nor the human sciences with classical philology as their center that were cultivated in German idealism up to Gadamer, but rather only the social sciences. This has inevitable consequences for the concept of philosophy, as demonstrated, for example, by his rejection of a sharp distinction between *a priori* and *a posteriori*, and in his sweeping defensiveness with regard to metaphysics—a discipline that is, however, now being seriously pursued again in analytic philosophy.

Habermas did his philosophical apprenticeship in the public eye; a fact that makes it easy to discover numerous changes in his positions, from those rooted in Marxism and Critical Theory—for example in *Erkenntnis und Interesse* (*Knowledge and Human Interests*, 1968), which does not do justice to the grandeur of purely theoretical contemplation, in whose preservation we have a legitimate interest—through his rejection of the consensus theory of truth, to his coming to terms with religion, whose positive social significance he increasingly recognizes, even if, unlike Kant and German idealism, he no longer has the intellectual resources to appropriate its content in a philosophical way (beyond noting its function as an antidote to naturalism, which he has always rejected.) His public debate on January 19, 2004 with Joseph Cardinal Ratzinger (whose election a year later as the first German pope since the Middle Ages gave Germans the feeling of having returned to the center of world attention) is an outstanding example of Habermas's curiosity and readiness to engage in conversation.

Habermas's most important work is *Theorie des kommunikativen Handelns* (*The Theory of Communicative Action*, 1981), of which I can only provide a succinct summary. In it he offers a comprehensive history of theoretical sociology and his own theory of society, developed in reflections inserted between the historical chapters—though they are much longer than the famed "intermediate reflection" (*Zwischenbetrachtung*) in Max Weber's posthumous *Gesammelte Aufsätze zur Religionssoziologie* (*Collected Essays in the Sociology of Religion*, 1920). Habermas seeks to solve two problems in sociology: on the one hand, he is concerned with the concept of rationality, which is not only the object of important theories of social development, but is also presupposed by sociologists on the methodological and meta-theoretical levels. On the other hand, he seeks to mediate between the two most important sociological approaches, that of theory of action and that of systems theory; the latter is based on the unintended consequences of actions that merge, for example in the market, in a system with its own logic. (However, Habermas ignores the

phenomenon of collective decision-making in corporate groups.)
His most important sources of inspiration are Durkheim, Weber,
Mead, Western Marxism from Lukács to Horkheimer/Adorno,
and Talcott Parsons (his debate with the latter is in many respects
a surrogate for the criticism of Habermas's rival, the defender of
systems theory, Niklas Luhmann [1927–1998]). According to
Habermas, the ultimate, indeed the only source of validity is the
communicative action that takes place in the life-world, which he
opposes to the construction of systems like the capitalist economy and bureaucratic administration. Communicative action is
sharply distinguished from strategic action, but Habermas does
justice neither to the fact that in the life-world these two forms
of behavior are interwoven (usually we communicate in order to
achieve goals), nor, unlike Apel, to the fact that there are situations in which there is no moral alternative to strategic action.
Habermas's complex attitude toward modernity insists that
modernity engages in a colonialization of the life-world through
the systems, and also that it both obliges the validity claims
implicit in communicative action to give reasons for the actions
and differentiates their original, religiously grounded unity. He
sees the colonization as negative, the giving of grounds, and the
differentiation as positive.

Habermas recognizes four validity claims inherent in every
speech act: comprehensibility, truth, truthfulness, and normative
rightness. In his main work he concentrates, taking his inspiration from Bühler, on the last three, which he connects with Karl
Popper's three worlds. Popper, after the worlds of the physical
and the mental, combines in his third world Frege's third realm
with Hegel's objective spirit, that is, something ideal with something real. Habermas follows Popper in that he does not conceive
the normative as a sphere of its own, and in consequence has to
normatively load the social world. Naturally, Habermas concedes
that an objectivizing approach to the social world is possible, but
this concession endangers the parallel he draws between his validity claims and Popper's three worlds. In addition, he does not recognize that normativity is also conceivable in a lonely rational
being's relation to itself (indeed, the nature of intentions alone
distinguishes a pretended from a real communicative purpose).
According to Habermas, the roots of modern science, art, and
morality lie in the three validity claims. An alignment of art and

truthfulness is implausible—the specifically aesthetic element has much more to do with the indirectness of the communication and, for instance, the relation between sound and meaning, the organic coherence of the fictive world, etc. No less unsatisfactory is the fact that Habermas connects rationality with a process of giving reasons that must eventually come to an end. Since he rejects both intuitionism and ultimate grounding, one has to ask what distinguishes a valid grounding from an invalid one—because some kind of reasons can be adduced for everything, and nothing guarantees that the justifications given by different persons will converge. (Naturally, unconscious background assumptions and social pressure work in this direction, but they are not free of domination, as ideal discourse presupposes they are.) In his metaethics, Habermas ranks values under norms, without adequately criticizing the opposite position, for instance, Scheler's; the status of values, which are supposed to be neither private nor as intersubjective as norms, remains unclear. Though Habermas acknowledges that the mythical experience of a unity of all validity claims was one of the most important sources of solidarity, he rejects as untimely attempts to derive theoretical validity claims from practical ones (as they are found even and especially in Kant, who interprets the world as the site of the realization of the moral law), while at the same time he also rejects, against Weber, a polytheism of values. To that extent, we cannot be surprised that the critical power of the new Critical Theory is quite modest: in the end, Habermas rightly warns against an excessive juridification of school and family, such as would lead to system-rationality undermining the life-world, but he offers nothing remotely like a comprehensive theory of the pathologies of late modernity, such as the destruction of capitalism by the encroachment of the principle of self-interest in the political system, which should instead limit capitalism. He lacks the relevant material principles to develop such a theory. His substitute criterion, the playing-out of the life-world, is not a functional equivalent of the old natural law, first because the expression "life-world" cannot be sharply distinguished from "system" (what is part of the system today is already part of the life-world tomorrow), and second because "life-world" is used homonymically: on the one hand as a sphere of reaching agreement, and on the other as a way of life that still has not been undermined by modern system-rationality.

Traditional wars are part of the life-world in the second sense, but not in the first. To be sure, Habermas understands the discontent of many people in the late modern age, who would like to have all the commodities that modern capitalism produces, and are at the same time becoming aware of the ever-greater cultural price that has to be paid for them. But nowhere do we find an injunction to choose between keeping intact certain traditions and personal values and the economic growth with redistributions that, according to Habermas, provides the social legitimacy on which late capitalism depends. Certainly we find in *The Theory of Communicative Action* a few references to social movements dedicated to environmental questions, but there is no mention of the insights of the Club of Rome, which have shaped modern environmental consciousness since 1972. It would seem that Habermas has neither a concept of intergenerational justice nor a philosophy of nature.

Two years before Habermas's *Theory of Communicative Action* came out in German, , however, in 1979, one of the most important books on modern environmental philosophy appeared: Hans Jonas's *Das Prinzip Verantwortung* (*The Imperative of Responsibility*). Jonas was almost a generation older than Habermas, but his work is in many respects more timely, because with this book he conceptualized the crucial problem of the twenty-first century. It is noteworthy that it finally won for Jonas, in the last quarter-century of his life, general recognition and even reverence. So far as I know, he is the only German philosopher of the twentieth century to whom a statue has been erected (in the city where he was born, Mönchengladbach). Paradoxically, part of the reason for the book's success was the archaic German in which it was written and which goes so well with its content. Jonas left Germany in 1933 with the declared intention of returning to Germany only as a soldier in an opposing army. In the years that followed he wrote mainly in English; which meant that he missed out on much of the development of the German language, and this did him more good than harm. But despite four decades spent in Palestine, Canada, and the United States, Jonas still needed much more time in order to write good English than he needed to write good German, and therefore he decided, in view of his advanced age, and even though he was not a remigrant, to return to his mother tongue. This was the right decision, because his thought was more essentially related to the German moral sensibility than to that of the United States, a country which because of its shorter history and more limited possibilities of comparison has a harder time seeing the ambivalence of modernity. The book rapidly became widely read in Germany, and it contributed to the articulation of that moral sensibility in wide sections of the population, so that today Germany is the most environmentally conscious industrial country. *The Imperative of Responsibility* was so successful because it deals with a contemporary issue—but on a level that can be achieved only by someone who has been reflecting for decades on the corresponding foundational questions. In fact, the success of this late book drew attention to Jonas's main work, which had hardly been noticed when it came out, namely *The Phenomenon of Life* (1966). This book contains one of the most important philosophies of biology. Jonas had begun his career as a historian of philosophy and religion, illuminating the history of late Antique gnosis by using his teacher Heidegger's categories to interpret it. But he soon realized that this was possible only because Heidegger's own approach sprang from an analogous historical situation—and for that very reason was not universally valid. This allowed him to move beyond Heidegger's historicism, and instead of focusing on the philosophy of history of the images of nature, to work again directly on the philosophy of nature. Plessner had already recognized that life has a more general structure than Heidegger's *Sorge* (care); but Jonas conceives the organic form of Dasein on the basis of metabolism rather than demarcation. For Jonas, the *Sorge* (of humans) is only a special case of a far more general structure, the organism's need to take in food. By constantly exchanging matter, the organism is independent of concrete matter (the cells we have now are not the same as those we had twenty years ago) and this makes it autonomous. But at the same time, the organism has to appropriate new matter by food intake; if it fails to do so, it dies. Jonas regards life as more than a regional ontological problem because the peculiar connection between matter and consciousness in life leads at the same time to a rejection of Cartesian dualism: life's central position between the inorganic world and the spirit forces us to correct the prejudices of both materialism and idealism. Thus Jonas argues for a realistic interpretation of ends in nature, and emphasizes that the apparent triumph of materialism in the theory of evolution in fact restores to life a dignity of which Christian Cartesianism had deprived it: "Thus after the contraction brought about by Christian transcendentalism and Cartesian dualism, the province of the 'soul,' . . . extended again . . . from man over the kingdom of life." Jonas rightly maintains that Darwinism is compatible with a hierarchy of forms of life, which he explores in his analyses of the difference between plants and animals (whose essential characteristics—the ability to move, perception, and feeling—are derived from heterotrophy) and in his phenomenological studies of individual sense organs. Like Aristotle and Hegel, Jonas discerns a continuity between the philosophy of life and the philosophy of the spirit, but he also discerns specific characteristics of human beings, such as the ability to paint pictures—and this sensomotor achievement also underlies creations that transcend mimetic representation.

Jonas's ethical work adopts a similarly ambivalent position with regard to Heidegger. The subtitle of *The Imperative of Responsibility*, "In Search of Ethics for the Technological Age," already indicates a break with Heidegger's rejection of a normative ethics. Contrary to what one might think, Jonas in fact follows Kant's central insights: according to both philosophers, the ethical law is irreducible to self-interest. In particular, Jonas recognizes that in the case of intergenerational obligations, reciprocity ceases to apply; indeed, that the current form of democracy does not provide for any representation of future generations. At the same time, Jonas rejects Kant's formalism (though he underestimates the scope of the formulation of the categorical imperative that speaks of ends in themselves), and he finds the material content in the ends that he sees realized in nature, in both organs and artifacts. Certainly, not every end is a good, but the ability to have ends is undeniably a good in itself: for even someone who wants to free himself from ends must at least set this end for himself. Jonas seems to defend the idea that it is not only humans that have intrinsic value, even if he clearly ranks their worth above that of other organisms—unlike radical ecologists who are less alarmed than Jonas at the prospect of humanity's self-destruction. Heidegger's influence is discernible not only in the first chapter on the changed essence of human action, but also and precisely in the phenomenology of responsibility, which Jonas sees as defined by totality, continuity, and futurity. The last two determinations have to do with temporality, but here it is not a question of rushing ahead toward death, but rather of care for the lives of children and of future generations. Jonas's God is a God of life, not of death, but life is essentially mortal because it is temporal—and only as such is it an object of responsibility. "The ontology has changed. Ours is not that of eternity, but of time. . . . It is in this context that responsibility can become dominant in morality." The most time-bound element in *The Imperative of Responsibility* is surely the conjecture that the way toward the necessary limitation of consumption might be shown by the Soviet Union, rather than by the capitalistic and democratic West; but since Jonas at the same time subjected the utopianism in Ernst Bloch's (1885–1977) *Das Prinzip Hoffnung* (*The Principle of Hope*, 1954–1959) to a brilliant critique, this apparent sympathy for communism on the part of a values conservative must have been surprising, but at the same time fascinating as the sign of a free spirit. Nonetheless, his failure to furnish economic and also concrete observations from the point of view of a philosophy of the state is a defect that might well mislead to the dangerous conclusion that the problem of the environment requires the abandonment of the democratic constitutional state. Jonas was no longer able to work out a concrete moral policy in response to the ecological challenge. This makes all the more noteworthy his essays on medical ethics in *Technik, Medizin, und Ethik* (Technology, medicine, and ethics, 1985), a book born of concern that not only the existence, but also the essence of human beings might be endangered by modern technology: a conception that he shares with Günther Anders's (1902–1992) *Die Antiquiertheit des Menschen* (The antiquatedness of humankind, 1956 and 1980). Especially classical are Jonas's essays opposing cloning and the brain-death criterion recognized in the United States since 1968.

The fact that a student of Heidegger's like Jonas, without really wanting to, had returned to German idealism's natural philosophy and Kant's ethics proves that the central ideas of classical German philosophy can be relevantly pursued further even after almost two hundred years of philosophical development. But as Jonas's death in New Rochelle as an American citizen makes plain, the most important thinking in the German language is no longer taking place in Germany. A person looking for justice in history might see in this a punishment for the near total obliteration of European Jewry, which since Mendelssohn had made such an essential contribution to the rise of German culture.

ᴥ 16 ᴥ

Why We Cannot Assume
That There Will Continue to
Be a German Philosophy

Anyone who is asked today which contemporary German philosophers are internationally known will react mainly with embarrassment—because there are no clear candidates under the age of eighty. This has to do both with philosophy's present situation in the world and with specific characteristics of German culture. To begin with the former, we can say that there is a striking decline of great names worldwide. This can be explained on three levels that reinforce each other.

On the level of production, there is a distinct decline in the number of minds with the complex weave of intellectual and stylistic qualities and character traits that distinguished past masters. This is in part due to the specialization required by the division of labor in the knowledge industry, which is almost lethal for the very idea of philosophy. The drying up of religious motivation is also a factor, for it has deprived philosophy of an essential source of strength—or, if one prefers, of a possible enemy whose opposition might prove invigorating. The increasing embarrassment of the arts is hardly a source of inspiration. And the defensive reaction against political ideas that represent more than the management of the status quo has more or less eliminated the need for public intellectuals.

On the level of distribution, the excess of information is the crucial problem. There are many too many intellectuals. It is hopeless even to try to keep track of all of them; and anyone who wants to have a career in science or scholarship is well-advised to quickly latch onto a network whose members mutually cite each other, invite each other to conferences, and organize university appointments for each other, even if that inevitably means that they have less time to read the classics and pursue their ideas further. One problem of the networker is that academic influence based on this kind of mutuality ends for the most part when one retires, and always with one's death. But given the triumph of small ambitions over great ones that characterizes this period, that is to be gotten over or at least repressed.

Finally, on the level of reception, not only the aristocracy but also the educated middle class that for centuries honored important intellectual achievements with sincere admiration have largely melted away. The modern inability to experience moral and intellectual superiority as uplifting, or even to recognize it, is gaining ground: the wish to interact only on an equal footing has even become the strongest argument for atheism.

The new media do not require the concentration demanded by a book like Leibniz's *Theodicy*, and there are now all too few princesses available to be its potential readers. Indeed, we witness the dispersal of even the Enlightenment's hope that philosophers would produce light and unity where religions had left behind only darkness and distortion. Discord between philosophical schools is far greater than it ever was between religions, whose representatives never, so far as I know, considered themselves zombies, that is, creatures without an interior life. However, everything is possible in philosophy today, and in fact the laws of the media world encourage people to draw attention to themselves by proposing theses that are as jarring as possible. The contrast between popular philosophy and serious academic philosophy is an old one, but today popular philosophers have access to television and to the pages of magazines and newspapers, and thus to a broader audience. At the same time, the formation of a popular philosophy is a necessary consequence of the fact that academic philosophy has become increasingly technical. This process, which was favored by analytic philosophy, was in part necessary. No one will fail to appreciate the gain in precision in the analysis of arguments that we owe to the transformation of logic since Frege. But it is just as true that this increased precision is by no means always useful. Instead, it is often superfluous and thus also harmful, because the time spent on its study diverts attention from more important philosophical problems. As a result, insofar as we consider a holistic theory of knowledge correct, we lack the genuine grounding that consists in the internal connection of the various philosophical disciplines.

The disastrous dualism between analytic and continental philosophy (which conceals the only interesting opposition, that between good and bad philosophy, which runs orthogonally to the former) has disadvantaged German philosophy, because it is located between the more or less Anglo-American analytic philosophy and the more or less French continental philosophy. But the decline of German philosophy cannot be reduced to this alone. Instead, it has to do with the world-historical situation, with the end of the German spirit, and with special problems in German universities, which will be examined below. So far as the world-historical situation is concerned, the age of nation-states may not be over, but the view is becoming established that global ecological, economic, and security-policy problems can be solved only internationally. Whether the European Union will fall apart or manage to take the next steps toward a deeper political union remains unclear, but globalization is irrevocable, unless a great war should intervene, which at the moment no one seems to want. But globalization depends on an international lingua franca, and that is English. Anyone who wants to have an international career as a philosopher or even desires to be perceived internationally is well-advised to write in English (because having one's work translated into English is expensive) and would also be wise to adopt the corresponding way of thinking. The twenty-first century will be not American, but Asian; however, the expected rise of the Chinese language will not free German from what is increasingly a niche position. All European cultures will suffer a loss of influence, and even if by cooperating they succeed in retaining a certain global importance, national differences will continue to erode, as they have, increasingly, since 1945.

If we now ask what distinguishes German philosophers from those of other European traditions, we can point to the following. The Middle Ages had already produced a rationalistic philosophy of religion that closely connected the individual soul with God. Pondering the essence of God, an activity that does not mesh well with being ruled by authorities, was one of the German spirit's greatest achievements; and since voluntarism was rejected, the attempt to understand certain characteristics of the world had to be made on the basis of God's reason—that is, *a priori*: in Leibniz, the German rejection of empiricism was theologically motivated. In Kant's ethics, this *apriorism* produced an alternative to ancient Eudemonism and to the British philosophy of moral sense, and this new ethics instilled in Germans a unique moral seriousness that made the German bureaucratic state possible, as well as an unusual submissiveness. When eighteenth-century Europe discovered the historicity of the world, a renewed Lutheranism took a gigantic leap from a naïve belief in revelation to a theology of the historical development of human culture. The result, which was elaborated in German idealism's systems, was philosophically grandiose but culturally unstable. In the course of the nineteenth century, the very high level of historical reflection largely corroded Christianity and led to a general relativism that during the political-social crisis of the period between the two World Wars solidified into one of history's most horrifying worldviews. At the same time, the challenge presented by German relativism elicited from thinkers from Husserl to Apel special efforts to provide foundations that were unknown in other cultures because other cultures had no need of them (for political reasons, we can add "fortunately"). So far as I can see, little has remained of these essential characteristics of the German spirit. Perhaps there is still a German thoroughness, and there may even be remnants of a German sense for systematicity in philosophy. But the philosophical form of religiousness that so strongly distinguished Germany from the United States, has evaporated, presumably because sadness and shame over the twelve cursed years has crippled appropriation of the spiritual treasures of the past, which can take place only with hermeneutic reservations, for example on the occasion of the anniversaries of classics. The trivializations of German dramatists that have to be endured in the Federal Republic's theaters are an expression of Germans' perplexity with regard to their own past, with which they are not capable of coping intellectually, but to which they at least want to appear superior by paying homage to what is politically correct. On the other hand, the Nazi period still has a special allure; its aftereffects and its prehistory are plumbed by some of the most successful current

German-language novels and films, from Bernard Schlink's *Vor-leser* ("The Reader") through W. G. Sebald's *Austerlitz* to Michael Haneke's *Das weiße Band* ("The White Ribbon"). In contrast, cautious reversions to the German tradition, and even to the German homeland, are breaking through in artworks, such as Ludwig Steinherr's lyric poetry and Hans Steinbichler's films.

It is well known that German scientific institutions are not at present in the best of shape: in *The Times Higher Education World Universities Ranking 2011/12*, only four German universities are listed among the best one hundred in the world, only three among the twenty-five best in Europe (Switzerland and the Netherlands also have three each in this category, while the United Kingdom has ten). In the new century, from 2001 to 2015, eight Germans have won the Nobel Prize, exactly the same number as the Israelis, whereas nineteen Britons have won it (of course, this is also in part because Britain is able to attract intellectuals from all over the world). As for the Kyoto Prize, which has been awarded since 1985, it has been won by three Germans, eight French, and eleven Britons. The country of Gauß and Hilbert has won a single Fields Medal, the highest honor in mathematics, while Belgium has won two and France twelve (here as before I do not count Germans who emigrated as children and were educated elsewhere). A comparison with the United States would be still more dramatic, but comparison with countries with a smaller population shows even more clearly that Germany has now become a second-rate scientific power. To be sure, most German prizes go to Germans, but the contrast between the illustrious figures of the past after which these prizes are named and today's winners is often striking, and so is the slender correlation between objective scientific achievement and academic influence. The weaknesses of the German system have been amply discussed over the past two decades, but it is unlikely that fundamental reforms will be undertaken in the foreseeable future, because too many interests would be adversely affected. Underfinancing cannot be corrected without tuition fees, the lack of appropriate compensation based on performance cannot be corrected without abolishing professors' status as civil servants, and the absence of competition (despite excellence initiatives, which precisely do not rely on the market) cannot be corrected without reducing the bureaucracy in the ministries of education: and the latter, as well as the professors and the students, would oppose all such measures. In short, institutionally, there is little reason to predict a great future for German philosophy.

And yet the works dealt with here are inexhaustible reservoirs of philosophical ideas. No matter where it takes place, philosophy will hardly be able to overcome its current crisis if the crucial ideas of Leibniz, Kant, and Hegel are not raised to the present level of awareness of the problems facing us. Therefore this little introduction has sought to provide a guide to reading the classics of German thought. The author cannot abandon the hope that when the cataclysmic natural, institutional, and mentality-related changes produced by our ever-increasing environmental problems will, in the course of the present century, have swept away most of the present-day culture industry, the ark of culture will carry these ideas to the salvific shore of a new beginning.

INDEX OF NAMES